GILBERT OF HOYLAND

Volume Four

TREATISES, EPISTLES AND SERMONS
WITH A LETTER OF ROGER OF BYLAND
THE MILK OF BABES

ꞇ

THE WORKS OF
GILBERT *of* HOYLAND
IV

Translated with an Appendix by

LAWRENCE C. BRACELAND SJ

CISTERCIAN FATHERS SERIES: NUMBER THIRTY-FOUR

Treatises, Epistles, and Sermons

with a Letter of Roger of Byland The Milk of Babes

and an edition and translation of the works of Master Gilbert, Abbot, from MS Bodley 87, The Bodleian Library

CISTERCIAN PUBLICATIONS, INC.
KALAMAZOO, MICHIGAN 49008
1981

This book has been published with the help of a grant from the Canadian Federation for the Humanities, using funds providing by the Social Sciences and Humanities Research Council of Canada.

The translation of Treatises and Sermons here presented is based on the edition of Jean Mabillon, Milan: Gnocchi, reprint of 1852, and checked against the reprint of J.-P. Migne, *Patrologia Latina*, volume 184. 'Master Gilbert, Abbot' has been edited and translated from the unique manuscript in the Bodleian Library, Oxford: Bodley 87.

© *Cistercian Publications, Inc., 1981.*

Available in Europe and the Commonwealth from

A. R. Mowbray & Co. Ltd. St Thomas House
Becket Street Oxford OX1 1SJ England

Library of Congress Cataloging in Publication Data
Gilbert, Abbot of Swineshead, Holland, Lincolnshire.
Treatises and epistles.

(The works of Gilbert of Hoyland ; v. 4)
(Cistercian Fathers series ; no. 34)
Bibliography: p. 207
Includes index.
1. Monastic and religious life—Early works
to 1800—Collected works. 2. Spiritual life—
Middle Ages, 600-1500—Collected works.
I. Braceland, Lawrence C. II. Series: Gilbert,
Abbot of Swineshead, Holland, Lincolnshire.
Works. English ; v. 4.
BX2435.G445213   1980   248.8'9   80-10808
ISBN 0-87907-434-5

Book design by Gale Akins at Humble Hills Graphics, Kalamazoo, Michigan
Printed in the United States of America

To the Monks and Nuns who Follow
The Cistercian Way

Haurietis aquas
in gaudio
de fontibus salvatoris.[1]
In caritate perpetua
dilexit nos Deus,
ideo exaltatus a terra
attraxit nos ad cor suum
miserans.[2]

The language of ecstasy
is a language of poetry and of love;
and in that language
a reciprocity is never omitted.[3]
What marvel is this, brethren?
Do you not regard this soul as blessed
which pierces and penetrates
the very heart of our Lord Jesus Christ
by its devout affections?[4]

1. Is 12:3. 2. Liturgy, Feast of the Sacred Heart.
3. Bernard Leeming in *Cor Jesu*, 1:604.
4. Gilbert of Hoyland, S 30:2.

CONTENTS

ACKNOWLEDGEMENT

The translation here presented of the minor works of Gilbert of Hoyland is based on the edition of Jean Mabillon, Milan, Gnocchi, 1852, of which the original Latin title is: *Sermones in Canticum Salamonis ab eo loco ubi B. Bernardus morte praeventus desiit.* Reference is made where advisable to the reprint of Mabillon in Migne, *Patrologia Latina,* volume 184, Paris, 1854, columns 11–298. Mabillon's edition has here been corrected against the manuscripts in the Bodleian Library, Rawlinson G. 38, and Bodley 24, from which also Gilbert's unpublished *Mira Simplicitas* was edited and translated in volume three of Gilbert's works (CF 26); for assistance in obtaining microfilm copies of these manuscripts, for permission to use them for this translation and to include the Latin original of *Mira Simplicitas* I wish to thank the Keeper of Western MSS, the Bodleian Library, Oxford. The translation of Roger Byland's letter, *Lac Parvulorum* is based on the edition of C.H. Talbot, corrected against the manuscript, Pembroke 154, thanks to the assistance of the Librarian and the permission of the Masters and Fellows of Pembroke College, Cambridge. The illustration for the dust jacket, from a colored miniature, folio 27, and likewise three pieces by Master Gilbert, Abbot, folios 89v–97r, in the Bodleian manuscript 87, are reproduced by permission of the Keeper of Western Manuscripts, The Bodleian Library, Oxford. The following abbreviations are used for these manuscripts in the notes: B–Bodley 24; R–Rawlinson G38; BR–when B & R agree; Mab.–Mabillon's edition, 1852; Migne–PL 184, ed. of 1854.

I am grateful for a timely research grant from the Research Board of the University of Manitoba, when current financial stringencies almost brought work on Gilbert to a halt. This volume has been published with the help of a grant from the Canadian Federation for the Humanities, using funds provided by the Social Sciences and Humanities Research Council of Canada. I am indebted to the Jesuit Fathers of St Paul's College, Winnipeg, for a large gift of patience and a smaller grant in aid of publication. Some others to whom I am indebted are mentioned in the notes, but two deserve my special gratitude: Fr Martinus Cawley of our Lady of Guadalupe Abbey for many helpful suggestions and Dr E. Rozanne Elder, the inestimable Editorial Director of Cistercian Publications.

L. C. Braceland, SJ

1

TREATISE 1
Written to a friend, a religious called R.[1]

CONTEMPLATION OF HEAVEN

*1. What kind of conduct becomes a religious?
2. To interrupt contemplation distresses a religious. 3. We must leap beyond the temporal to
behold the eternal. 4. Here we must fight to
attain peace there. 5. Here we have a lamp,
there we shall have the day. 6. We aspire to the
beatific .vision. 7. We long for a happy and
divine intoxication. 8. Each of us is the moon
but he is the sun. 9. We long for the triple
ray of eternal day. 10. After his resurrection he
appeared at dawn, for high noon is his eternal day.*

N OW DO YOU THINK I have woven a
discourse lengthy enough to make up for
what was cut short in previous dispatches? Perhaps in length I have gone to
excess and burdened you with my prolixity, though
previously you chided me for conciseness. Yes, you
complained of my brevity, my dear R., saying you
received not epistles but jottings snipped off before
they formed a pattern.* You added that you would
be delighted if a rather expansive page would compensate for the rarity of our friendly chats. When
I suggested your preoccupations as a pretext for my
brevity and confessed that I should spare a fastidious
correspondent, however, you on your part bade me
be reassured.

To speak frankly then, nothing is more pleasant,
nothing more appealing to me than this exchange,
provided we take as the subject of our talk the one
who is the object of our love. If he is the sound on

Is 38:12

our tongues, may all be calm in our hearts. May he
give birth within to what he may utter without.
In Peter also you read: 'let whoever speaks utter as it

1 P 4:11

were, words of God',* given by God and related to
God. For from him comes our eloquence; he is our
topic; with him is matter most abundant. Who will
exhaust this matter? Not to mention his essence for
the moment, who will explain his benefits and his
judgements? Here no discourse is too long; no discourse is long enough. 'Exalt the Lord', says Sirach,

Si 43:33

'as much as you can, for he is greater still.'* This
material is a treasure indeed and this task is a treat.
For what is a greater treat? What occupation is more
attractive than this? This alone decks and adorns our
picture both of the angels now at play and of the
occupation we shall inherit.[2] 'It is good to give
thanks to the Lord', says the Psalmist, 'to sing praise
to your name, Most High, . . . for you make me glad
O Lord, by your deeds; at the works of your hand

Ps 91:2, 5

I rejoice.'* If your magnificent deeds cause such
delight, cause such joy, what emotions will your
essence arouse? If you delight us in your words,
how attractive to us will you be in yourself?

2. Happy are they who can have a foretaste of

Ps 45:11; 33:9

this, who can attend and see how sweet is the Lord!*
Woe is me, that my years do not glide by on this one

Horace, Odes
2:14:1-2

course unimpeded.* Woe is me that, gnawed until
half dead, my spirit distracted with mordant cares,
I approach so holy a sight and cannot boast with
the prophet of an uninterrupted watch: 'Upon the
lookout of the Lord I stand continuously by day

Is 21:8

and at my post am I stationed the livelong night.'*
His years were not flowing into a void. No, he was
not a wandering minstrel eloping with time,[3] but he
kept his hours captive, expending them in watchfulness over himself or on the lookout for his Lord.
Watchfulness over oneself is healthy but the lookout
for the Lord is more pleasant. Note that Scripture
compares watchfulness to the night, the lookout to
the day.

What does the apostle say? 'But we all with faces
unveiled, reflecting as in a looking glass the glory of

the Lord, and being transformed into his very image
from glory to glory.'* It is unquestionably excellent   *2 Co 3:18*
to keep oneself unsullied and not to be 'conformed
to this world',* but it is far superior to be reformed   *Rm 12:2*
for the future world and to be transformed from one
glory to a greater glory.* To be unremitting in so   *2 Co 3:18*
looking out is to stand on the lookout of the Lord
and to stand throughout the day. 'Standing continuously throughout the day', says the prophet.
What happened to him? Did your knees not grow
weak, O blessed prophet, from standing continuously? Were they not weakened from fasting? But
looking out in this way in reality is not fasting but
delightful feasting. In Scripture, to the man who
dwells on the tower, bread is given and his cisterns
never run dry.*   *Is 33:16*

3. 'Who will give me the wings of a dove',* that   *Ps 54:7*
I may fly to an outpost so secure and so fruitful,
where there is rest and refreshment? For me access
to rest is rare, if indeed there be access at all, rare but
perhaps also immediately interrupted and 'withdrawn
like a shadow at sunset', until 'I am again startled
into a sudden leap like a grasshopper'.* Good indeed   *Ps 108:23*[4]
is the leap one reads about in the Psalm: 'let me
know my end, O Lord, and what is the number of my
days.'* Is not this Psalm entitled, 'for Idithun', that is   *Ps 38:5*
for 'one leaping the wall'?* He had leapt over all   *2 S 22:30;*
that is transitory, travelling in his mind to what is   *2 Ne 4:3*
real and permanent.

That number of days is numberless; that 'end' is
endless, an end exterminating misery but not ter-
minating happiness. 'For Christ is the consummation
of the Law unto justice for everyone who believes.'*   *Rm 10:4*
The same Christ is also the consummation of the faith
unto happiness for everyone who contemplates, since
he the true wisdom 'reaches from end to the very end
mightily and governs all things sweetly'.* 'Reaching'   *Ws 8:1*
as a highway from end to end, from faith to hope,
and 'governing' as life, for he says: 'I am the way and
the truth and the life.'* 'I am the way', leading;   *Jn 14:6*
'the truth', teaching; 'the life', delighting. 'Now this
is eternal life, that they may know you, the true

Jn 17:3

Ps 15:11[5]

Ps 4:9

Is 65:23

Gn 4:12

Jn 16:21[6]
1 Co 11:7

1 Jn 3:2

Rm 8:22

Ws 3:5

God.'* This 'knowledge' is full of delight. 'You will give me unbounded joy with your countenance and at your right hand delights to the very end.'* In this end we shall be gently governed, when God will be our all in all. When the last traces of the old man are effaced, our mortality will be swallowed up by his life, our weakness by his power, our blindness by his truth and the concupiscence of our flesh by the abundance of his spirit.

4. Now since as long as life lasts here, flesh and spirit are at odds, we must fight bravely that we may rest blissfully and that war may be changed into peace as it is written, 'in peace in the self same, I shall sleep and take my rest'.* O true peace, perfect peace, so much the more true the less it is transient, so much the more perfect the more it is everlasting! The 'self same' banishes diversity as 'peace' banishes adversity. 'They shall not labor in vain nor bear children for calamity.'* As if the prophet were to say: they shall not labor without harvest nor shall the harvest cost them labor. But on earth no harvest is without labor and labor without harvest is frequent. When you shall have tilled the soil, it will not yield its harvest.* Now we are in labor and we mourn, then we shall rejoice over offspring. A woman does not remember her travail, when she has brought forth a son,* for she has brought forth a man, in whom 'is the image and glory of God'.*

But when will that take place, when will the Scripture be fulfilled? 'We know that when he appears, we shall be like him, for we shall see him as he is.'* Advancing towards this vision every creature is in anguish, yearning and travailing together until now.* That is truly wisdom which guides us gently towards the divine image. Harassed now in many things, then we shall be well governed in all things,* then indeed not through the changes of the seasons, nor the grades of perfection, not from virtue to virtue, not from splendor to splendor, but once and for all in every virtue and in all truth.

Did not Isaiah say precisely this? 'Before she came to labor, she gave birth; before labor came upon her

she delivered a male child.'* Who is this woman who
with so much haste and without any weariness brings
to birth? Yes, she is that very wisdom of which we are
speaking, for she says: 'I am the mother of fair love
and of recognition.'* She will then bring us fully to
birth, in love and recognition without labor,[7] when
without difficulty in eternity we shall contemplate
truth; we shall be minted into charity. 'My little children, with whom again I am in labor until Christ be
formed in you'!* So now the apostle is in labor, but
then Christ himself will bring to birth. 'Shall I who
make others give birth, not give birth myself? Shall I
who grant generation to others, be sterile myself, says
the Lord.'* Nay more, we shall all be called the taught
of God,* conformed to God.†

5. Scripturally, in this conformity born of the
vision of God, we are renewed into the male offspring, if indeed 'the man is the image and glory of
God'. Wherefore 'a man ought not to cover his
face',* to anticipate by unveiling his bodily countenance, what later will take place in his spirit, when
with the countenance of the mind unveiled, looking
at the glory of the Lord, we are transformed[8]
into the same image without the struggle for perfection or the fear of defection. Is it about this then
that Isaiah asks in wonder? 'Who ever heard of such a
thing? Or who ever saw its like? Can a nation be born
all of a sudden? Can the land give birth in one day?
Because Sion has brought forth children?'* For in
truth, the Sion which is called a lookout, gives birth
in a day, yes, in that one day in the courts of the
Lord which is better than a thousand.* Of this day
another prophet says: 'and there shall be one day
which is known to the Lord, not day and night.
And at the evening hour there shall be light,' since
assuredly 'your sun shall no longer set nor shall your
moon wane, for the Lord shall be your everlasting
light'.*

This is the day which is known to the Lord, for
this day is the Lord. 'No one knows the Father
except the Son and the one to whom the Son
chooses to reveal the Father.'* His revelation of

Marginal references:
Is 66:7

Si 24:24

Ga 4:19

Is 66:9
*Jn 6:45
†Rm 8:29

1 Co 11:7

Is 66:8

Ps 83:11

Zc 14:7[9]

Mt 11:27

himself will make us also 'days'; we shall be like him
when he appears.* 'The days shall be listed', says the
psalmist, 'and no one of them omitted',* yes, no one
of those to whom is said 'you are the light of the
world'.* You now have 'the prophet's discourse, and
you will be right to pay attention to it as to a lamp
until the day dawns'.* Rightly the lamp is hidden,
when the morning star rises.* The discourse of the
prophet will disappear; the discourse and the interpretations of the apostle will likewise disappear, for
the apostle says: 'We know in part . . . . What is but
partial will disappear, when what is perfect has
come.'* Hence Philip says: 'Lord, show us the
Father and it is enough for us.'* You and the Father,
he says; no other than you, no other reality than
God, 'and it is enough'.

6. For your 'invisible attributes, understood
through the things which have been made, are clearly
seen . . . your power everlasting also and your
divinity'.* It is one thing to see you with no inter-
mediary, another thing to see you thanks to some
intervention. Why have I lit a lamp for myself?"[11]
That I may behold the sun? A lamp is good, but for
weak eyes. Breasts are good, but for infants in Christ.
A looking glass is good, but a kiss is better. Then kiss
me with the kiss of your lips, with your lips* I say,
not with your works. The lips are within, the works
are without. 'Who would grant me', says the bride,
'that you my brother' nursing at my breasts, 'I might
meet out of doors with a kiss.'[12] He whom the bride
desires to meet out of doors and to kiss, she also
represents as nursing at her breasts, to make some
allusion to the outpouring of his Incarnation. Wisdom
the Craftsman, though in a different way and still in
the unity of his person, through the signs of his work
shines as a light out of doors. He gives delight[13] out of
doors pleasantly enough but not fully enough. Do
then what is enough: show yourself!

Relentlessly I seek you out of doors, slowly I
find you, with difficulty I hold you, and somehow
as you take flight and vanish I blow you the fondest
kiss. Good are these kisses but as in a looking glass, as

1 Jn 3:2
Ps 138:16

Mt 5:14

2 P 1:19
*Jb 11:17;
2 P 1:19 10

1 Co 13:10
Jn 14:8

Rm 1:20

Sg 1:1

in shadow. Good are these kisses; they refresh for a moment, but are not enough. Do what is enough. Kiss me with the kiss of your lips, with the kiss of the Word, not of the flesh; the kiss of Truth not of its image; a kiss gratuitously granted, not snatched under duress; the kiss of your epiphany which likens me to yourself, that matched with you and joined with you, I may be in one spirit with you. Indeed 'he who cleaves to the Lord is one spirit with him'.* *1 Co 6:17* This undivided embrace of love and union with you is rightly understood in the word 'kiss'. Therefore I delegate to you the office of the kiss; I assign you the initiative, where all springs from your action and not from my effort, from your indulgence and not from my diligence, from your epiphany and not from my search.* *2 Co 4:2; Is 4:28*

7. Therefore I say: reveal yourself to me through yourself, just as you are and it is enough for me. 'I shall be satisfied when your glory has appeared',* *Ps 16:15* when you shall fill me with that wine, new wine, which you drink yourself and broach for others in your kingdom. That wine I desire neat and not diluted, pure and without milk, for milk is the drink of babes. Whatever belongs to babes will be banned. Better indeed are breasts than wine, but not better than your wine; rather your wine is by far the best, beyond breasts. In Scripture, breasts do not inebriate, but wine intoxicates and immerses the state of the mind in some novel and extraordinary perceptions. Breasts in giving suck are emptied, but your wine which inebriates continues to overflow. I do not wish that its fervor be tempered with the chill of milk. I long for your wine, pure and perpetually flowing. For so we read in the psalm: 'They shall be inebriated in the overflow of your house . . . for with you is the fountain of life and in your light we shall see light.'* Surely extraordinary is this inebriation *Ps 35:9-10* which results from light and not from liquor, from serenity and not from strong drink.*[14] *Lk 1:15*

Then 'send forth your light and your truth',* your *Ps 42:3* plentiude and not some pledge which delays your presence, dilutes your grace, overshadows your light.

May what is promised in the dark, be granted in the light. In the dark is what is promised by the prophet: 'Without you, O God, the eye has not seen what you have prepared for those who await you.'* But even the daughters, who in the book of Numbers have no inheritance but seek their father's inheritance, were called the daughters of Zelophehad, that is, his 'shadows'.† For neither could Zelophehad, neither could 'shadow' beget males, in whom is 'the image and glory of the Lord'.* This will occur as long as we live by faith but when we shall enjoy the vision, 'we shall be like Him'.* Wherefore we who exist in the body, 'pilgrims far from the Lord',* seek our inheritance with the daughters of Zelophehad. 'What we should seek as we ought, we know not.'* We seek a paternal inheritance, for 'the Lord is my allotted portion'.* We seek with Philip: 'Show us the Father and it is enough for us.'* I insist on no more, I can subsist on no less. Herein I set a limit to my desires and put an end to my vows. What at last is that end? The apostle tells us that end: 'but your end is life everlasting.'* What is this life everlasting? What Christ tells us: 'This is eternal life, that they may know you, the true God, and Jesus Christ whom you have sent.'*

8. To this end, as if to the ending of all things, he had crossed by desire, for he prays in the psalm: 'Make known to me my end, O Lord',* the end of evil and the end of good; of evil because it is consumed; of good, because it is consummated. He speaks rightly, therefore, of an end purified, plenary, and perpetual; purified of evil, plenary in good, perpetually purified and plenary; pure affection, complete satisfaction, and both without deficiency. The psalmist asks a further question: 'what is the nature of the number of my days'. A good question indeed, for those days exist simultaneously; they do not succeed one another for the psalmist. The total number of those days is not diminished, is not changed. Therefore the psalmist asks: 'what is the nature of their number'? How does my day decline into night, if my 'sun does not set'? Your sun will not set', says Isaiah, 'and your moon will not wane'.* I am the moon and He the sun.

Is 64:4

†Nb 27:1-6, Zelophehad had seven daughters but no son.
*1 Co 11:7
1 Jo 3:2

2 Co 5:6

Rm 8:26
Ps 16:5
Jn 14:8

Rm 6:22

Jn 17:3

Ps 38:5

Is 60:20

Therefore the moon will not wane, because by the perennial and ever present Sun, the moon is not moved.

In a new kind of mathematics, there will be no limit to my days, but there will be a number. There we shall enjoy a continuous and unfaltering everlastingness, though not that absolute simplicity conformed to the unity of God. All other than God, though they be everlasting,[15] are in no way simple. For in all others, 'to be' is not the same as 'to be this or that', because in all others 'to be this or that', is not the same as 'to be whatever each one is'.[16] For things which in themselves are infinite, in a spiritual creature are infinite because of an illimitable continuity, and in relation to each other they are somehow limited and finite, because of some fixed diversity of their natures and affections.

As the Lord says: 'In my Father's house are many dwellings':* dwellings obviously of lesser lights, because God himself 'dwells in light inaccessible'.* So what the psalmist calls the number of days, John understands as a multitude of dwellings, not because there is one dwelling for each spiritual creature, since for some one or other there are many dwellings, as the Lord says in Luke, 'and you shall have authority over ten towns'.* 'For star differs from star in splendor.'* Yes, as the number of virtues increases, so the gift[17] of splendors is multiplied, as the prophecy in Isaiah indicates: 'and the Lord shall fill your soul with splendors'.* Blissful surely is the soul, which will be filled not only with one but with many splendors, those indeed of which it is said: 'Yours is princely power in the day of your birth, in the splendors of the saints.'* The most blissful splendors are those which the Lord pours upon his saints; the beginning of eternity, the day of truth, and the virtue of charity.[18]

9. Who will grant me that my spirit may be enlightened with a ray of this triple splendor? that this most blessed number may complete, yes complete and contain my days?[19] Who I ask, will grant me that my days may stretch out to that line of eternity,

Jn 14:2
1 Tm 6:16

Lk 19:17
1 Co 15:41

Is 58:11

Ps 109:3

may shine in the splendor of truth and be inflamed with the spirit of charity? Unlike the dispensation which prevailed at the first creation of the world, when an alternating return of dawn and dusk set limits between the many days, then indeed there will be one unending day, one unbroken high noon. There at the first creation, only between morning and evening, so to speak, inauspicious night was banned, but in this new day high noon will replace dawn and dusk; the two limits of the day will no longer grow dim. As Zechariah says, 'in the evening there will be light',* for then there will be no temporal 'variations, no shadow of change'.* Yet when, oh when, will this occur? When, O good Jesus, will you manifest yourself as you are in your high noon? For in you we shall see the Father, and it will be enough for us.*[20] How sluggish are our years, how slow our hearts! slow to see, quick however to believe!

10. Approach us, O Lord, in person, that we may be able to say: 'Hark! my lover! here he comes springing over the mountains, leaping across the hills.'* Approach and anticipate our snail's pace. In Scripture, we have just read how you approached that pair on their way to Emmaus, chiding them for their laggard faith and explaining yourself from the Scriptures; disclosing within and appearing without but disappearing too quickly, perhaps because you manifested yourself not at high noon but at dusk when the day was far spent.*

Scripturally, in each and every appearance after your blessed Resurrection, I do not recall ever having read of your appearance at midday. You appeared either when the day had hardly begun or was already ending, that one might understand that here below all light of truth is obscured by some shadow of ignorance. At the same time, a pleasant distinction should be noted in the fact that in the dawn's early light he showed himself at the tomb to the women seeking him anxiously, but that late on the same day, the first of the week,[21] he showed himself to the disciples huddled at home.*

Oh that you would appear to us also, O Lord,

Margin references:
Zc 14:7
Jm 1:17

Jn 14:8

Sg 2:8

Lk 24:13; 35

Lk 24; Mk 16;
Jo 20

here in our dawn or in our dusk, for you are above dawn and dusk, the brightest high noon. In that high noon we shall recline at table in your fatherland. Meanwhile as we are journeying on, let us pray, O Lord, that you may warm us with the last ray of evening light. Now we are concluding our discourse with the onset of a day but we do not exclude you; rather we close with you as we opened with you. In the morning let us give thanks, breaking into that song of the Canticle: 'I rested in the shade of the one I longed for.'* Farewell.[22]

Sg 2:3

1. The editions of Mab. and Migne, have been checked against a microfilm copy of the mss. Bodley 24 and Rawlinson G. 38; these are here abbreviated B and R, or BR when, as usual, they are in agreement. I am grateful to Martinus Cawley, OCSO, of Our Lady of Guadalupe Abbey, for painstaking assistance with the Treatises and Letters. According to Mab., G.'s correspondent, called simply R, may be Roger of Byland to whom Treatise 7 is addressed. The date is near Easter, year unknown.

2. BR *Quid hac occupatione gratius, quae sola feriationis (fruitionis,* Mab, Migne*) angelicae et futurae conversationis superinduit et vestit imaginem?*

3. RB 1:10-12. The Prophet of Judah whose lookout was Jerusalem, G. seems to be contrasting with the *gyrovagi*; his words seem reminiscent of the Archpoet's *Confession: Aestuans intrinsecus ira vehementi . . . ;* note especially: *similis sum folio / de quo ludunt venti . . . stultus ego comparor / fluvio labenti, / sub eodem aere / nunquam permanenti. / . . . Feror ego . . . ut per vias aeris / vaga fertur avis.* The Archpoet (died 1165) and Gilbert (died 1172) were contemporaries and the former's *Confessio* 'is one of the hardiest things in medieval literature'; see Helen Waddell, *Medieval Latin Lyrics* (London: Constable, 1929) 170-183, 338-40, her *Wandering Scholars* (London: Constable, 1927) 147-60 and the bibliography there, especially pp. 282-85.

4. BR omit *forte*, perhaps, and read *excutiar* vs. *excutiat* of Mab. and Migne.

5. BR *usque in finem;* Mab. and Migne *usque ad finem.*

6. BR *pepererit;* Mab. and Migne *peperit.*

7. BR *In his sine parturitione nos ad plenum pariet;* omitted by Mab. and Migne.

8. BR *transformamur;* Mab. and Migne, *transformabimur.*

9. BR: *De qua et propheta alius: 'Et erit dies una, quae nota est Domino';* Mab. and Migne, *propheta alias . . . quae nostra est.*

10. BR: *Jure;* Mab. and Migne: *Iam.*

11. BR: *accendi;* Mab. and Migne: *accendis.*

12. BR: *fratrem* for *fratrum*, with Mab; quoting Sg 8:1, G. writes *ubera mea* for *ubera matris meae* of Vulg.

13. BR: *delectat;* Mab. and Migne: *delectatur.*

14. For *sobria ebrietas*, see Jean LeClercq, 'La liturgie et les paradoxes chrétiens' (Paris, du Cerf, 1963) pp. 37-57.

15. BR: *licet sempiterna sint;* Mab. and Migne: *. . . sunt.*

16. *Cetera enim omnia licet sempiterna sint, simplicia tamen nequaquam sunt, quibus non hoc est esse quod hoc vel illud esse, nec hoc vel illud esse quod quidlibet quod sunt esse. Sic* BR.

17. BR: *munus claritatum;* Mab. and Migne *numerus claritatum.*

18. BR: *Serenissimi splendores isti quos in sanctos suos refundit, eternitatis principium, veritatis dies, et virtus caritatis;* Mab. and Migne omit *quos . . . veritatis.*

19. BR: *compleat, compleat et contineat?* Mab. and Migne; *expleat, compleat et contineat?*

20. See F. Chatillon, 'Hic, ibi, interim', RAM 25 (1949) 194-199.

21. BR: *die illo uno sabbatorum;* Mab. and Migne *illa una.*

22. BR end with *Vale*, which Mab. and Migne omit.

TREATISE 2
HERE WE SEEK, THERE WE SEE
ACCORDING TO MEASURE[1]

*Here we seek, there we find. 1. How should
Christ be sought? 2. Why did Christ allow himself to be anointed before but not after his
resurrection? 3. How does contemplation differ
among pilgrims and among the blessed? 4. Why
is the reward of beatitude said to be given
according to measure? 5. Open my heart,
O Lord, as a faithful pilgrim along the way.*

OUR BELOVED HAS TURNED ASIDE
a little amid the shadows of the night.
Where then shall we seek him? What
kind of person do we seek? The one
indeed who says: 'I am the flower of the field'.* If
then we seek him, let us go out to the field, or rather
let us go into the garden, if indeed he 'has come down
to his garden, to the garden-bed of spices'.* Yes, and
when Mary sought him in the garden she found
him.† She sought him weeping; let us seek him
singing his praises. Delightful is the task, but more
delightful the reward. What kind of reward? That
mentioned in the psalm: 'His offering of praise will
glorify me, and to one chanting along my way I will
show the salvation of God.'* So Jesus ought to be
revealed to those who sing his praises.

Let us seek him with praise but let us seek him in
the garden. In a garden he was betrayed, in a garden
he suffered, and in a garden he reappeared. In the
Canticle, because the bride saw him, she also ex-
claimed: 'O you who dwell in the gardens, friends are

Sg 2:1

Sg 6:1[2]

†Jn 20:1-16

Ps 49:23

Sg 8:13

Jn 15:14,
Lam 18, n. 75

Sg 2:14

Jn 20:17

Mt 28:9

Ps 132:1-2

listening for you; let me hear your voice!'* Friend?
Yes, Peter and John. Friends? Yes, the disciples
who hear his words: 'You are my friends'.* Make me
hear what news I should bring them.[3] They are in the
field and I am in the garden. As men they put their
hands to hard tasks, I to an easy task. Happy the
woman who deserved to hear you, happier the woman
who saw you, for 'your voice is charming and handsome your face';* happiest of all would she have been
if she had touched, clasped and held the One toward
whom she had stretched her hand;[4] but at once she
hears his word: 'Do not touch me!'* What one woman
could not, many could do, those to whom he said:
'Hail! And they approached and embraced his feet'.*
What singularity can not embrace community does,
charity does embrace. Let us seek then in union of
hearts and we shall seek in unity of action. In the Gospel the women who came with ointment, came upon
him. Good is the ointment mentioned in the Psalm:
'Behold how good and how pleasant for brethren to
dwell in unity! like ointment upon the head'.*

2.   Perhaps the Lord did not so much allow himself to be come upon, as intrude on his own. 'His
feet', says Matthew, 'they embraced', but did not
anoint with ointment. They discovered him alive,
whom they sought among the dead. They were coming to bathe the Christ, to anoint the Anointed, and
he was coming to them, his whole person breathing
forth the vital fragrance of immortal spices. Before
his passion he willed to be anointed and afterwards,
awaiting burial, he permitted his anointing; but risen,
he needed no anointing, for he was overflowing now
from the anointing not only of immortality but also
of royal and supereminent power, as he also testified:
'All power in heaven and on earth has been given to

Mt 28:18
Ph 2:9
Sg 1:2

Sg 5:1

me',* and as Paul says: 'God . . . has given him a name
above every name'.* So it is said in the Canticle:
'Your name is oil poured out',* and he invites the
bride to enjoy his ointments: 'Come into my garden,
sister, my bride; I have gathered my myrrh and my
spices.'* What I have sown, he says, I have already
reaped. I have sown weakness; I have reaped immor-

tality. I have sown in tears; I reap in exultation. I have sown in your garden; the harvest I gave garnered from mine, for myself but not less for you, for myself in fact for you in hope.[5] Hence my invitation stands: 'Come into my garden, sister, my bride.' Pleasing are her titles and filled with sweetness, for they mean a relationship either of nature or of grace. Having become a sharer of your nature, in turn I share my grace. So I call you sister, but in the flesh; and spouse, but in the Spirit; in the flesh, because in the flesh humanity was assumed intact; in the Spirit, because through the Spirit charity was infused. Come then sister, my bride, redeemed at so great a pledge, assured of fulfilment.[6] 'I have gathered my myrrh with my spices.'* *Sg 5:2* Myrrh for my sister, spices for my spouse; myrrh for the flesh, spices for the Spirit; the myrrh of incorruption, the spices of truth. You shall know the truth but when my anointing shall have taught you.* You come *1 Jn 2:27* with ointments but I have others which you know not,* new ointments but also old; for all both new *Jn 4:32* and old I have accumulated for myself. The beginnings of the future resurrection at the end of the world have already blossomed in me, and the glory of that pristine eternal splendor abides. For the Father has glorified me 'with the splendor I had before the world' was made.* *Jn 17:15*

3. Yes Lord, these ointments are the finest and their fragrance has already reached your spouse. So she says: 'Behold, the fragrance' of my Beloved 'is like the fragrance of a fertile field.'* For as she says *Gn 27:27* in the Canticle, where you lead the bride follows: 'Draw me after you; we shall run in the fragrance of your ointments'.* O blessed times, when they shall *Sg 1:3* hear this question asked about them: 'Who are they who fly like clouds?'* Now the spirit is willing but the *Is 60:8* flesh is too weak;* my weakened strength cannot *Mt 26:41* match my will. Wherefore 'draw me after you; in your fragrance we shall run'.* To run is good, but to be *Sg 1:3* drawn is more effective. Await the straggler; draw on the struggler. I shall run more ardently, if you run with me; we shall run together, you in anointings, I in their fragrance.

Happy the soul which after labor rejoices at last in
ointments, for into it flows the anointing of your
acquaintance and your love. Or rather the torrent of
pleasure and the excess of delight ravish and absorb
the soul into themselves. Happily hidden indeed is
one who there finds himself lost, buried with Christ,
or better in Christ, as Isaiah says: 'his sepulchre will

Is 11:10
be glorious',* glorious indeed for 'his abode has been
Ps 75:3
built in peace, and his dwelling in Sion.'* There the
inhabitants contemplate you from a lookout. But what
do we see save in a looking glass, the looking glass of
1 Co 13:12
creatures and the riddle of the Scriptures?* We look
out on figures and shadows, but they on truth and
Ps 45:11
brilliance. They rest and behold,* they stop and listen, and in joy rejoice at the voice of the Bridegroom,
Jn 3:29
at the countenance of the Bridegroom.*
Sg 2:14
Yes, 'his voice is gentle and handsome his face'.*
Therefore continuous longing and unwearying zest for
so sweet a sound and sight pervade the souls who
share his anointing. For 'oil poured' over them is
Sg 1:2
'your name'.* Oil it is rightly called, for your name
and your acquaintance is illumination and joy, pro-
Rm 5:5
fuse joy, joy 'poured into the heart'* not of those
who still believe but of those who already behold. In
heaven exist not heart and heart but one heart of all.
'O how good, how delightful for brothers to dwell in
unity, like ointment upon the head'. How delightful
Ps 132:1-2
it is,' I say, 'to dwell in unity',* for there the Lord
dispenses and disperses; dispenses openly and disperses abundantly; he pours his blessing with largess
Ps 132:2-3
and his life forever and ever.*[7]

4. Woe is me that I do not pour out fully whatever abundance I hold! Woe for the dryness of my
discourse and still more for the dryness of my interpretation! Neither does my discourse measure up to
my affection, nor my affection to my faith; for my
faith does not suffice, since it does not fully refresh.
We shall be satisfied, says the psalm, 'when your glory
Ps 16:15
appears'.* So when vision arrives hunger will depart,
the hunger of our present want, not the hunger of our
future plenty; the hunger of our fast, not the hunger
of our repast. Good is the repast which destroys

distaste and whets the appetite; good is the hunger
which satiety begets. 'Who devour me', says Sirach,
'will still hunger.'*   *Si 24:29*

What does a banquet mean if not contemplation?
'The just will banquet . . . in the sight of God',* that   *Ps 67:4*
is, in beholding God. But what does it mean, to
hunger, if not always to seek? 'Seek the Lord and be
strengthened; always seek his face.'* 'Always seek his   *Ps 104:4*
face', for you see him face to face; we who are in the
body, what do we behold but his back?* 'Draw us   *Ex 33:23*
after you.'* Draw us from your back to your face,   *Sg 1:3*
from faith to vision, from fragrance to anointing, 'for
through faith we walk'* but in fragrance we   *2 Co 5:7*
run.* Happy they who have so run as to have   *Sg 1:3*
arrived already* and need run no further but stand   *1 Co 9:24*
in truth;* they do not waver, steeped in every kind   *Eph 6:14*
of ointment of immortality, drenched with the
myrrh of immutability. There they praise you with
greater exuberance to match their greater freedom.
'You shall know the truth', says John, 'and the truth
shall make you free.'* So at the dawn of truth, vanity   *Jn 8:32*
will vanish, 'for creation was subjected to vanity not
of its own will',* and the heavy yoke of corruption   *Rm 8:20*
will become smooth and light from the gleam of oil',*   *Is 10:27;*
and the profusion of ointment. Indeed good measure,   *Mt 11:30*
shaken together and overflowing, shall be put into
your lap.* You will be the donor, O Lord, and you   *Lk 6:38*
will give yourself, for my share is the Lord.*   *Ps 15:5*

What does it mean that you give yourself in
measure, you who are great and measureless? You do
not, do you, pour in oil also apportioned to the
capacity of our jar? Why then do you say overflowing? Because you pour out more than our capacity?
Not even if with all our effort we extend ourselves
to full capacity to receive you, do we grasp you in
your entirety. Mighty is God to create beyond the
measure we seek and understand;* how much more   *Eph 3:20*
does what he is and what has not been created[8] sur-
pass the measure of our desire and the limit of our
understanding! Behold, he says in Isaiah, I bend over
them like a river of peace and a flooding torrent of
glory!* Will a man be able then to swallow 'the river   *Is 66:12*

whose stream gives joy to the city of God?'* Will he
be able to empty the Jordan so that it flow fully into
his mouth?* Truly we are not restricted in you,
O Lord, for you give profusely. Nor do you give only
to a few, nor only a few gifts, nor in a parsimonious
or niggardly way, but anticipating our merits and sur-
passing our desires. No, in you we are not restricted
but we are restricted in our inmost affections.*
Possessed of promises so great,* my most beloved,
let us also extend ourselves; let us extend ourselves to
desire, that we may be extended to receive.

5. Or rather come to expand our hearts[9] with
the calm, smooth flow of your bounty, O Lord, since
I ran the way of your commands, when you expanded my heart,* and since you stretch out the sky
like a hide,* now smoothly stretch out the hide of my
heart grown old and shrivelled in an idle breast. Un-
fold its wrinkles, draw out its hiding places, enlarge
its vessels, that without measure I may yearn for
you, without measure contain you, and that this holy
yearning may give me greater capacity! For thus, with
a slight foretaste of experience, where faith beckons
affection will take wing and fervent eagerness will
not await the prompting of reason; so along the
harsh and protracted ways of temptation, the perseverance of holy resolution will experience less
travail, if it be lured on by the expectations of forth-
right desire and pious hope.

Let us wait here awhile to catch our breath,
sparing our weary spirit, that refreshed by a brief
respite our spirit may rise with greater fervor.[10]

Ps 45:5

Jb 40:18

2 Co 6:12
2 Co 7:1

Ps 118:32
Ps 103:2.
Miquel, 153, n. 8

NOTES ON TREATISE 2

1.   G. writes throughout for his beloved brethren, *charissimi*, par. 4.

2.   G. *aromatis*, Vulg. *aromatum.*

3.   BR: write *quid* instead of *qui.*

4.   BR: *ad quem manum tetenderat, tetigisset, tenuisset et retinuisset.*

5.   BR: *Quod, inquit, seminavi, jam messui. Seminavi infirmitatem, messui immortalitatem. Seminavi in lacrimis; in exultatione meto. Seminavi de tuo sed de meo messui mihi, imo et tibi; mihi in re, tibi in spe.* The passage is marred by omissions in Mab. and Migne.

6.   1 Co 1:22, 5:5; Ep 1:14, for the pledge of the Spirit. See also the antiphon for the Feast of St Agnes: *Anulo suo subarrhavit me Dominus meus Jesus Christus.*

7.   The ointment and oil are blessing and life forever.

8.   Mab. and Migne: *quanto magis id quod ipse est et factum non est;* B: . . . *et factus non est;* R: . . . *et facta non est.*

9.   BR: *Tu autem, domine, tu potius dilata...;* Mab. and Migne omit *dilata.*

10.   BR: *Vale.*

TREATISE 3
HOW JOY DIFFERS ON THE WAY
AND IN THE FATHERLAND!

1. How God is both light and darkness; God hides himself that he may be sought more eagerly. 2. How joy and tears accompany our pilgrimage; here there is no joy free of tears. 3. The blessed have an unflagging desire to praise God. 4. Thanksgiving for the bliss of the blessed, consolation and hope for pilgrims and exiles. 5. An exhortation to desire eternal happiness. 6. In this life joy is only a drop or a spark, 7. comparable to morning dew; man is more prone to things of earth than of heaven; Christ pretends to be leaving us, that we may constrain him to remain.

REFRESHED BY YOU, O Lord, in the quiet of night, it becomes us[1] 'to stand by you at daybreak'.* 'To stand by', or to follow you? Happy the man who finds you seated at his gates at daybreak, that he may stand by, stand by until evening and not seek you with wandering gaze amid the light breezes, should you have taken wing in sudden flight![2] For you make darkness your hiding place.* Light you are and a hiding place, since 'you dwell in inaccessible light'.* Therefore to us you are darkness, to us inaccessible; inaccessible to our vision, yes, but not to our voice; for where reason does not reach, prayer penetrates. 'My cry in his sight', says the psalmist, 'entered into his ears.'* Therefore let our cry also enter into your sight that you may emerge into our sight and even

Ps 5:5

Ps 17:12
1 Tm 6:16

Ps 17:7

23

consent to be seen, though you do not permit our embrace. 'Return, return, that we may gaze upon you!' 'That we may gaze upon you', until we may embrace you!* Return my Beloved and 'be like a gazelle or a young stag upon the mountains of spices'.*

Sg 6:5

Sg 2:7; 8:14

'Be like a gazelle', says the bride. You may be seen and then bound away; you may be near and then far off; you may be near to our sight and far from our touch. As you say to the woman in John, 'Do not touch me'.* Do not grope for me with a hand that puts faith in experience. Behold, O Lord, I restrain my hand and train my eyes. 'At daybreak I shall stand by you and see you.'* Woe is me, should I hear the words of the Beloved: 'Turn away your eyes from me, for they have put me to flight.'* Or perhaps while you elude our gaze, you enkindle our longing, since you are more eagerly sought until you are more fully loved.[3] In these verses, your flight lures us more keenly to pursuit.

Jn 20:17; Miquel 152, n. 7

Ps 5:5

Sg 6:4

2. Who will give me the footing of hinds,[4] that nimble and keen I may be able to pursue this young hind and that, unlearning my household chores, I may range the forest in heavenly solitude? It is good to shed the heaviest burden, the burden of oneself, and to be reduced imperceptibly to the nimbleness of wild goats.[5] Hence the prophet says: 'I was not fatigued, for I pursued you, O Lord.'* True is your boast, blessed prophet, true is your boast, but not the whole truth; not to be fatigued does not suffice, unless you also rejoice. So what you left unsaid another prophet articulated: 'They shall sing in the ways of the Lord, how great is the glory of the Lord',* and likewise: 'Your statutes were the subject of my songs in the place of my pilgrimage.'*

Jr 17:16; Is 40:31

Ps 137:5

Ps 118:15

All is enacted within, for the song is sung in his heart, for there too the race is run. 'In his heart he planned ascending steps in the valley of tears.'* Now what is the meaning of a mountain climber with lament and of a pilgrim with a song?[6] For one can neither lament in one's fatherland nor rejoice in a foreign land. 'How shall we sing the Lord's song in a

Ps 83:6-7

foreign land?'* Well perhaps, yes certainly, they weep who sit and wait by the waters of Babylon, but they who depart exult.* He who climbs up in the valley of tears also climbs out of the valley of tears. Though he climbs from tears, he does not climb with tears. It is indeed more pleasant to be on the mount of joy than in the valley of sorrow. But if the ascent is with tears, this is because the ascent is sluggish and arrival not yet near. Because 'in his heart' one plans 'ascending steps',* it does not follow that he immediately completes them. 'When the legislator shall have given his blessing', then 'shall they mount from virtue to virtue, that the God of gods may be seen in Sion',* because they hasten and hurry in joy of heart towards the prize,* like one who to the accompaniment of the pipes reaches the mountain of the Lord, the mountain spoken of by the prophet: 'On this mountain the Lord will make . . . a feast of fatlings and a feast of the wine press, one of rich marrows and one of vintages from the lees'.*

The joy of the mountain climber is diluted and still cloudy and blended with tears, for 'the chalice of pure wine in the hand of the Lord is blended with a mixture'.* The blended wine is for those hastening upwards, the pure for those reaching the top, and the dregs for the laggard. Here on earth Wisdom diluted wine in a mixing bowl, but in heaven she will strain the new vintage.[7] But only one preoccupation engages the blessed spirits there, one celebration of a year of jubilation, to rejoice with the Lord and to praise him, for joy shall be found in Sion, thanksgiving and the song of praise'.*

3. Rejoice Jerusalem, burst into hymns of praise.* Praise his Majesty, be grateful to your Benefactor! This yearning to praise is always being discharged by you and always demanded of you. It is promptly discharged and piously demanded. The demand in itself is a joy. Your yearning to grasp blessed truth is its own commendation and the breath of peace settling over the affections brings joys along with the light. 'Light has dawned for the just and joy for the upright of heart. Rejoice in the Lord, you just.' What exchange

Ps 136:4

Ps 136:1

Ps 83:6

Ps 83:8

Ph 3:14;
2 Co 9:24.

Is 25:6

Ps 74:9

Is 51:3
Is 54:1

shall they make for this rejoicing? 'And remember to
praise him for holiness.'* So delight flows from the
light and thanksgiving flows from delight. Delight ex-
panding bursts into praise, and our hearts overflowing
cannot but bubble over with the happy intoxication
of luminous truth, and inebrated with the flow of
sweetness cannot refrain from song. This sweetness
indeed whets our appetite, largess provides satiety,
and eternity guarantees unending bounty. In Scripture,
this sweetness and abundance and eternity is assured:
'in anyone who drinks the water I give, it will become
a fountain of water leaping into life everlasting.'*

4. O blessed spirits and souls of the just! O
Church of the first-born enrolled among the inhabitants of heaven!* You were truly the first-born
because you foretasted the firstfruits of final bliss.
'Eat and drink, my friends, and be inebriated, my
dearest beloved!'* Drink from your cistern;† let the
streams of your well rise and overflow;let the waters
of your delights tumble and spread through the
squares of your heart. Let not the estranged share
with you, let not all of your household be welcomed.*

Indeed we are 'fellow citizens of the saints'; we
belong to 'the household of God'.* We are citizens
enrolled but not yet welcomed.* We are citizens in
exile,[8] citizens on pilgrimage,* citizens wandering
and fugitive,* 'for our iniquities, like a gale, have
swept us away'.* You blessed, however, are enthroned 'in the beauty of peace and in the tents of
trust and in the repose of prosperity'.* Woe to the
earth-dwellers, where peace is rare and security
non-existent, where labor without respite gives birth
only to indigence.* 'For the life of man upon earth
is a warfare',* as long as flesh lusts against the
spirit,* and 'our adversary, like a . . . lion, goes about
seeking whom he may devour';* 'in the sweat of our
brow we eat our bread',* and the soil of our heart
produces 'thorns and thistles for the laborer'.* Consequently, routed and wounded and faint of heart, we
still have at hand more cogent reasons to groan with
anguish over ourselves than to be carefree and
rejoice in the Lord.

Ps 96:11-12

Jn 4:14

Heb 12:23

*Sg 5:1
†2 K 18:31;
Pr 5:15

Mt 10:36

Eph 2:19
Ac 15:4; Lk 10:8
2 Co 5:6
Gn 4:12; Jg 20:45
Is 64:6

Is 32:18

Qo 5:13
Jb 7:1
Ga 5:17
1 P 5:8[9]
Gn 3:19
Gn 3:18

Yet fair hope anticipates our goal from the evidence of our firstfruits and from the presses of tribulation extracts the oil of consolation, for when our faces gleam* and our heads glisten with oil,† with the apostle we may boast in sufferings* and in insults be content,* 'knowing that suffering brings patience, and patience brings perseverance, and perseverance and endurance bring tried virtue and tried virtue brings hope'.* But what does hope seem to be, but the present foretaste of some early joys of the glory destined for us? 'For in hope we have been saved', says Paul,* and we are 'rejoicing in hope'.† For a devout faith knows how to fly ahead of our dawdling days and from the present day to be swept onward to what our faith pictures for itself with unshaken confidence. But that is a hope which not presumption but the purity of a chastened conscience brings to birth.

5. 'Be washed, brothers; be cleansed.'* Be washed and be purified by fire,* that when you have been chastened and refined by the practice of penance and suffering, as if in a furnace,* then your upward gaze may refresh you like dew with a spindrift of relief as you proceed to burst into a cry of joyful exultation: 'matching the number of griefs in my heart, your consolations have gladdened my soul.'* Be washed and rejoice; be washed the more frequently that you may rejoice the more fervently. Practise more often now what you cannot yet perform eternally! O unhappy mountains of Gilboa cursed with perpetual dryness, you have not been drenched with this gratuitious rain,* nor has a drop of predawn dew fallen upon you!* Wherefore neither are you the 'fields of firstfruits' nor is a late harvest expected from you.* O that 'my head were drenched with your dew', O Lord, 'and my locks with drops of the night'!* For where but under the cover of night is our activity, until the day dawns and the shadows end?*

Yet in the high noon which we await, no shadow is feared, no dewdrop desired. Here a drop flows from 'the bucket of Jacob', but there 'his seed

*Ps 103:15
†Ps 22:5
*Rm 5:3

2 Co 10:9-10

Rm 5:3-4

*Rm 8:24
†Rm 12:12

Is 1:16 [10]

Ps 16:3; 65:10

Pr 27:21 [11]

Ps 93:19

Ps 67:10

2 S 1:21

Js 5:7

Sg 5:2

Sg 2:17

Nb 24:7
Gn 2:6-7, 10-14

Jg 1:15
Ps 83:3
Ezk 16:30¹²

Is 58:11

Ps 35:9-10

Ps 35:11

Ps 50:14

Ps 18:9

Is 9:3
1 Co 9:24-27
*Heb 12:1-2
†1 Co 9:24-27
**Ph 3:14
††2 Tm 2:10

Rv 1:15

Ps 105:4-5

will be upon many waters'.* O happy times, when the whole face of the earth will be irrigated,* irrigated from on high, and when the barren desert will have no part; yes, irrigated both from above and from below,* when my flesh and my heart shall leap towards the living God!* Good clearly is the fountain which will then arise and inundate our hearts,* a fountain better than the fountain of the first paradise, because it cannot dry up.* We¹³ 'shall be intoxicated with the largess of your house; from your torrent of pleasure you will give us to drink. For with you is the fountain of life and in your light we see light'.* Good certainly is the fountain, from which flow four such streams: pleasure, fruitfulness, life and truth.

6. Rain down upon us dew from your fountain; shed mercy on us who know you,* though not all of you. Shed mercy, pour in grace, pour your Spirit upon us to renew the spirit of our inmost being, your steadfast Spirit to reform and conform us to himself,* to conform and strengthen, to gladden and enlighten. 'The precepts of the Lord are upright, joy for the heart; the command of the Lord is clear, light for the eye',* as far as here upon earth we may be enlightened and gladdened. Elsewhere, of course, 'we shall rejoice in your presence as those who rejoice in the harvest, as victors rejoice at the capture of booty, when they divide the spoils'.* There we shall rejoice as those in possession;* here we rejoice setting the goal before us,* anticipating the prize† and in pursuit** until we achieve our goal.†† There the joy is in possession, but here in the promise; there in fulness, here in a part.

What is sprinkled upon us from above is a drop not the stream, a spark not the fiery furnace.* Alas, how quickly even this spark goes out and this drop evaporates! 'Remember us, Lord, as you favor your people; visit us with your saving help, that we may see the prosperity of your chosen ones, rejoice in the joy of your people and glory in your inheritance.'* Visit us to let us behold, rejoice, praise; visit us in salvation and light, in rejoicing and praise. Wonderful are these tiny drops, however rare, and falling like dew. 'Rain down dew from above, you heavens';* 'send sprays of sweetness upon us, you eternal mountains';* 'fruitful soil will rejoice in your gentle rain'.*

Is 45:8

Jl 3:18; Am 9:13

Ps 45:8; 65:11

7. Be to us, O Lord, 'like the dew' that we too may 'blossom like the lily'.* Your word once sent knows not how to return without profit; your word will be fruitful wherever it is sent.* As Isaiah adds: beneath the freshness of this dew, 'in place of the thornbush the cypress will grow, instead of nettles, the myrtle.'* All the while your dew lifts and exalts the downcast; it softens and tempers the provocations of the flesh; it employs those who have lost hope and engages them in the business of heaven;* it softens the harsh and makes them like the meek.* A delight is your visitation, but 'like a mist of morning and a passing dew at dawn'.* While we are in the flesh, rightly likened to a dew at dawn is any contemplation and any rapture of the mind, for it retains some, or rather a lot, of the chill of night, thanks to our less fiery affectivity, and again a lot of the gloom of night, thanks to our somewhat darkened understanding.

Ho 14:6

Is 55:11

Is 55:13

Ph 3:20

Si 43:24

Ho 6:4

But if this be the meaning of a dew at dawn, what is the meaning of a passing dew? Does the dew pass from us, or does it pass into and penetrate through us? 'The word of God is alive and active, and more penetrating than any sword',* so that it not only marks the flesh on the surface, but pervades the interior, penetrates the marrow and soaks the bones,* for his words, though 'softer than oil', still pierce like arrows.* Is this the reason why, if the heart of man be stretched like the parchment of the sky,* it will fold shut like a book* and condense like a mist?*[15] Let each one interpret this according to his own view as he experiences it is his conscience: the perfect, saying that the word flows in and inundates him; the proficient, saying that the word passes through and flies by. It passes through and beyond us to attract us after it, and makes us pass over to it, as if by its flight it should say: 'Pass over to me, you

Heb 4:12

Jb 21:24[14]

Ps 54:22

Is 40:22; 34:5

Is 34:4

Is 51:6

Si 24:26

who long for me'.*

Perhaps, O Lord, we pass from you more frequently than you from us,[16] since indeed you light a
lamp and sweep the house and search for us accord-

Zp 1:12; Lk 15:8

ing to the prophet,* wherever you find us lurking
amid squalor, immersed in vanities and vagaries, in
enervating and irritating cares and counsels, not only
giving half our spirit to God and half to the world,
but even more inclined and more ready for the
worldly half, if not by design at least in practise. For
even tasks which are admitted for a useful purpose
boldly impose upon us, and when the need is no
longer urgent, the superfluous still preoccupies us.
Scripturally, we seem to be running from the waters
of Siloe which flow in silence, and to chase the

Is 8:6

waters of Babylon.*[17]

Well, at least we have chatted a little with you,
O Lord, and about you, and have been tastily
refreshed, like the whelps, from the crumbs which

Mk 7:28

fell from your table.* If you so treat us, when you
are passing and strolling by, what do you do when
you stay as a lingering guest? Woe is me, that we are
unworthy of so pleasant a stay! 'Stay with us, Lord,
because it is towards evening and the day is now far

Lk 24:29

spent.'* Yes, the day is really far spent, when you
withdraw yourself. Constrain him, brothers, by the
urgency of your prayer. The two making their way
to Emmaus put pressure on him, when he pretended
to be going further. Why does he who is the truth
pretend what he does not perform? He pretended to
be going away, though he was constrained to stay but
not to stay forever, for he disappeared in the midst
of dinner. His pretense of going away is an occasion
for him to stay. He pretends, as it were, to be going
away, diminishing joy of the spirit, but he stays on
disguised, increasing justification and adding to humility.

NOTES ON TREATISE 3

1.   G. addresses his brethren, *fratres*, and everywhere quotes or alludes to Scripture.

2.   BR: *Felix qui te assidentem foribus suis matutinus invenerit, ut astare possit, et astare in vesperum, ne subito elapsum volatu, vago vulto tenues inter auras quaeritet;* Mab. and Migne: *matutinis . . . quaereret.*

3.   BR: *An forte dum fugis aspectum, accendis desiderium, ut avidius quaeraris, dum amplius amaris;* Mab. and Migne: *accendes . . . ut anxius.*

4.   See S14:3; Morson 164 on *cervus*, White 37–39 on *cervus* and *hinnulus.* Isidore 12:1:12. See Dimier, 'Ménagerie Cistercienne', *Cîteaux* 24 (1973) p. 22.

5.   See S14:3, S23:2; S27:3. See Morson 161–2, 154, on *caprea, caper,* and White 40–43.

6.   G. may be quoting some accentual verses: *Quae est tamen ista ratio / ascendentis cum lamento / et peregrinantis cum cantico.*

7.   BR: *Hic . . . ibi;* Mab. and Migne: *Hic . . . ubi.* See Chatillon, Jean, 'Hic, ibi, interim', RAM 25 (1949) 194–99.

8.   Reading *exsulantes* for *exsultantes,* despite BR, Mab. and Migne.

9.   BR: *transvoret;* Mab. and Migne: *devoret.*

10.   BR: *Lavamini, fratres, mundi,estote;* Mab. and Migne omit *fratres.*

11.   BR: *camino;* Mab. and Migne: *gemino.*

12.   BR: *et inundabit cor nostrum;* Mab. and Migne *mundabit.*

13.   G. lists four streams of the new Paradise. BR: *inebriabimur;* Mab. and Migne: *inebriabuntur.*

14.   BR: *et fiat irrigatio ossuum;* Mab. and Migne: *ossium.*

15.   See illustration and note about the so-called 'bréviaire de St. Bernard', PL 185 bis: 1730–34.

16.   See Miquel 155, n. 18. BR. and Mab: *Fortassis nos frequentius transimus;* Migne: *Fortassis non . . . .*

17.   BR: *videmur mihi Siloam refugere;* Mab. and Migne: *silvam;* see Ps 136:1, *abjecit populus iste aquas Silue, quae vadunt cum silentio.*

TREATISE 4
ON CONVERSATION AND COLLOQUY,
THE SHADOWS OF SUBSTANCE[1]

*1. Can a discussion about divine mysteries be
called a chat? All such discussion is unequal to
the task. 2. How languor and passion differ;
fervent desire for truth is refreshed in the
shade of symbols; conferences on divine mysteries may well be called chats. 3. From the
abundance of the heart flows good spiritual
conversation. 4. Spiritual colloquy leads some
to ineffable joy. 5. Meditation is the tinder and
affectionate love is the flame. 6. How even faith
and virtues are called vanity by comparison with
love. 7. All is vanity save the truth and the love
of God. 8. How we quarrel and wrangle for
temporal goods and forget the everlasting Good!*

YOU HAVE YOUR REQUEST but you
have it enriched with interest of a kind.
This interest I list as a credit and count as
a gain. Whatever the occasion, I cannot
but count it my good fortune as often as an opportunity arises of chatting with you. You may cavil
perhaps at my use of the word chatting. Because we
are wont in fact to speak only on a serious subject, by
the word 'chatting' I have done an injustice to the
sublimity of our insights.[2] Or do you think it is not
chatting when we speak of what we have not seen and
testify to what we have not heard?* 'Eye has not   *1 Jn 1:1-3*
seen', says Isaiah, 'any god but you, O God, doing
such deeds for those who wait for you', yes, hoping
and on the lookout but not looking at!* 'For why   *Is 64:4*

33

Rm 8:24

1 Co 13:12

does anyone hope for what he sees?'* Now if what
we see, we see reflected in a looking glass and in a
riddle,* how much more what we talk about? For
discourse, however eloquent, cannot fully explain
the mysteries beyond our own insight.

Now to communicate my own insight, every
parable with figures to hint at the reality to come
seems like chatter in comparison with that reality.
Granted that all creatures in the universe are fair
to behold and fashioned in unity and suited to our
needs and powerful in their effect, still what are they
all in comparison with the immense and simple and
eternal unity of the divine essence, in comparison
with the beauty of divine wisdom, the depth of divine love and the might of divine power? To Moses
God introduced himself as 'I am who am',* and 'to
his wisdom there is no limit',* while the fullness of
divine charity surpasses wisdom.* And 'who will
speak of the powers of the Lord'?*

Ex 3:14
Ps 146:3
Eph 3:19
Ps 105:2

All things adopted in discourse, to give us a hint
somehow about the divine powers, are incalculably
different by reason of their nature and are nothing
in comparison with the divine. Gold from Ethiopia
can not be compared with the divine, nor can the
purest dyes match the divine.* Nevertheless, through
gold and dyes, through flowers and fruits, and
through all created beauty, that Beauty which is
beyond all things beautiful is presented to us colorfully and imaginatively, in such a way that although
the divine Essence completely eludes us, because it is
hidden deeply within, yet through the borrowed
colors of imagery, what is deeply hidden somehow
shines through the shade. Good indeed is the shade
and for a moment it refreshes. Therefore the bride
exclaims: 'I sat in the shade of him whom I longed
for, and his fruit was sweet to my palate.'*

Jb 28:17-19

Sg 2:3

2. O with how much more delight, with how
much more affection, would she have reclined not in
the shade but above the shade upon your breast,
good Jesus, and, having reached this goal of her
longing, been at rest! Now, however, does she really
recline in the shade? Does she really refresh herself

in the shade? What kind of refreshment is this, which
ends in relapse? 'For we know in part . . . but when
that which is perfect has come, that which is in part
will pass away.'* Meanwhile, these are crutches for
persons who are tottering, nourishment for persons
who are languishing. In the Canticle the bride adds:
'Prop me upon flowers, encompass me with fruits,
because I languish with love.'*

Happy the one whose holy love is a langour and not
a passing passion. Some may be so suddenly wounded
by charity[3] that straightway they are healed, like the
vine of Jonah which dried up within the very hour it
blossomed.* Now passion is a sudden feeling of longing but languor is a lingering affection. O falsely
healthy or rather truly unhealthy is the heart which
knows not how to be smitten with this wound!
'Wounded have I been', says the bride, 'with charity.'*
Charity not only wounds it slays, for 'stern as death
is love', says the Canticle.* Indeed the apostle says:
'You have died and your life is hidden with Christ in
God.'* While life is hidden, longing also is heightened;
while truth lies hidden,[4] courage languishes; the heat
of fretful longing is cooled in the shade of images and
propped upon spring flowers.

Quite beautiful are these figures and they refresh
an exhausted affection; they revitalize with delicacies
meant for children, in order that through these
familiar and sensible pleasures we may seize upon experiences of extraordinary joys.* Your squares, O
Jerusalem, will be paved with pure gold.* 'I shall lay
your stones row on row and I shall set your foundations on sapphires.'* I shall 'change your deserts into
oases of delight and your solitudes into a garden of
the Lord'.* How many other verses of prophets and
apostles have been spoken about this city which is a
prototype of the heavenly Jerusalem! When its gates
and squares, its walls and its metals, its precious
stones and woodwork, its foundations and streams
are described, how deeply the descriptions affect and
delight us! How joyfully the words are heard, yet
how obscurely they are spoken! Something is left to
our imagination, something incomprehensibly dif-

1 Co 13:9-10

Sg 2:5

Jon 4:6-7

*Sg 5:7. Mab. refers
to Sg 5:8 in LXX.*

Sg 8:6

Col 3:3

*See Miquel
154, n. 12
Tb 13:22

Is 54:11

Is 51:3

ferent, something incomparably greater than is presented in the likeness.

Jon 4:6
'Jonah rejoiced exceedingly in the shade of the ivy tree',* but that ivy withered and the figure disappeared. Wherefore when likenesses are woven together from figurative passages, I would readily call this chatter, not because of the eternal truth adumbrated within but because of the figures of fancy displayed without, for 'what is imperfect will pass away'.* Consider the remark in Luke about the two walking to Emmaus: 'they were chatting and questioning together', perhaps because they were seeking and not yet grasping, faltering and not yet steadfast in faith. So they were said to be seeking and comparing, walking and chatting. Nevertheless, as they were so chatting, 'Jesus himself drew near and went along with them'.*

1 Co 13:10

Lk 24:15

3. Do you not joyfully recall[5] how frequently our hearts also were burning within us thanks to Jesus, when we were speaking about him on the way? For what we said about him, he first said within us. O that this might fall to my lot more often: to seek and compare and chat together with you[6] about him, about him yes, and with you, but not so much to speak myself as to listen to you speak. Though your discourse is compressed, still you express well what you think. Few are your words but full of insights. You seem to summon every word before a law-court, so true is it that no word escapes you unquestioned. As the Beloved says: 'your lips are a dripping honeycomb.'* Your remarks are spaced and measured as if weighed one at a time, so that you might be thought to be not pouring water but distilling honey. Your words fall measured, subtle and condensed, so they seem to be a distinct and tasteful distillate extracted from inmost cells.

Sg 4:11

Therefore your words are like a honeycomb, 'milk and honey beneath your tongue'.* 'Beneath the tongue', says the text and not 'on the tongue'. For what lies hidden beneath the tongue is greater than what is brought to light upon the tongue. What

Sg 4:11

if it were also above and beyond the tongue? 'Under your tongue, milk and honey.' Now this means not only in discourse, nor wholly in discourse. Though you have no pretense in your voice, still much lies hidden in your heart. On the tongue is what you speak openly; beneath the tongue is what anyone, however eloquent, becomes tongue-tied in explaining, for here the only art of communication is silence.

4. I remember, if I mistake not, that sometimes in the very act of speaking, you checked your discourse, alert and astonished at the light and gladness flaring in your heart. Your voice broke off and was changed into a sigh which became audible. Now though your tongue is evidence enough,[7] still interior astonishment and love and amazement at the light radiating from above attracts and ravishes and completely captures your mind which had been expressing itself in words and as with Moses* cloaks   *Ex 24:15* your mind in a cloud of the spirit, makes a cloud its mantle, makes darkness its retreat, so that your mind becomes stunned at what is happening within, and dumb to what is happening without. So honey beneath your tongue and sweetness beneath your voice is nowise inferior but somehow more interior; or rather this is too deep for your understanding, as long as your mind—not yet master of the sweetness conceived within—cannot either fully explain or even endure the experience of joys multiplying within. Though your attention yields itself entirely to joys, it does not entirely possess them.*   *Miquel 153, n. 11*

'My eyes were worn out watching for your promise', says the psalmist.* Not only toward your   *Ps 118:82* promise, but also for your promise; towards your promise by yearning for it, for your promise by conceiving it; towards your promise wherein it is partly enkindled,* for your promise because it is a   *Ps 17:31* raging fire. Indeed 'your word is a raging fire'.*   *Ps 118:140* Therefore my soul melted when my beloved spoke. 'I sought him.'* My soul melts, unable to bear what   *Sg 5:6* it hears, and, becoming more eager at the sweet sound, my soul does not cease to yearn for it. So the bride adds, 'I sought him'. Though the ear is not sated with hearing, the ear is not yet equipped to hear.

5. So not only were my eyes worn out looking towards your promise, but also my soul melted, despising itself, and hastened towards your promise to gaze and marvel and love and woo it on all sides, powerless either to reach the fullness of desire or to retain all it receives.[8] How then is one's breath not cut off as one speaks, when one's interior insight is swallowed up as one meditates? Just as solid and tougher logs offer greater resistance to the power of fire, while tinder that is fine and dry and light is more quickly kindled and consumed in the devouring flame, so spiritual and refined meditations more quickly welcome but do not endure very long the sweet violence of enkindled love. 'Your spirit', says Isaiah, 'will consume you like fire.'*

Is 33:11. See Lam 185, n. 9, and S 5:8, S 26:7.

For my part I have regarded meditation as the tinder and love as the flame. 'And in my meditation a fire will blaze out'.*[9] If a fire rages in a more violent conflagration, it transforms and consumes within itself all the effort of the mind, so all that was meditation becomes wholly affection, and reason can not retain its self control, after it has been swallowed up by the power of love, for reason's job is to dig out what is hidden, to distinguish ambiguities, to rethink and recollect what it devoutly knows. 'I fell silent far from the good and my grief was renewed; hot grew my heart within me.'* 'I fell silent', says the prophet, I grieved, I grew hot. I grew hot from some grasp of interior goodness; I grieved over my imperfection, and so I fell silent. Divided, distracted, absorbed by this twin suffering, 'I fell silent far from the good'. But from what good? Perhaps the good of which the psalmist speaks: ' believe I shall see the good of the Lord in the land of the living.'*

Ps 38:4

Ps 38:3-4

Ps 26:13

6. Rightly then the psalmist falls silent,[10] even far from the blessings still unseen. But if he falls silent in prophecy, he does not fall silent in prayers of petition.[11] So he continues: 'Let me know, O Lord, my end and what is the number of my days, that I may

learn what is lacking to me.'* When then is lacking? *Ps 38:5*
What indeed is not lacking? Listen to what the psalmist says: 'My life is as nothing before you; yes, all vanity is ever living man.'* What then is not lacking, when *Ps 38:6*
all is either nothing or undoubtedly vanity? Does it
follow that faith itself and the virtues are vanity? Has
this interior life of man been called vanity, because it
has also been called death? 'For you have died and your
life is hidden with Christ.'* What if even the life of *Col 3:3*
faith is vanity[12] because it is only partly living, as we
read—for 'that which is partial will pass away'*—and *1 Co 13:10*
since 'the just man lives by faith',* and since the goal *Rm 1:17;*
Hab 2:4.
which he longs for is beyond faith, will is faith therefore
disappear? His justification which is through faith* will *Rm 1:22*
not disappear, will it? How then does charity never
fail,* which is really the only justification? What if we *1 Co 13:8*
should admit that all things which exist in the present
life are vain, all unrelated to that future good or all
vanity compared with it? All things then are vanity,
either through their useless use or through their
fleeting passage or in relation to the future.

7. But if the necessities of life are vanity, what
are life's superfluities? If that is vanity which in the
present life is truth, what is vanity itself? 'All vanity
is every living man.'* Not only vanity, but adversity! *Ps 38:6*
'For in vain is man made restless.'* In vain does he *Ps 38:7*
rejoice, in vain is he disturbed; in both joy and sorrow is vanity, either because their motives are
worthless or because their existence is brief. And
now amid these evils and vanities 'for what do I
wait? Is it not the Lord? My substance is in your
keeping.'* 'My substance is as nothing before *Ps 38:8*
you',* but my substance 'is substance in your *Ps 38:6*
keeping'.* 'Make known to me my end, O Lord, *Ps 38:8*
. . . that I may know what is lacking to me.'* Human *Ps 38:5*
vanity is sufficiently familiar to me from personal
failure, but let its flavor be fully experienced in contrast with my personal taste of goodness. When will
our longing be filled with goodness, O Lord, 'with
the goodness of your house'?* When, I ask, shall we *Ps 64:5*
be filled with your truth, that no taste or scent of
vanity may remain in us, as we read of Moab that 'he

Jer 48:11
Ps 38:3

Ps 143:13

Gn 27:28
Gn 49:25
Rm 8:18

Jb 38:8

Is 11:9

Rm 1:18
Ac 14:26
Jn 10:7
Jn 10:9[15]

Gn 26:20

kept his taste and his scent was not lost'.* There we shall not 'fall silent far from goodness',* but we shall be like bins, not empty but full, overflowing and 'spilling over from one crop to another'.*

8. I have spilled out some thoughts for you from my empty folly. Would that I also deserved some wisdom distilled for me from your fulness,[13] from 'the dew of heaven',* and from the well lying beneath* but not yet gushing fully, from that well of 'future glory which will be revealed in us'.* This glory exists then in us, not yet revealed but rather concealed[14] and hidden as in a seed, enclosed in some rich veins of faith and closed behind the doors not only of fleshly affections but also of bodily phantasies. Behind such gates was the sea enclosed; when confined, 'it leapt tumultuously as if from the womb'.* Good is the sea about which Isaiah says: 'the earth will be filled with the knowledge of the Lord, as waters fill the sea.'* Good is the sea but heavy the door. Scripturally, the first Adam by a kind of breakwater of disobedience constrained this sea, and by his action imprisoned by his wickedness the waves of God's truth once surging and breaking.* The first man excluded us by the door of his wickedness; the second man removed that door,* became himself our door,* when 'anyone who enters' through him 'will be safe' and find pastures.* Wickedness has been broken down but still there remains a heavy door, the wickedness of our own day.

A door cloudy enough is our habit of using imagery in thought as well as our anxiety about the necessities of life. To develop a mentality of this kind is really to dig in the ground, to dig a leaky cistern and a well which cannot hold water. Yet how men come to blows, how they infest the courts, how they spread calumnies against us for such wells of the Philistines, for waters of transitory necessity, not to say pleasure!* Happy the man who like the patriarch Isaac[16] abandons wells of this kind, abandons occasions for lawsuits and cases of personal enmities, to dig in the riverbed and there find a rich vein of living waters, if only he may not enclose the water behind

heavy doors!* Personally I should have believed   *Gn 26:14-22*
these doors more open to you and access to hidden
chambers more familiar and frequent. Only do not
stand outside looking in through the window and
gaping through the door. Well, I shall shut the door
of my lips at last that, according to the proverb, the
shepherd's pipe may be handed to you, while I
catch my breath.

1. The treatise throughout is addressed to a friend in the second person singular; though we do not know his correspondent, still *vestra* suggests a brother abbot, n. 13, and perhaps Aelred of Rievaulx, n. 7.

2. Gilbert puns on *fabula* and *confabulatio,* fable and confabulation; fable and fable-talk might suggest his play on words.

3. BR: *vulnerentur;* Mab. and Migne: *vulnerantur.*

4. BR: *veritas latet et virtus languet;* Mab. and Migne: *veritas jacet . . .*

5. BR: *Annon suaviter recolis . . .* Mab. and Migne: *Unum suaviter recolis . . .*

6. BR: *tecum;* Mab. and Migne: *totum.*

7. BR: *evidentiam* for *erudiendum.* Remembering this vivid experience, G. continues in the present tense. A comparison with S41:4–6, G.'s eulogy after the death of Aelred of Rievaulx, January 11, 1167, where G. speaks about Aelred in the same terms, may suggest that G. is here addressing Aelred and that this treatise was written before 1167, the date of Aelred's death.

8. BR: *capit;* Mab. and Migne: *cepit.*

9. Ps 38:4. See Lam 185, n. 96, where this passage is linked with S29:3, S24:3, S24:5. See Anselm Le Bail, 'Les Exercices spirituels dans l'ordre de Cîteaux', RAM 25 (1949) 265.

10. BR: *Jure ergo silet;* Mab. and Migne: *silui.*

11. BR: *Si silet a predicandis, non tamen silet a deprecandis;* Mab. and Migne: *precandis . . . deprecandis.*

12. BR: *Quid si et ista vanitas est;* Mab. and Migne omit *et.*

13. G. uses *vestra,* your fulness, perhaps a respectful plural for a brother abbot, though G. uses *tibi* in the preceding sentence and throughout.

14. BR: *occultata;* Mab. and Migne: *occulta.*

15. BR: *ut . . . salvabitur;* Mab. and Migne: *et salvabitur.*

16. Reading *Isaac* for *Jacob,* as suggested by the text, Mab. and Migne. BR: *Jacob.*

TREATISE 5

EVERY BEST GIFT AND EVERY PERFECT GRANT IS FROM ABOVE, COMING FROM THE FATHER OF LIGHTS*[1]

Jm 1:17

1. Preoccupation and the difficulty involved have delayed Gilbert's answer to a friend's problem. 2-3. The difficulties of the text are noted but the problem is not solved, since the larger part of the letter or treatise is missing from the manuscript.

YOU ASK INSISTENTLY for what I had casually promised, little realizing the difficulty of the subject. Here occurred a kind of double burden, because we underestimated both the time required and the number of texts to be compared: the time, of course, for other tasks were to have a prior claim; and any comparison with other writers on this subject, which I seemed to have undertaken with too little foresight, I prudently disavow.[2] I shall attack the problem, however, for I am under an obligation to solve it. Now your role will be to anticipate me by petitioning for me the favor you ask for me, that from above, thanks to your prayers, grace may be poured into me, which I may channel to you more abundantly.

'Every best gift and every perfect grant is from above, coming down from the Father of lights.' Does it follow then that what are not perfect, what are not the best, do not come from above? Whence do they come, if they are not from above? 'What have you which you have not received?'* It is indeed *1 Co 4:7* not true that the best are from God, and the

43

Rm 11:36[4]

less good from elsewhere, but as the apostle says: 'all things are from God.'* Or is it true perhaps that by these words nothing has been excluded, because all are perfect and the best, since all things are from above? If that be true, then by these words 'best' and 'perfect', no distinction is made between what are more and what are less good and so the two words are simply an expression of 'each and every good'.[5] And how is it that each and every good is not the 'best' and 'perfect', since every good is from above? What is the meaning of 'from above'?[6] 'Descending from the Father of lights,' says James. For what reason can anything imperfect be considered to be with the Father of lights? Or perhaps did 'every best gift and every perfect grant' descend from above but not exist there? But how could what existed in him, that is, in the Father of lights, descend and depart from him? For descent does not seem to suggest a migration from place to place but rather a virtual diminution.

2. In Scripture, the Lord himself seems to distinguish between what is perfect and what is less perfect: 'Do this and you shall live', he said.* How-ever, 'if you wish to be perfect, go sell all you have and give to the poor and come follow me'.* And the apostle says: 'each one has his own grant from God, one in this way, but another in that';* and likewise 'as to little ones in Christ, I gave you milk to drink, not solid food',* and earlier, 'wisdom, however, we speak among the perfect'.* For what reason then does James state distinctly that every perfect grant is from above, since neither is every grant perfect, nor is any grant not from above? Or if every gift is best and if every grant is perfect, because it is from above, why should we not say one and the same, gift and grant, rather than each and every one?[7]

Lk 10:28

Mt 19:21

1 Co 7:7

1 Co 3:1-2
1 Co 2:6

Indeed everything which is with the Father of Lights must be considered simple and uniform, not multiple. What if everything with the Father of lights is both the best and perfect, but descending to us from the Father of lights is less good and less perfect? But this will be to subject that immutability to the condition of things mutable. For how can it be that 'to become less' is not 'to be changed'?[8] For what reason then can what exists in the Father descend from him?[9] But again on what grounds can what does not exist in the Father be said to descend from him? Or if it descends from him, how is it not perfect? And since even the authority of Scripture holds that some things are more perfect and others less perfect, what does it mean that only the best and the perfect grant is said to descend from above, when it seems rather that each and every grant should be said to descend from above? Then what does it mean to use two sets of words, gift and grant, best and perfect? Through these sets of words some distinction is suggested. Or were they spoken only for vividness and emphasis?[10]

3. The words of this verse create the above difficulties for me. But now let us return to the sequence of words in the verse, praying God that he be kind enough to unbar the door and grant us a worthy explanation of his gifts. 'Every best gift,' and so forth. In the first place, between gift and grant it seems to me some distinction may be made as follows: Something is called a gift, because[11] you do not have it from yourself, but a grant, because it does not come from your own merit. It is a gift, as long as you are receiving it; a grant, as long afterwards as you deserve it; a gift, as long as you have it for your use; a grant, as long as you retain it for your enjoyment.[12]

1.   True to his promise to a friend, G. attempts to solve a problem of interpretation. The larger part of his answer is lost. See Cornelius à Lapide, *Commentaria in Scripturam Sacram*, 20:63–69.

2.   BR: *Tempus quidem si aliae praeripuerint causae, comparationem cum
aliis de hac ˙materia scribentibus prudens diffiteor, quam minus considerate
praesumpsisse videbar;* Mab. and Migne: *. . . si aliae proripuerunt causae, . . . de
materia sic habentibus.*

3.   Rm 11:36.

4.   BR: *Neque tamen optima ab illo sunt, et minus bona aliunde;* Mab.
and Migne: *Neque tantum . . .*

5.   BR: *Quod si est, non est per haec verba "optimum et perfectum",
magis et minus boni facta distinctio, sed omnis boni expressio;* Mab. and Migne:
inter magis et minus bona facta distinctio, sed boni expressio.

6.   BR: *Et quomodo omne bonum non est "optimum et perfectum", cum
omne desursum? Quid est desursum?* Mab. and Migne omit *non* from the first
sentence, and *est* from the second.

7.   *. . . quomodo non magis unum et idem, datum et donum, quam omne
dicendum est?*

8.   BR: *Minorari enim quo modo non mutari est?* Mab. and Migne:
minorari enim quodam modo mutari est.

9.   BR: *qua ratione ergo quod in ipso est, ab ipso descendere potest?*
Mab. and Migne: *qua ratione ergo quod in se est, ab ipso descendere potest?*

10.   BR: *An solam dicta sunt ad expressionem et commendationem?* Mab.
and Migne: *An solum . . .*

11.   BR: *Datum est quia . . . ;* Mab. and Migne: *Datum est quod . . .*

12.   The remaining paragraphs are missing from the manuscripts. I had
translated *donum, dum possides ad fructum* as a metaphor from banking. As
David M. Stanley has pointed out to me, however, G. says that gift, *datum,*
always remains in the possession of the donor, while by contrast the grant,
donum, can be 'consumed', 'used up', *ad fructum,* precisely because the donor
has surrendered his rights as possessor to the beneficiary. Whether or not we can
conclude from G.'s failure to refer to the Greek version that he did not know
Greek, or that he had an unquestioned reverence which attempted to save the
Vulgate version of his day, I would hesitate to say. Otherwise, I might conclude
with Fr Stanley: 'Poor Gilbert (I realize that the extract is not complete) if he
had only known Greek, he would have been spared some of his speculations! The
Greek line is a hexameter, and the introduction, "Mé planasthe!" might seem to
indicate a quotation, "Datum optimum" in Greek is "dosis ágathē", a *nomen
actionis* rendered by the NEB as "all good giving". Here James is presenting an
argument against blaming "temptations" on God. The argument is from creation,
specifically of the stars, "lights". God as creator is viewed as "Father". He has
set the stars on their courses to fix divisions of time, to light up the darkness, and
stars are so much more brilliant in the Near East. These stars are subject to cer-
tain laws: *parallagē* is a term from astronomy for "variation"; *tropēs áposkiasma*
is a "shadow cast by variation" in the position of these heavenly bodies. God
himself as creator is subject to no such laws or change in his being and in what he
does; hence he cannot be the cause of anything evil or imperfect, such as
"temptations".'

TREATISE 6
ON THE OCEAN, THE CHALICE AND
THE NAVEL-CUP OF OUR REDEMPTION
Written to a friend

*1. G. redirects the affection, reliance and zeal
of a friend. 2. Though demurring at the task,
G. distills drops of wisdom for his friend.
3. The ocean of Majesty ebbs from our hearts
and lips but returns in the tiniest drops.
4. The divine Simplicity is hidden in the mys-
stery of the Incarnation. 5. Wisdom cries aloud
its existence in the works of creation, but
hidden in the Incarnation and in us does not
shout aloud. 6. God became incarnate for our
sake; Christ's wounds are compared to breasts
and to clusters of grapes. 7. Faith conquers
both the world and death, for which we receive
the palm of victory. 8. We will be assumed into
the palm tree. 9. With the wheel and the scalpel
each should shape a well-rounded mixing bowl
which never lacks wine, that he may not need
to draw water from the well of someone else.*

YOU HAVE WRITTEN me a letter quite
sparing in words but, I believe, full of
affection. Certainly I rejoiced at the good
will you show me but I was less pleased
at your singing my praises. It is a mark of honesty to
blush at praise which one knows one does not
deserve. To tell the truth, thanks to a kind of
friendly trustfulness, your better judgement about
me went astray. That faith is slower to believe, which
devoted affection does not inspire. The reason why
you believed me so implicitly was because what you

believed, you embraced with so much partiality. Now
for me three features are reflected in the countenance
of your little page. I would like to see the first flourish in my regard, the second moderated concerning
myself, the third diverted from myself but not
diminished in you. These three are: affection, reliance and zeal, a devoted affection, a gracious
reliance, a pious zeal for learning the word of God. I
welcome your affection, but reprove your reliance
and encourage your zeal. Develop your love, withdraw from your reliance on me, direct your zeal
towards another. Briefly, you will discover in me
much less than you presently suppose. Perhaps in
speaking to you I may be proven a barbarian, though
previously my silence made me a philosopher.*

*Pr 17:28. See OB
3:138 and CS 28,
p. 150 and n. 30.*

2. Hence I have reason first to applaud your
zeal for learning, but I decline the task of teaching.
'I am not a physician and in my house there is no
Is 3:7
bread.'* I have not the resources either to cure the
sick or to sustain the needy; but you are neither sick
nor needy, so you require neither my art for your
healing nor my bread for your sustenance. Of course,
you are requesting neither of these but rather some
drops of a more hidden wisdom, drops refined and
mellow, delicious and tasty. Do I appear to you to be
in any way one of the mountains 'which distill
Jl 3:18; Am 9:13
Ps 67:17
Jl 3:18
sweetness'?* Do you suspect that I am one of the
granulated mountains?* Would that I were even a
hillock! Yes, for 'the hills flow with milk'.* Now
though the word 'flow' suggests plenty, still the word
Heb 5:13
'milk' dilutes the value, since milk is for little ones.*
On the contrary, though 'to distill' suggests the limitation of one drop at a time, still the abstract word,
'sweetness', directs us beyond any limitation.[1] Indeed, what else but infinity is expressed by an
unending distillation? The more this unlimited sweetness is free from the limitation of any specific quality, the more it surpasses every limited sweetness.

'The mountains will distill sweetness', says Joel,
Jl 3:18
'and the hills will flow with milk.'* Though milk is
sweet, milk is not sweetness itself. Sweetness is not
only sweet but also sweetness itself, and from sweetness

all things sweet are sweet, however different they be
in kinds of sweetness, however differentiated they be
in degrees of sweetness. Now whatever is sweet by
participation in sweetness, still is not sweet by comparison with sweetness itself. Wherefore sweetness
itself is not qualified, but stands alone in its simplicity, in order that the immensity of its reality may
be linked with the very use of that word.[2] This
reality Isaiah understood as something absolutely
unlimited and profound which he sought to hint at
but was unable to explain:[3] 'Eye has not seen any one
but you, O God, doing such deeds for those who
await you.'*   *Is 64:4*

3. The measureless ocean of divine Majesty ebbs
away from the narrow straits of human hearts and
lips, and from the ocean as if through tiny fissures,
some drops barely trickle back to us. How then can
one emphasize[4] in speech what one cannot reach
through the senses? For even if in some persons the
spirit is spoken of as 'scrutinizing all things, even the
profundities of God',* still the spirit is not spoken of   *1 Co 2:10*
as also penetrating all things. It is beyond either my
leisure or my talent to reach that profound mystery,
to penetrate into that immensity, to immerse my
head in that abyss of hidden light, and with 'locks
drenched with the drops not of night'* but of light,   *Sg 5:2*
'for your dew is the dew of light', says Isaiah,* and   *Is 26:19*
then to sprinkle upon you some sweet drops from
that ocean.

Scripturally, such drops as you request of me are
few in quantity but precious in quality, and your
request is prudent enough. You are aware, of course,
that almost throughout Scripture, preference is shown
for fine goods* rather than course, for sprinkling   *Is 19:9;*
rather than pouring, for the lean rather than the fat.   *Ezk 16:10.*
The law of sacrifices in Leviticus commands that the
blood of animals be poured,* but that the blood of   *Lv 4:6-7;*
birds be sprinkled,† that the altar outside and its   *16:18-19.*
foundations be soaked but that the altar within and   *†Lv 5:7-10*
its veil be either touched lightly or sprinkled seven
times.* We read in Exodus that the manna was fine   **Lv 4:6-7;*
as hoarfrost,† while incense was crushed to   *16:18-19.*
                                                           †Ex 16:14.

50

Gilbert of Hoyland

Ex 30:34-36

powder,* so that what objects you find in Scripture small and minute, you may apply in spiritual and mystical senses.

4. Towards such objects then, your very keen thirst drives you. Good is this thirst. But would that the inebriated, as we read in Deuteronomy, might welcome the thirsty.* He is the inebrated who is called 'full of grace and truth'. He is the inebriated 'from whose fullness we have all received'.* He is at once inebriated and inebriating. He is the toastmaster and the chalice. He is at once the goblet and the wine, wine pure and wine mixed, for wisdom mixed wine in his mixing bowl.* How sparkling you are, O inebriating mixing bowl! Sparkling indeed, radiant in truth, intoxicating with delight! As Paul says, 'in him are hidden all the treasures of the wisdom and knowledge of God'.*

Dt 29:19

Jn 1:14, 16

Pr 9:2

Col 2:13

Good is the mixture where grace blends with truth, knowledge with wisdom, the human with the divine. What belongs to Divinity is pure through and through, where nothing is either composed of parts, or materially subordinate, or formally affected;[5] therefore nothing is diverse, whether treated simultaneously or treated successively, but all things which in us and according to us[6] are separate in name and in notion here convene in one indistinguishable and essential simplicity, a blending which nothing can divide. These then are the really pure and simple attributes of Divinity. But they are blended with human attributes into the unity of the person through the mystery of the Incarnation. In Christ Jesus see how there exist unity of person and Trinity of essence: outwardly his body, inwardly his spirit, in the depths, God. In him both eternity begins and immensity grows! In him might failed and opulence becomes empty![7] In him wisdom knows not and the word is silent! As Isaiah says: 'he will not cry out . . . nor will his voice be heard outside.'*

Is 42:2

Pr 1:20

5. What is the meaning, good Jesus, of what we read in Proverbs: 'Wisdom cries aloud outdoors; in the squares she raises her voice'?* Are you not the Wisdom which came forth 'from the mouth of the

Most High'?* How then does she cry aloud outdoors,   *Si 24:5*
while you do not cry out? Is your voice not heard
outdoors, while she raises hers in the squares? Are
you not the Wisdom of which the apostle speaks:
'Christ has become for us God-given Wisdom'?* Yes   *1 Co 1:30*
indeed, for us he was made Wisdom, for in himself
he was born Wisdom; for us he was made Wisdom or
rather we have been made wise in him, for we have
been created in Christ Jesus not only in good works
but also in feelings of devotion.*   *Eph 2:10*

Still more, we are in him and he is in us. 'My little
children', says Paul, 'with whom I am in labor again,
until Christ be formed in you.'* May he be formed in   *Ga 4:19*
us unto life! May he be formed in us unto truth! 'I
live, now not I', says Paul, 'but Christ lives in me.'*   *1 Co 2:20*
Why could Paul not follow up and say: I am wise, now
not I, but Christ is wise in me? Christ is all things in
me: redemption in me, holiness in me, wisdom in me.[8]
No one savors wisdom in me, O Lord, but yourself.
But you do not savor wisdom in me, unless you savor
yourself, if only I seek in you and savor in you 'the
things which are above'.*[9] 'For their glory is in their *Col 3:2*
shame, whose taste is only for things of earth.'* Let   *Ph 3:19*
him who glories', rightly says Jeremiah, 'glory in this,
that he knows and is acquainted with you.[10] Since then
you are yourself the wisdom of God,* and since you are   *1 Co 1:30*
also wisdom, O God, wisdom in yourself and wisdom
in us, wisdom known and wisdom knowing, wisdom
without and wisdom within, acting without and
inspiring within, why is it, I ask, that 'wisdom cries
aloud outdoors' and you 'do not cry out'? Is your
'voice not heard outdoors' and why does 'wisdom
raise her voice' through the squares? Or do you cry
out through the witness of your work,[11] but are not
yet heard with full understanding? Outdoors you cry
aloud while you teach us through signs that you
exist, and likewise you do not cry out, while in
reality you hide what you are in yourself. Outdoors
you cry aloud by manifesting your good works; and
likewise you do not cry out by hiding your essence.
Happy the ear which can perceive the rich veins of his
whisper! Rich veins they are, for they are life-giving

and hidden and enclosed, and therein whatever
lightly escapes us is more like a whisper or rather like
silence than like a shout.

6. Surpassingly pure is the essence of divine
Majesty,[12] both too hidden and too subtle to be
grasped by a coarse heart. For capturing the divine
essence, every created heart is certainly coarse. Therefore the divine essence must as it were be filled out
and fattened with many a riddle,* and must be
blended with a mixture of shadows and perceptible
actions, and at last be clothed in the garb of the
Incarnation,[13] that the divine essence may be more
easily grasped by us, be more frequently recalled,* be
longer embraced, and be reviewed with greater devotion.* For all things which exist concerning
Jesus* are found subtle if they are explored and useful if they are observed; pleasant on the lips, fruitful
in action, attractive in meditation, though in imitation some things are somewhat hard. Indeed our harsh
exterior affliction itself is bedewed and sprinkled
with his interior grace of heart, so that it may be
roughly smooth, bittersweet, an oasis in a desert, and
as if roasted on the gridiron[14] of the cross may be
still sprayed with the oil of fair hope, as Paul writes:
'rejoicing in hope, being patient in tribulation.'*

Likewise in the Canticle we read: 'I have drunk my
wine with my milk.'* There too the breasts of the
bride are likened to clusters of grapes.* Good is the
cluster pressed in the winepress of the cross, that
the wine of his Passion, full of gall and vinegar, may
be sweetened for us to drink like milk, and that his
wounds may be transformed into breasts. For one
who contemplates, his wounds are breasts; for one on
his daily rounds, they are wine; for one who meditates, they are sweet fruit; for one who imitates him,
they are somewhat bitter. In his breasts, by fore-
tasting, we savor some knowledge of things to come;
in his clusters, by a kind of inebriation, we drug the
uprisings of the flesh. In his breasts, we are engrafted
upon him unto life;* in his clusters, we are buried
with Christ unto death.* For us his wounds are
breasts, as long as through the merit of the Lord's

1 Co 13:12

Ph 2:71
Lm 3:21

2 S 14:14
Lk 24:27

Rm 12:12

Sg 5:1
Sg 7:8

Rm 6:5
Rm 6:4

Passion and his gift of grace, we live in hope of everlasting blessings; for us his wounds are clusters, as
long as through zeal for imitating his Passion, we
separate our spirit from the rebellious feelings of the
flesh. Through his breasts, we are in part reformed
into what we shall be; through his clusters, we are
gradually transformed from what we are until we are
fully conformed to the image in which we were
created,*[15] for 'when he shall appear, we shall be like
him'.†

Rm 8:29; Col 3:10,
2 Co 3:18
†1 Jn 3:2
**1 Co 13:9

7. Now undoubtedly 'we know in part'.** Wherefore until he fully reveals what now for our welfare
he withholds from our understanding, let us review
with devotion either the blessings he conferred or the
woes he endured, contemplating not only the delights
but also the tribulations of the Lord. The time will
come when delight will dethrone all things else and
when 'death will be swallowed up in victory'.* This is
anticipated in the Canticle: 'I shall climb the palm
tree and I shall grasp its fruits.'* Truly one climbs
into the palm tree when 'death, the last enemy, shall
be destroyed'.* The palm is perfect for crowns of
victory. 'Your stature was like a palm tree.'* In faith
we stand fast, in faith we triumph: 'the victory which
conquers the world is our faith.'* Good is the victory
which conquers the world; better the victory which
conquers death. By faith we conquer the world, by
our goal we conquer death.[16] 'You have your fruit
unto sanctification', says the apostle, but you have
'as your goal, life everlasting'.* For this is life everlasting, that we should know the true God.* Therefore our goal is knowledge but our beginning is faith.
In faith we stand fast but at the last we ascend. In
faith we stand ever erect and firm, neither swayed by
the allurements of this world nor broken by its
threats. At the goal we ascend,[17] relieved of burdensome corruptibility, neither needing the service of the
world nor travailing in torment.*

1 Co 15:54

Sg 7:8

1 Co 15:26
Sg 7:7

1 Jn 5:4

Rm 6:22
Jn 17:3

Mt 25:6

8. We should not overlook a distinction in this
passage. Our likeness to a palm tree is mentioned
first and then our assumption into a palm tree; in
the later verse, it is not our likeness which is suggested

but our union which is expressed.[18] As Paul says, 'he

1 Co 6:17

who cleaves to the Lord, is one spirit';* and he is wholly spirit, drenched and soaked in light and delight, losing himself entirely and grasping only the spirit, yet in no way losing himself by this healing affliction, since

Mt 10:39

there 'he who loses his life for my sake, will find it'.* He will find himself for a more blissful reason, neither overreaching nor underreaching himself through vain curiosity, nor going in circles in isolated satisfaction. There the mind will be engaged and absorbed in gazing on God. The mind will enjoy tranquility in utterly perfect freedom from cares. The mind will be irradiated with clearest light and inebriated with sweetness. There will be security without peril, clear light without cloud, sweetness with inexpressible jubilation.

9. But these joys belong to those who, once

Is 28:9

weaned from milk,* have solid food from their

Ps 67:4

entrance into glory.* Those banquets are too heady

Ps 138:6

for us; we are not ready for them.* Therefore, excluded from those banquets, let us return to his breasts, from the banquets of contemplation to the breasts of consolation, to the breasts and to the clusters; from that undiluted and festive simplicity to this blended cup which Wisdom mixed for us in that mixing bowl wherein dwells all the fullness of the

Col 2:9

Divinity.* Of this mixing bowl also the Canticle sings: 'your navel is a well-rounded bowl with no lack

Sg 7:2

of wine.'*[19]

Therefore let the navel of your soul be like a well-rounded mixing bowl, refined and purified and made fine and capacious by the scalpel of penance and discipline, that you may be filled to the brim and inebriated, that the verse may be rightly applied to you: 'your navel is a well-rounded bowl with no lack of wine.' In Ezechiel, the following is spoken to the faithless bride: 'your navel cord was not cut on the

Ezk 16:4

day you were born.'* How many today, on the day of their birth and at the hour of their first conver-

1 Co 7:18; Dt 10:16; Jr 4:14; 1 M 1:16.

sion,[20] have cut their navel cord, but in later days act as if rejoined to the world by their navel;* though beginning in the spirit they are consummated in the

Ga 3:3

flesh!* So let your umbilical cord be not only cut but

trimmed and rounded in unending evenness, that with
all corruption, or rather corpulence, excised, the well
of your spiritual cup, as it were, may overflow with a
continuous stream of living waters and so for the
future you may no longer come here to draw
water.* Farewell.[21]

Jn 4:15

NOTES TO TREATISE 6

1.   BR: *indeterminata dulcedo nos mittit ad immensum*; Mab. and Migne: *nos nutrit.*

2.   *Propterea dulcedo non haec vel illa, sed simpliciter ponitur: ut ex modo vocabuli pendatur immensitas rei.*

3.   G. plays on the words *intimum* and *intimare. Valde infinitum quiddam et intimum intellexit propheta, intimare volens, explicare non valens.* The prophet wishes to intimate the intimate, to hint at profound mysteries.

4.   BR: *excluditur;* Mab. and Migne: *concluditur.*

5.   *ubi nihil est vel partibus compactum, vel materialiter subjectum, vel formaliter affectum.*

6.   BR: *secundum nos;* Mab. and Migne: *per nos.*

7.   BR: *In ipso et aeternitas incipit, et immensitas crescit, et potentia deficit, et opulentia ianescit, et sapienta nescit, et sermo silescit!* Mab. and Migne: *... incoepit ... defuit ... !*

8.   BR: *Omnis in me Christus: in me redemptio, etc.;* Mab. and Migne omit *Christus.*

9.   BR: *Non sapit in me Domine, nisi tu; sed non sapis in me nisi te, si tamen in te quae sursum sunt, quaeram, si quae sursum sunt, sapiam;* Mab. and Migne omit: *quaeram ... sunt.*

10.   Reading *sis* with BR. and Migne.

11.   BR: *An forte clamas per operis evidentiam;* Mab. and Migne: *perperis (i.e. indoctis) evidentiam.*

12.   BR: *Mera vehementer est majestatis illius essentia;* Mab. and Migne write: *Mira ...*

13.   See *Sermones Inediti B. Aelredi Abbatis Rievallensis,* ed. C.H. Talbot, 'Series Scriptorum S. Ordinis Cisterciensis', Vol. 1, pp. 20-23.

14.   For the gridiron, the *craticula* of St. Lawrence, see S 40:6.

15.   BR: *donec ad quam creati sumus imagini plene conformemur;* Mab. and Migne write *imaginem.*

16.   BR: *fine vincimus mortem;* Mab. and Migne: *fide vincimus mortem.*

17.   BR. and Mab. in *fine ascendimus;* Migne: in *fide.*

18.   BR: *in quo* [Sg 7:8] *non similitudo innuitur, sed exprimitur unio.*

19.   G. applies to the Bridegroom what the chorus sings about the bride.

20.   BR: *primae conversionis tempore;* Mab. and Migne: *primo conversionis tempore.*

21.   Only R concludes with *vale.*

TREATISE 7, Part 1
To Abbot Roger[1]

*This treatise has two parts. In the first, Gilbert
confutes the ambitious and the presumptuous.
In the second, commending Roger for talents
suitable to a prelate, he encourages him to persevere in his present position.*

*Part one: 1. Ambition needs no provocation,
2. for it multiplies even in the desert and in
paradise, 3. and even in heaven; an apostrophe
to the prince of pride. 4. Ambition is a rampant
weed, a Sibmah 'exulting in its height'.
5. Worldly ambition must be pruned. 6. The
monastery is not a market. 7. Presumption
likewise needs no advocate.*

YOU ASK, MY DEAR ROGER, that you be
persuaded to continue to hold your present
office and that your fear of the risks of
power be diminished by my recommenda-
tions. Of course, you are ordering me 'to throw oil on
the fire',[2] and on your account alone to enflame with
the bellows of my discourse the ambitions of many
already white hot within. Why do I mention bellows?
'A breath', says Job, 'will kindle the embers' of the
ambitious.* Whomsoever you appoint to plead this   Jb 41:12
case will be thought quite an eloquent orator. He will
easily persuade his audience. On a subject to which
the hearts of all men are almost irrevocably enticed,
we can all add some attractive word of persuasion.
But when one comes to discuss the right thing to do,

57

the orator must labor and pour words into a sieve. In
Scripture, the prophet, with reproach, makes this
very point derisively: 'speak to us what is flattering,
conjure up illusions for us'; speak not 'to us of righ-

Is 30:10

teousness'.*³ Good is this case, which itself plays the
orator's role and, without the aid of art, lures and
melts the hearts of the audience.

Superfluous will this persuasion be; it will achieve
nothing but to turn the ambitious into rogues. It will
remove the light cork of modesty, which seems to be
the only stopper of ambition and, as it were, bottles up
its bubbling action like a surging sea in the bosom of
the heart.⁴ This means to open not a window but
double doors and to apply the blasts of bellows to a
raging furnace. Wanton enough is the shrub of ambition; if the shoots are unpruned, in pleasant soil it
will not so much grow fruit as grow rank.⁵

2. This is the root of bitterness, which sprouting

Heb 12:15

above ground entangles and poisons many.* Nor can
it be eradicated. Why then do you ask me to irrigate
it? In the very hands of those who try to uproot it,

Jb 14:7

the plant revives and multiplies.* Do you request that
I cultivate it by some careful exhortation? Though
the root of this weed is dead in yourself, still it springs
up everywhere around you. If a word of encouragement were sent for your profit, it might well fall
among others to their harm. This plant is as ubiqui-
tous as tamarisks in the desert. I know not where it
blossoms more luxuriantly than in a soil parched and

Is 17:6

brackish.* Examine with me those whose skin is
weather-beaten, whose countenance is pale from fasting, whose toil-worn hands are hard with callouses,

Ps 54:8
Jon 3:8

who keep aloof and remain in solitude,* who are
clad in sackcloth* and whose hide is covered with
rags. See whether in their land of squalor and solitude
the roots of ambition do not spread luxuriantly. In
Scripture, amid the trees of life in paradise and their
joyful foliage, where man did not have the folds of
his garments wherewith to hide his sins, in the best

Gn 2:8–3:23

soil, this cursed weed sprouted.* Yet exceedingly
good was everything God created.

3. But why talk of the garden of Eden?⁶ The

heavenly retreat and the mountain fastness of the
angels, towering aloofly above our human life and
society, proved disastrously fertile in producing the
weed we are discussing. Witness the fall of the angels
who were planning a preposterous uprising. Listen to
the proclamation of their prince: 'Above the stars of
heaven I will plant my throne; I will ascend above
the heights of the clouds; I will be like the Most
High.'* This he continued to proclaim not aloud but   *Is 14:13*
in his heart. Nor did he say 'among the stars and
the clouds' but 'above the stars and above the
heights of the clouds'. Created, alas, among the
morning stars and one of the sons of God, not satisfied with the lot of others, he wanted to inherit
without rival the sanctuary of God and be enthroned
upon 'the mountain of the testament' with the title
of God's heir, for by the testament is conferred the
inheritance of paternal right.

 'I will be enthroned upon the mountain of the
testament.'* Whither does your unrighteous brash-   *Is 14:13*
ness hasten? Why do you usurp what belongs to the
Only-begotten? In person he alone is the Son, the
Only-begotten, the 'image of the invisible God',* the *Col 1:15*
splendor of God's glory and the mirror of God's
essence,* and do you say 'I will be like the Most   *Heb 1:3*
High'? If you will be like him, then you are not now.
But the Only-begotten is forever and wholly alike,
and in this likeness he is not adopted but born, and
the rights of his Father's power he did not receive by
grace but possesses by nature. Firm and immovable
and eternal is the testament of the divine essence and
unchanging its unity, and do you try to purloin for
yourself the mountain of the testament?

 'I will ascend above the stars and above the
heights of the clouds.' Let it be outrage enough for
you in your rash daring to have conceived a discon-
tent with the common lot of others. Here you might
have set a limit to your pride and checked the level of
your climb. 'I will be like the Most High.' Do you soar
above the level of the clouds and compare yourself
with the Most High? Do you prefer yourself to your
fellow creatures and compare yourself with the

Creator?[7] You have broken ranks; you have usurped a rank above you. Therefore you have been cast down from your own rank and your own position and your pride has been plunged to the lowest depths.*

The Lord planted you as a chosen vine, wholly of good seed,* but 'on the day of your planting' you immediately became a wild vine and before harvest lost all your blossoms.* O yes, you blossomed, but the buds were scattered, not kept for harvest, not brought to maturity, but, as the prophet adds, 'a perfect plant budded and withered before being ripe'. Therefore your branches were pruned; sterile and fruitless, your branches were trimmed by the pruning hook of divine justice.* According to the taunt of the same prophet, you yourself, like a useless root,* have been cast from your place of contemplation and glory and your sojourn has been cabined in a milieu of guile, in a milieu of grief. A sprig of pride could spring up in paradise, but it could not last, for 'every plant which my heavenly Father has not planted will be uprooted'.* You wanted to plant yourself in a plot not your own; hence like a hybrid, you did not thrust your roots down deep. 'No one assumes an office but the one summoned by God';* but since you usurped an office not your due, you lost an office already conferred.

4. Alas, how true it is that no place is sheltered, no region immune from this shrub! The root, the root of cupidity, thrives almost everywhere and bears its fruit. It spreads over the face of the earth and, as if mindful of its first place of origin, it spreads particularly among those who bear the image of heaven.* When, O Lord, will you uproot this faithless plant, this alien weed?* When will be fulfilled the words of the prophet: 'The vineyard of Sibmah has become a desert; the lords of the gentiles have cut down its branches'?* Sibmah means 'exulting in one's height'. What else is this than to magnify one's merits? 'I am not', said the Pharisee, 'like the rest of men.'*

Christ taught us otherwise: 'When you have done

Margin refs: Is 14:11-15; Is 5:1-2; Jr 2:21; Is 17:11, 18:5; Is 18:5; Is 14:19; Mt 15:13; Heb 5:4; 1 Co 15:49; Mt 15:13; Is 16:8; Lk 18:11

all things well, say "we are unprofitable servants"."*   *Lk 17:10*
He taught me not to magnify but to minimize the
heights of virtues and good works. So he taught and
so he acted, as it is written, 'Jesus began to act and to
teach'.* For 'though he was in the form of God . . .   *Ac 1:1*
he emptied himself out'.* He became like the rest of   *Ph 2:6-7*
men. He lowered his height, and are you exalting
yours? What then is meant by the vine of Sibmah but
the attitude of a sotted spirit, an attitude which
exalts itself above the attitude of God of which the
apostle speaks, 'have this mind among yourselves[5]
which was in Christ Jesus' and so forth up to the   *Ph 2:5*
words: 'he emptied himself out';[8] likewise 'do not
be haughty but associate with the lowly'.* Now hear   *Rm 12:16*
of an attitude of overweening wisdom, wisdom
exalting itself and vanishing like smoke in its own
subtlety: "'I will punish," says the Lord, "the arrogant boasting of the King of Assyria and his haughty
pride. For he said, 'by the strength of my hand I have
done it and by my wisdom, for I have understand-
ing","* and elsewhere, 'Is not this the great Babylon   *Is 10:10, 12-13*
which I built'?*   *Dn 4:27*

5. You have heard of this attitude, this boastful
attitude vaunting itself; you have understood the
meaning of the vine of Sibmah, the vine which I wish
were sterile with no one to cultivate it! Listen now to
the apostle; listen to the teacher and doctor of the
gentiles: indeed 'the lords of the nations have cut
down its branches'.* Hear how Paul prunes the   *Is 16:8*
tendrils of Sibmah: 'Do not become proud but stand   **Rm 11:20*
in awe',* and 'command the rich not to be proud'.†   *†1 Tm 6:17*
The branches they pruned, he said, the root they
could not prune; they cut down what rose above
ground, what lay concealed they could not cut. The
root itself is cupidity; the branches are honor and
exaltation. Concupiscence, as it were, is the root and
anxieties the branches. Note how imaginatively Isaiah
writes. We suppose there are pleasures in high posi-
tions, but the prophet calls these high branches
scourges. For surely they scourge and flay the spirit
and scar a tender affection devoted to Christ.
Unhappy surely is he who in the active life has

become so hardened that he feels these cares not
as scourges but as pleasures. 'They have scourged me'
and I felt it not.*

'The vineyard of Sibmah has become abandoned.'*
It was really abandoned by our Fathers who knew
how to cultivate not property but piety, how to
attend not to their goods but to their good life. 'Alas
for the times, alas for the customs!'* Now almost all
persons develop in themselves a worldly attitude.
They rejoice to possess the spirit of this world, 'the
wisdom of this world which is folly in the sight of
God',* for this spirit knows not, and knows not how
to be subject to, the law of God. Indeed, cupidity
cannot be the servant of charity. Cupidity knows
not how 'to bear others' burdens',* but rather knows
how to lay its burdens upon others. The greedy are
the sharpest beggars but the most niggardly bursars,
so that in them Saul surely seems to have been born
of Cis.* For as Cis means Harsh,[9] so Saul means
Petition, so from harshness beggary is born,[10] from
greed, avarice, and from miserliness, importunity.
Harsh is the north wind for by it the waters are
frozen; gentle is the south wind for at its breath flow
the perfumes of mercy and charity.* A harsh father is
Cis, but gentle is he of whom Jesus Christ says: 'that
you may be the sons of your Father, who makes his
sun rise over the good and the evil.'*

6. What contradictory attitudes are manifest in
those who esteem possessions too highly, when on the
one hand they engage in and take part in good works,
and when on the other hand they barter and traffic
in merchandise. With what an astute double standard
they draw from their store of yarns a pennyworth or
a pound's-worth.* They seem to have been born and
bred not in a monastery but in a market. While in
business experience they are healthy, in their experience of Christ they are quite thin, emaciated and
scrawny. So the prophet asks: 'And to whom has the
arm of the Lord been revealed? For he grew up before
him like a young plant and like a root out of parched
soil.'* In them is nothing sturdy and tall; all is feeble
and stunted. Beyond the root of simple faith, they

have scarcely any experience of a higher and divine wisdom. Paul speaks of 'bearing fruit in every good work and increasing in the knowledge of God'.* On the contrary, not content with their own lack of skill, they contemn the knowledge of others, and in their invidious estimate of others they interpret the pursuit of wisdom as obtuseness, and they blacken with the mark of folly or of vainglory what is cautious subtlety, while personally they labor for the food which perishes and does not remain unto eternal life.*

Col 1:10

Jn 6:27

Whenever they return home from the fields, they are angry at the music and dancing and grunt like swine at the joy of their younger brother.* This is a fine young brother of whom the apostle says: 'put on the new man who has been created according to God',* and of whom likewise Paul says: 'if there be in Christ any new creature, the old things have passed away, all things are made new'.* Imprudent was the elder brother, for he knew the fatigue without knowing the joy. He is rightly called elder, for he perseveres in the old way and frets about what concerns the old man. He takes care of the flesh, if not in riotous living, at least in longing for it, and at least in his preoccupation for acquiring abundant wealth if not for squandering it.

Lk 15:25-32

Eph 4:24

2 Co 5:17

Those who yearn to become not wanton but wealthy, says the apostle, fall into many senseless and harmful desires.* There the desire is senseless and harmful, where one feels the pinch of necessity but goes to extremes in its cure. A cursed thirst is the lust for wealth.[11] Greed then is a parched soil from which the root of piety and faith puts forth a weak and creeping vine, which with difficulty raises its head but a little above the ground. The root of faith, according to Scripture, cannot but languish where worldly desires spread riotously and where their worthless offshoots luxuriate.

1 Tm 6:9

Happy the man who has uprooted these desires from his soul. Happy the man in whom the vineyard of Sibmah is left uncultivated, the vineyard, of course, which exalts its height, the height of its

'life-style' to the stature of prelacy. For Sibmah also
means a kind of conversion or change of 'life-style';
indeed, those who seem to have approached somewhat the beginnings of a conversion, these I am sure,
like the topmost branches, are more swayed by the
wind of ambition. This plant grows wild enough by
itself; it sprouts on its own where it is not sown, and
shoots up while it is being cut down. Therefore it
needs not planting but pruning, not cultivating
but cutting.

7. What I have said should now suffice to show
how inexpedient for others would be my composi-
tion of the exhortation you request. But because
I have already spoken at some length against ambition, it is not fitting to be altogether silent about
presumption. I have partly checked those who are
swept aloft by their own cupidity; let me disconcert
or rather warn those also who, under the pretext of
obligation to their brothers, claim that they are
bound to remain in office. For them, and laudably of
course, business is burdensome and contemplation a
delight. But likewise[12] they are moved by an empty
or rather an arrogant and pompous fear, lest if they
relinquish the post of master, there may be no one
on whom they might justifiably confer the honor.
They are wise in their own eyes and prudent in their
own presence.* Not content with this position of
vanity, with Elijah they seem to be abandoned and
left to themselves alone.* Each considers himself a
kind of Moses but a better than Moses, for while
Moses said, 'If you please, Lord, send someone
else',* they say: 'there is no other, Lord, whom
you may send'.

'A man will seize his brother', said Isaiah, 'in the
house of his father', saying 'You have a mantle, you
shall be our leader.'* What did the other reply? 'I am
not a physician and in my house there is neither
bread nor a mantle. Do not make me a leader.'* His
reply might be worded as follows: 'it is not sufficient
for me to have a mantle, unless it be ample enough
to be shared with others.' To become a prince, it is
not enough to have the mantle of discipline, the

Rm 11:25; 12:16

1 K 18:22; 19:10.

Ex 4:13

Is 3:6

Is 3:7

mantle of external deportment and observance, to
keep well-ordered the outer man, whom, as it were,
I make use of as a mantle in every act and gesture, for
that is not sufficient for myself and much less sufficient for others. What is praised in me is but a trifle;
greater gifts must be sought. It is trivial that I am
personally in good health, unless I can also heal
others. Therefore as Isaiah records: 'Do not make me
a leader; I am not a physician and in my house there
is neither bread nor a mantle.' While Isaiah said, 'I am
not a physician', our presumptuous man says, 'I am
the only physician'. So wherever the latter casts his
eye, he sees only either inexperience or impurity or
guile or idleness, so that he alone is the prudent and
faithful servant.* Consequently, in his own con-   *Mt 24:45*
science he may say: 'do not appoint another your
leader, lest perchance a child be given as your
prince and effeminate persons be your lords.'*   *Is 3:4*

Such men do not need the inducement you
require of me. For though they may not be delighted
by their superior rank, still they console themselves
with the results of their labors; their fondness for
peace and contemplation makes them shy away from
work, while on the other hand they are not shy about
the success of their activities. Here I am reining in my
galloping discourse, for you are already being dragged
off to other concerns, or rather as often happens, you
are distraught by many concerns.*   *Lk 10:41*

NOTES ON TREATISE 7, Part 1, to Abbot Roger

1.   In answer to a request not necessarily by letter, from Abbot Roger G. writes twice, the first and second parts of Treatise 7. Roger was Abbot of Byland, 1142–1192. See Mikkers, 273 and n. 93, and Talbot, 221. If we remove the first two sentences of Part 1, like a detachable dedication to Roger, one sentence of transition at the beginning of paragraph 7, and the final sentence which lacks the usual word of farewell, we then have a treatise on ambition and presumption without thought of Roger.

2.   Horace, *Sermones*, 2:3:321, *Adde poemata nunc, hoc est, oleum adde camino.* In the few personal lines to Roger, Gilbert had no need to attribute to Horace two words of what must have become a very common proverb. Did G. intend Roger to read Horace's Satire to see how absurd the poet considers ambition? According to Horace, all but the wise are absurd, but especially the ambitious; indeed Horace allows himself to be considered no less absurd: a puny midget, who puffs himself up like a frog and writes poems, indeed *sermones*. If G. were to contribute to the absurdity by writing a *sermo* to encourage the ambitious and presumptuous, that would indeed be to add fuel to the fire.

3.   BR: *propheta exprobrando subsannat;* Mab. and Migne, *se exprobrando.*

4.   Perhaps a reference to Horace, *Sermones*, 2:5:98.

5.   BR: *et tamquam in laeta non tam fructificat, quam luxuriat humo.* Mab. and Migne read *homo.*

6.   B: *Sed quid ego de paradiso retexeo?* R: *retexio;* Mab. and Migne: *retexo.*

7.   BR: *concreatis praefers,* rather than *praes.*

8.   Reading *vobis* for *nobis.* BR: *usque (ad) semetipsum exinanivit, et item, non alta sapientes . . . ;* omitted by Mab. and Migne.

9.   The etymology becomes a memorable satire on miserly Cistercian bursars, for in them Cistercians become Harshtercians.

10.   BR: *de duro petitio;* omitted by Mab. and Migne.

11.   *Mala sitis, ardor habendi.* See Vergil, *Aeneid*, 3:57, *auri sacra fames,* and Horace, Ep. 1:18:23, *quem tenet argenti sitis importuna famesque.*

12.   BR: *sed item;* Mab. and Migne: *sed tamen.*

TREATISE 7, Part 2
To Abbot Roger

Gilbert commends Abbot Roger as one endowed with qualities suitable for a prelate and bids him to continue in office; however, he first exposes for Roger the difficulties and burdens of office. 1. After Gilbert wrote the first part of this treatise, he encountered some storm making it difficult to reconcile administration and contemplation, making him unlike Jacob who reconciled Leah and Rachel. 2. An abbot must provide the milk of babes despite the opposition of princes. 3. Roger must not resign his mantle, as Joseph and David and Gilbert were tempted to do. 4. All the evidence tells against his resignation; the onus of office is not substantially different from the early days but is more burdensome. 5. His minor officials are his support and his consolation. 6. The skill and grace required in an abbot to govern well four classes of religious are presented in an apostrophe to Roger's monastic city. 7. The qualities an abbot should have, in action and contemplation, for the good of his flock, in virtue and prudence. 8. An abbot must be not a Laban or a Rachel but a Jacob. 9. The vanity of a Laban, the weakness of a Rachel, must yield to the strength of a Jacob. 10. The vanities of a swashbuckling Thraso, a parasitical Gnatho, of one who imagines himself a Cato in chapter, a Cicero in court, a Virgil among the poets, are no substitute for the prudence and strength of a Jacob. 11. G. omits further comparison with the virtues of Jacob; Roger must not resign, both for his own good and for the good of the Church.

I N A PREVIOUS DISCOURSE, I took pains to check the presumptuous along with the ambitious but in this I wish to encourage those who are more than duly apprehensive. Good Lord, what a distance separates this from the previous discourse! What a raging tempest of worldly calumnies dashed the quill from my fingers and swept my hand and my mind alike far from their subject matter![1] Yes, 'I launched upon the depths of the sea

Ps 68:3
and the tempest overwhelmed me'.* When, O good
Ps 54:9; Lk 8:24
Jesus, will you save me from the storm?* Or if not from the storm, at least from my own craven spirit? On all sides the tempest rises and intensifies, while I remain pusillanimous and dispirited. Nor with the calm breeze of my reflections can I counteract the onslaught of the whirlwind[2] and the rage of the gales. I cannot blend spiritual joy and civil lawsuits in the one mixing bowl of my heart.

'Narrow is the couch', as Isaiah says, 'so that one of the two must tumble out and a scanty mantle cannot cover both.'* The holy patriarch Jacob em-
Is 28:20
braced his wives by turns, and since he could not embrace both at once, under constraint he used to quit the chamber of Leah for the marital rights of Rachel.[3] By his own reckoning he would obviously have been happy could he have yielded unreservedly
Gn 29:31
to the possession of Rachel alone.* Overwhelmed with frequent obloquy, my spirit might have become callous and by custom grown hardened to adversity. Frequently indeed a thick skin is drawn over my spirit and it becomes callous to violent attacks. Ah, how often do I consider myself steadfast in enduring the onslaughts of the world! Not that I would now prefer to take shelter and, as Isaiah says, to hide myself from the wind and seek cover from the
Is 32:2
tempest.* But if ever my mind begins to dally in the soft embraces of Rachel, I slip back straightway into

my wonted tenderness and become unskilled and
unaccustomed to the endurance of tribulations. With
Isaiah, I find no better alternative than to dodge the
arrows of insult by stepping down to a humbler
position,[4] and from the menace of my own fear
to fly to the clefts of the cliffs.*   *Is 2:21; 7:19*

2. Alas for those with child and for those who
give suck especially in these days!* Blessed indeed   *Mt 15:19*
are 'the breasts which have not given suck';* for one   *Lk 23:29*
who needs milk as nourishment is an infant whose
spirit is too feeble to bear scarcity and 'the plunder
of his possessions'.* For such weak spirits, another   *Heb 10:34*
must appear in court,[5] attend councils, coax rulers,
thwart rustlers, refute prosecutors, pay judges' fees,
reconcile with the world those whose conversation,
like Paul's, has been in heaven.* There were times   *Ph 3:20*
when we used to drink the milk of the nations and be
nourished at the breasts of kings;* and see, now they   *Is 60:16.cf. S 31:3.*
importunately demand a recompense for what we
imbibed perhaps a little too freely. While nations and
kings squeeze barren breasts too violently, they draw
blood with the milk of their temporal subjects,* not   *Pr 30:33*
this blood of the flesh but blood of the soul, that
vital interior blood which runs in the veins of the
spirit, that blood of which the prophet sings: 'Bless
the Lord, O my soul; and all that is within me bless
his holy name.'* That blood, I insist, they siphon and   *Ps 103:1*
drink, and so cause excessive anguish. Alas, how our
world is turned upside down! In warfare is our peace,
in peace our warfare. 'In peace is bitterness most
bitter',* especially for us who are obliged to engage   *Is 38:17*
in worldly business, whom an Egyptian wife[6] keeps
imprisoned in the mantle of a prelate and bound
by the obligation of providing for others,* for we are   *Gn 39:6-23*
still subjects in the flesh, to whom the apostle says:
'Let every person be subject to the governing
authorities.'* Yet 'the spiritual man judges all things   *Rm 13:1*
and is himself to be judged by no one'.*   *1 Co 2:15*

3. But why these lamentations? Is it to have you
abandon to the hand of an Egyptian wife the mantle
of office you accepted? You may abandon it, I say,
and with Joseph escape from it as something fraught

with peril.* Or with David you may lay it aside as a
burden. That David might join in the dance unimpeded, he frequently[7] disrobed and shed the mantle
which covered him.* Heavy enough for the body is its
own slothfulness and its own weight is burden
aplenty. Have I any wish to strip you of the cloak of
office you accepted? That is far from my intention.
I have undertaken to persuade you not to cast aside
the pastoral charge which you have duly undertaken
and aptly administer. For though you undertook
this office with little inclination, you are always
inclined to retire either from fear of danger or in
search of peace. A man so disposed, however, was
bound to have misgivings, lest while his mind as it
were wavered in the balance, some carelessness might
infiltrate into his administration. But how shall I
attempt to persuade you of what now I have almost
dissuaded myself? The basis of argument is much different for each of us; in short, as an unskilled artisan
I must toil in sweat and tears with difficult material,
while all things run to enlist under you at your nod
and promptly follow your advice.

4.   You cannot disguise what the real evidence
proclaims. Your material resources, should you make
an inventory, you would find extensive and well
established; herein no scarcity embarasses you, no
inequities disturb you. The site of your monastery is
secluded, cultivated, irrigated, and fruitful. Your
wooded valley in springtime so echoes with the sweet
melodies of songsters that it could charm a dead
spirit back to life, dissipate the distaste of a delicate
soul, and soften the hard-headedness of a mind devoid
of devotion.[8] These signs, in scriptural terms, either
display for you the harbingers of future beatitude or
manifest some vestige of the pristine beatitude which
our unfallen human nature was allotted amid the
beauties of paradise. But to merits of this kind, you
will say, no moral value is attached. This I cannot
deny, since they are only means; yet as they are negli-
gible only in acquiring merit, so they are no small
blessing in contributing to peace of mind.

Herein we do not much disagree with the ancients,

who transmitted to us their experience of religious
life, for their authority is more ancient and their
purity more perfect; we do not disagree, I say, to
such an extent that what they considered impediments to perfection, we proclaim the means of virtue.
They defined fertile and beautiful sites as obstacles
to a braver spirit; we call them an encouragement for
a weaker spirit and for one who cannot yet say: 'My
soul refuses to be comforted; I remember my God
and I am filled with joy',* and 'I can do all things in   *Ps 76:3-4*
him who strengthens me', Christ.* The ancient   *Ph 3:14. See*
fathers sought out thorny and desert regions to have   *Miquel 150.*
an opportunity to practise abstinence and to avoid
distracting the soul with worrisome occupations.
They applied themselves more diligently to manual
labor not only to win freedom of heart but also to
avoid the inconstant frivolity of a nomad and the
dishonesty of a beggar.* More in handicraft than in   *See Lam 1 75,*
agriculture, they spent their lives relieving the con-   *nn. 27, 29.*
straints of impoverishment, not to say of destitution,
by a wealth of contemplation, for they were content
with bare subsistence that they might either chastise
the body or refresh the mind. Indeed with anxiety
and distress the heart is wearied and distracted, if it is
overwhelmed with the obligation of providing abundant supplies for an extended time.

They were servants of their era, let us be servants
of ours.* Our age, fallen into decline, has introduced   *See Lam 196,*
other ways. We must now provide[9] abundance for   *n. 171.*
permanent residents and delicacies for transients. Nor
by transients do I mean lay folk; for why should I
pass judgement on outsiders?[10] Among them, how-   *1 Co 5:12*
ever, the usual moderation may not be observed, for
they can scarcely tolerate rationing where they
imagine the existence of supplies of all kinds. But
why should I advert to those whose god is their
belly?* Why, the very ones who profess and preach   *Ph 3:19*
abstinence, the very primates of the Order, how
finicky they are in the houses of others! What an eye
they have for banquets of rare foods prepared for a
gourmet!* How they wrinkle their foreheads, turn up   *Horace*, Odes,
their noses, and look askance, if anything is served[11]   *3:1:18-19.*

Horace, Satires,
2:2:126; Epistles,
1:5:23.

with less taste and less festivity!*

5. But since such are the facts of life, thanks to
the degradation of our time, your hand can cope with
both, for it can handle at once ostentation and need,
both the necessities of the poor and the vanity of
the rich. Is there a further consideration? What kind
of officials have you as colleagues? How vigorous are
they and how diligent? How solicitous and, a capital
point, how loyal? Thanks to them, it is almost superfluous that even a summary of the administration of
temporal affairs be referred to you. For practically no
other destination do you depart from the tabernacle

Lv 10:7 of the Lord.* Though your officials are occasionally
seen in councils, in conventions, at the entrances of
the squares where but recently 'the stones of the

Lm 4:1 sanctuary were scattered',* you are seen most infre-
quently. Herein is valid evidence that disturbance is
not pleasant to you, and that there is no need for
you to make a public appearance. Neither your hand,

Mt 8:8-9 nor your eye, nor your foot is a scandal to you.*
Were it otherwise, one would have to sever and
remove, however painfully, the member from the
head rather than the head from the body. So in your
officials you have no pretext for relinquishing office.

Perhaps I may seem insulting to you[12] and to
adduce consolations too soft and unworthy of a
scholarly spirit practised in virtue. But what if impoverishment should strike? if insults? if calumnies?
if dire want in the house, nay more in the community, and plunder on top of dire want? if on your
flank should break the perilous revolt of false

2 Co 2:11 brethren?* Then should a brave and loyal man
surrender? Should he retreat from his position?
Should he abandon the community contrary to
Paul's warning?* On the contrary, the more perilous

Heb 10:25 the crisis impending, so much the more should the
community be guarded and defended. Like Paul, you
have already run through almost all of these forms of
trials;[13] when you have run over rocky roads, will

Ps 72:3 your footsteps falter on the level?* When you have
learned to suffer want, will you not know how to
live in plenty? Having kept fast with Paul, will you

not know how with Paul to keep festival?*[14] Rather,   *Ph 4:12*
in good fortune and ill, you have given proof of a
spirit well formed,[15] without hesitation following a
way of life once accepted, as if following the thread
of an uninterrupted career. On the contrary, not
mentioning your braver deeds, I preferred[16] to travel
a middle road and to recall facts which would relieve
you of reasons for anxiety, although[17] we have
always heard that in gravest impoverishment you
were ever calm, relying more on faith and manual
labor than on shameful beggary or degrading barter.

6. But since I have spoken at length about the
effortlessness of administration there, it follows that
I should not overlook your skill in administration.
Should I call it skill, or rather grace? I mean both skill
and grace. Material however suitable will be awkward
in the hands of an unskilled craftsman; his skill will
be either harmful or helpless in the absence of guid-
ing grace, for unless the Lord build the house, the
builders labor in vain.* The talents conferred on you,   *Ps 126:1*
perhaps you will camouflage; but what humility
camouflages, achievement heralds. Why should I now
make an inventory of the farmlands, the resources,
the utensils, the clothing, the buildings, the men,
an inventory of all that emerged and thrived in your
hands, of all that pertains to external possessions or
to religious life? From the time the Lord harnessed
you to plough in his place and after him to leave in
furrows the unbroken soil of the valleys, what an
abundant harvest of devout souls has sprung up!
How rich in grain are your valleys, grain of which the
prophet speaks: 'What is its wealth or what is its
beauty but the grain of chosen young men and the
wine to make maidens flourish.'* An administrator   *Zc 9:17*
without grace you cannot be, because through your
effort the crop has so grown in glory. Obviously
glorious deeds have been done in your city,* but   *Ps 86:3; Ws 3:15.*
through your hands. In exchange for a city aban-
doned and held in contempt without a soul to visit
her, see how she has been founded for the admira-
tion of the centuries,* though once she was toppled   *Is 60:15*
by   impoverishment   'and   tempest   blast,   and

left inconsolable'.*

See, O city, how 'your stones have been laid row on row and how you have been founded on sapphires'.* If your foundation is upon sapphires, how high is your citadel? Well, you were founded on sapphires. The foundation means humility and the sapphire purity, humility of conscience and purity of doctrine, the humility of your way of life and the purity of your contemplation. You were founded, let me repeat, on sapphires. Therefore it is said: 'Your Nazarenes were purer than snow, whiter than milk, more ruddy than coral, more beautiful than sapphire.'* In the snow, they are contrite; in milk, nourished; in coral, strengthened; in sapphire, purified. In snow, they are penitents; in milk, innocents; in coral, lovers; and in sapphire, contemplatives. Again, in the snow they are mortified, in the milk vivified, in the coral enkindled, in the sapphire enlightened. And all this, O city, because you were founded upon sapphire.

But you personally fulfil the function of a foundation, by your example and by your providence. You show yourself sapphire, by your word and your wisdom. In the words of the Canticle, 'your voice is mellow and handsome your countenance',* the voice of your word and the countenance of your example, the voice of your preaching and the countenance of your daily life. Therefore the young maidens love you exceedingly.* But if you depart, to whom else will they be able to say, show us your countenance, 'let your voice sound in our ears'?* On whose example will they be able to rely? Whose advice will they heed? Who is your peer in summoning, proclaiming, and explaining the Order?[18] Who can lay another foundation, O Abbot Roger, to match the foundation you have already laid?* 'Your sons are like vigorous new plants; . . . your daughters are carved in marble, caryatids dressed for a temple; your barns are full; your sheep prolific, multiplying as they leave the sheepfold.'* How shall we fail to call a man happy and holy when these are his possessions? How shall we fail to call the Lord his God, when such

Margin references:

Is 54:11

Is 54:11

Lm 4:7

Sg 2:14

Sg 1:2

Sg 1:4

1 Co 3:11

Ps 143:12-13

are his riches?* *Ps 143:15*

7. These are signs which give clear evidence that the Lord has 'chosen you and not cast you off' in your ministry.* These prompt you to hold what you hold with so much success. When your awareness of so many good works consoles you, why will you require my persuasion? The virtues of your own house persuade you to hold office, lest another welcome your position. The diligence of your house will persuade you as well as the idleness of another. Your auspicious success will persuade you as well as your inauspicious successor. Well do I know your spirit, your interests, your character, whether conferred by nature or acquired by practice. I know how readily you would be relieved of this burden, if another could be found on whom you might worthily confer it. Your feelings and your reason are at odds, your feeling of humility and your reasonable account of success. You would consider it pleasant to have time for yourself and for God. But it is likewise a serious matter to retire and leave your post vacant. Vacant assuredly, for who will fill it? *Is 41:9*

Who will give us another Jacob, who with only his staff crossed the Jordan and now recrosses the river with many companies?* Who, I may ask, will prepare us a person who knows how to shuttle with discretion between Leah and Rachel, balancing the ugliness of the former with her fertility, and cloaking the sterility of the latter with the charm of her beautiful form?* There is no one like you, so caught up in contemplations without becoming remiss in good works; for despite the preoccupations of wisdom, you do not neglect the occupations of provident government. Under the guise of service, you do not transgress the rights of contemplation; you do not so commend Leah as to condemn or at least contemn Rachel, for to you is neither Leah sterile nor Rachel ugly. There is no other, who day and night is so scorched by heat and by cold* in his anxiety to avert harm from his flock, and is in still greater anxiety, if his flock has suffered some harm, to make reparation at his own cost, to make reparation by tears, to make *Gn 32:10*

Gn 29

Gn 31:40

reparation, by fasting, compassion, prayer, and exhortation. Who else in his revenues has no truck with the false gods of greed? Who else, though he discover them in his retinue, does not discover them in his religion? Who else, though he discover them among the baggage, does not discover them among the sacred vessels? Who else is the servant of piety and not of pennies and pounds, as Scripture notes: 'all things are subservient to money'.* Paul also notes that 'greed is the service of idols'.*

Qo 10:19
Col 3:5

There is no other, who neither courts greed in his business dealings nor contemplates idols of bodily shapes in his contemplation of eternal forms, but within and without lets his intention and his insight be pure and prudent. You will see many a man of tender affection toward God, of a noble countenance, in appearance as pure and beautiful as Rachel either in deportment or in thought, but still of a weak and effeminate purpose, needing guidance under the firm judgement of another Jacob. Indeed, when Rachel did not consult Jacob about her conduct, she secretly carried off the false gods of her father Laban.* She carried off, I repeat, the false gods of Laban, carried off some symbols of worldly honor, of worldly charm, or worldly whiteness, for Laban means Whitening.

Gn 31:19

8. Now do they not seem to you to have carried off on their journey some false gods of Laban and some symbols of worldly vanity, who overlay religious life with some superfluous charms? who modify the rules of the ancient observance with novel dispensations[19] and dilute their wine with water? who exchange the toilsome vineyard of the Fathers for easier truck gardens,* and the ruggedness of monks for the delicacies of the world? For just as Paul says: their god is their belly,* similarly it can be said: their god is vanity, their god is a hypocritical humanity, their god is scurrility,[20] and so on through every species of worldly whitewash and distraction. How much I dread lest in returning from Mesopotamia we should import with us many similar false gods of Syria, not in a saddlebag but on a standard, not without Jacob's knowledge but with his full consent. Some of her father's idols which Rachel

1 K 21:2;
Rm 14:2

Ph 3:19

avidly filched, she cautiously concealed because she
cherished them with a woman's tender affection,
offering as a pretext for hiding them the infirmity of
a woman.* What were treated with honor by Laban   Gn 31:35
and with affection by Rachel, were discovered with
horror by Jacob. But what Laban adored and Rachel
concealed, Jacob did not know.* So what Laban   Gn 31:34, 32
worshipped openly and Rachel concealed for a time
at her own risk, Jacob buried forever. 'He buried', let
me quote, 'and interred the strange gods beneath a
terebinth',* beneath the tree of faith as a memorial of   Gn 35:4
empty ambition and worldly pomp.

9. To the faithful soul after temptation, Isaiah
speaks in a promise: 'it will remain in evidence like
the terebinth and like the oak which spreads its
branches',* and again in Genesis, 'under the tere-   Is 6:13
binth which is beyond the city of Shechem'.*   Gn 35:4
Shechem means shoulders. Good are those shoulders
of which it is said, 'the pinions of its back are
covered with the sheen of gold'.* Good is the   Ps 67:14
shoulder of Christ Jesus, 'for power was laid upon his
shoulder'.* Beyond this city of Shechem was placed   Is 9:6
the terebinth; it was planted in the passion and faith
of Christ. Happy the one who in this tree triumphs
over all principalities and powers,* and beneath its Col 2:15
root inters collectively every idol of vanity, for their
idol is but 'wind and the void'.* Hence the pomp of   Is 41:29
the world is rightly compared to idols. Such a victory
is not characteristic of an infirm, effeminate, and
fragile soul, but rather characteristic of a wrestler
who throws his adversary.* So victory does not   Gn 32:24-26
belong to Rachel but to Jacob, and though there is
many a Rachel there is not many a Jacob.* Rare is   1 Co 4:15
the man who knows how to supplant Esau, to cozen
Laban, to inter Laban's deities; I mean who knows
how to inter and bury the old man,* the image of the Eph 4:22
world, conformity to the times, so as to be 'conformed to this world' no longer but 'reformed in the
newness' of a loving piety.* Such a man has been   Rm 12:2
'sown once and for all in the likeness of the death of
Christ' that simultaneously he may 'be made in the
likeness of the resurrection of Christ'.* This is   Rm 6:5-6

indeed to condemn, to destroy, to bury the idols of
Laban, if the image we bear of the old man and
earthly man be despatched into hiding and if the
image of the new and heavenly man be displayed like
the terebinth.

10. These careful distinctions I make on purpose,
lest perhaps man be discharged and woman put in
charge, lest the strong be occupied with contemplation and the weak be preoccupied with the active life,
lest Jacob retire and Rachel succeed. But your new
little brood who in recent times have begun to emerge,
shapely, well-groomed and washed white, are some
progeny of Laban who is called Whitened, but otherwise are no match for the modesty of Rachel. For the
appearance of worldly vanity she hid and concealed
under the pretext of womanly weakness, but their
traffic in worldliness and superfluity, men of the new
brood overlay and cloak with the coloring of ur-
banity; they do not 'purge out the old leaven'* but
rather show off as merrymakers with imported dishes
of food and are thought worthy of praise for the
bountiful display of their banquets.

1 Co 5:7

It would be a tedious performance if I should
wish to mention even cursorily their many species of
vanity and to compose a list of their acts of ostentation. Each of these characters you will recognize as a
[swashbuckling] Thraso in gesture, an innkeeper in
merrymaking, a [parasitical] Gnatho in a brawl.[21]
Each wishes to appear as a Cato in chapter, a Cicero
in court, a Virgil among the poets. Finally, in familiar
conversation they are mummers but not monks. Their
discourse overflows with salty witticisms yet not as
the apostle advises: 'let your speech always be gracious, seasoned with salt';* but as the Lord warns:
'but if your salt become insipid and lose its savor,
wherewith will it be salted'?*

Col 4:6

Mt 5:13

11. Thanks first to such characters, it seems to
me that you should be unhesitatingly retained in
office and not changed, but thanks secondly to others,
if there be any, among whom linger traces of what
men call our ancient rustic behavior, lest if we toss
away the good salt, we may gather salt without savor

and suffer what Isaiah threatened: 'harvests will be
destroyed in drought and women will come to
instruct them'.* I could colorfully apply to you each   *Is 27:11*
and every virtue of the Patriarch and through the
person of Jacob continue my comparison in extend-
ing my recommendation. But I refrain, lest in blessing
my friend at the top of my voice, I should be
likened to someone pronouncing a curse. Though
sometimes you weigh these blessings in private, still
unless I thoroughly misread you, you do not attribute them to yourself.

Let these remarks suffice then, not only on the
ease of administration and the abundance of graces,
but also on the scarcity of suitable successors. What
else can one say, if you can manage and are
splendidly administering the office entrusted to you,
and if I know not whether any of the younger men
could manage as well? Now I see no further stumbling blocks, unless perhaps you promise yourself a
more abundant grace of merits in a lower rank; yes,
for yourself but not for others, for yourself but not
for the Church of Christ, and therefore not for
yourself either; for in you alone, Christ cannot compensate for what he loses in many others. But if it
seem worth while, let us reserve this topic for another
occasion; for now we have buried our charmer[22] and
our discourse must yield to our psalms.[23]

NOTES ON TREATISE 7, Part 2

1.   The storm might have broken over G.'s head as a result of the first part of this treatise; G. mentions however, lawsuits, the opposition of princes and other difficulties for the administrator.

2.   R: *aura leni;* B: *auralem;* Mab. and Migne: *aura.*

3.   BR. and Migne: *ab unius thalamis in alterius jura difficile transibat;* Mab. *thalami.* Rachel became a symbol of the contemplative, Leah of the active life.

4.   Gilbert returns to thoughts of his resignation below, par. 3.

5.   BR: *exsequenda sunt jurgia;* Mab. and Migne: *exercenda.*

6.   In allusion to Potiphar's wife and the patriarch Joseph.

7.   BR: *frequentem;* Mab. and Migne: *frequenter.*

8.   See Jean-de-la-Croix Bouton, *Fiches Cisterciennes, I: Histoire de l'Ordre de Cîteaux,* 139; Lam 10, n. 34.

9.   BR. and Migne: *providenda;* Mab: *providentia.*

10.   See Bouton, *Fiches Cisterciennes,* I:140.

11.   BR: *apponitur;* Mab. and Migne: *apponatur.*

12.   BR: *Forte injuriosus tibi videar;* Mab. and Migne omit *tibi.*

13.   BR: *temptamentorum genera;* Mab. and Migne: *testamentorum genera.*

14.   BR: *cum Paulo esuriens, sed cum Paulo saturari nesciens?*

15.   Mab. and Migne: *utroque in genere bene instituti animi documenta praebuisti;* BR: *bene instituisti.*

16.   Adding *volui* with Mab. See Lam 174, n. 25.

17.   BR: *quamvis altissima in paupertate;* Mab. and Migne: *cum altissima . . .*

18.   G. may refer to the letter of Roger written to G., *Lac Parvulorum* below.

19.   BR: *quique antiquae observantiae regulas novellis dispensationibus temperent;* Mab.: *qui . . . disputationibus temperent;* Migne.: *qui . . . dispensationibus.*

20.   BR: *quorum deus simulata humanitas est, quorum deus scurillitas est;* omitted by Mab. and Migne.

21.   These three are characters in Roman comedy; Thraso and Gnatho, from Terence's *Eunuchus,* seem to have become standard names for the braggart, *miles gloriosus,* and the parasite, *parasiticus,* perhaps a Falstaff and a Bardolph. Horace mentions both Gnato and Cato, in *Satire* 1:2:20-21 and 31-32: *Terenti / fabula quem miserum Gnato vixisse fugato inducit . . . ; 'Macte / virtute esto,' inquit sententia dia Catonis.*

22.   *Charam nostram sepelivimus.* Probably 'we have buried our dear Rachel', in preferring Jacob.

23.   See Giles Constable, *Monastic Tithes from their origins to the twelfth century,* (Cambridge: CUP, 1964) 195-6; the author refers to this letter

'deploring the cupidity of his age and especially his order' in the context of monastic reformers who 'tended to consider the acceptance of clerical revenues by the new monastic orders, especially the Cistercians, as a sign of avarice and moral decline'.

A SERMON ON THE WORD OF GOD
AS A SEED

TO MISQUOTE in your presence the words of the apostle which you have just heard: 'Gladly you put up with a fool, because you are wise yourselves.'* Paul's word's were a reproach; mine are a eulogy. I commend you for keenness, I commend also your humility, for passionately you strive to hear the word of God and respectfully you stoop to listen to me, to one scarcely up to it. As was written in the old testament, although you have drunk enough yourselves, none the less you welcome a thirsty man.* So to requote: Gladly you entertain a foolish man, for you are so full of good sense, although you do not so much entertain me as wring the word out of me. From you I received the order, from you I learned the topic, as if in any soil I could divine rich 'veins of living water'* and make seeds sprout upon all its rivulets,* and as if in an instant words would blossom for me at will![1] Oh, then be it done unto me according to your faith,* and may all my limbs dissolve into speech,[2] and may I be able to say with the prophet: 'all my bones will proclaim: "who is like unto you, O Lord?"'*

2. Well, I shall strive to do my best on the spur of the moment and 'shall not restrain my lips'.* On one point beware, lest to me or rather to him, the word of the Lord return in vain.* Nor will it return in vain, provided it falls not by the wayside, not on rocky ground, not among thorns.* From these three places, watch out for yourselves: from the wayside, from the rocks, from the thorns. The reason for the first obstacle is the dexterity of the enemy;* for the second, the duplicity of our hearts;* for the third, the multiplicity of our anxieties. By the wayside, we guard ourselves

2 Co 11:19

Dt 29:19

Jr 17:13
Is 32:20

Lk 1:38

Ps 34:10

Ps 39:10

Is 55:11

Mt 13:3-8 18-23.

Gn 3:1
Si 1:36

83

imprudently; on the rocks, we cultivate ourselves indolently; amid thorns, we busy ourselves too diligently with the goods of others. By the wayside, we resist weakly; on the rocks, we abandon our project; amid thorns, we insist fretfully on trivialities. By the wayside, our thought is malleable; on the rocks, changeable; amid thorns, irritable; rather, amid thorns our thought is at once malleable, changeable, and irritable: malleable amid sensual pleasures, changeable amid ephemeral riches and opportunities, irritable amid our anxious and fretful cupidities. Yes, fretful and irritating are anxieties and passions for ephemeral possessions, since their quest is difficult, their passing swift, and their reward vain, not to say reprehensible.

SERMON ON THE WORD OF GOD AS A SEED—NOTES

1.   See Lucretius, *De rerum natura,* 1:187, 220-30.

2.   Perhaps a reminiscence of Eurydice in Virgil's *Georgics* IV, or Ovid's *Metamorphoses,* X, or better still of Echo in *Metamorphoses,* III:396-99.

EPISTLE 1,
To Brother Richard

Gilbert praises Richard who was previously offended by some reprimand or harsh word but has been reconciled.[1] 1. One should test and not trust too easily a prospective friend. 2. Brother Richard has been tested and merits friendship. 3. Gilbert apologizes for some fault and is ready to welcome Richard with open arms.

YOU ARE ACTING, my dear Richard, according to a proverb as true as it is ancient: 'all things should be weighed with a friend but he should be weighed first of all.'* 'Put no trust in a friend', says the prophet; 'have no confidence in a leader; against her who lies in your bosom, guard the portals of your mouth.'* Feigned friendships make true friendships suspect and the rarity of this virtue makes one question its sincerity. Happy the man who veers towards neither extreme, showing himself prudent enough in winning friends without going to excess in anticipating their loss. As it is impractical to sow seeds in sand,* so it is much more desperate to sow no seeds at all with a weather eye on the winds and the clouds.* In matters of the least value, we are solicitous owners; in ownership of the most precious kind, in friendships I mean, we are altogether remiss.[2] Though no one would fail to underpin a collapsing house,[3] who is practically the only one to shore up a faltering friend? These remarks I make

Seneca, Epistolae Morales, *3:2.*

Mi 7:5

Ovid, Heroides, *5:115.*

Qo 11:4

87

intentionally, that its very rarity may commend this virtue in you, and that there it may stand out the more brilliantly in comparison with the number of those who neglect it.

2. In scanning your letter I straightway recalled the saying of a philosopher; 'even after a bad crop one must sow again'.* It seems to me that you burn so avidly for the exchange of friendships that, where a short while ago you suffered shipwreck, you may again put out to sea.*[4] With prudence obviously, the more successful results of a single hour may perhaps balance the losses of a longer time.* And to interject a remark from our familiar philosophy, in you I am conscious of the saying of Peter, 'charity covers a multitude of sins'.*

The mistake of a friend you chastise with such restraint that you might appear to be offering an excuse rather than proffering a complaint. Scripturally, you chew me out with such sharp-toothed kindness that I feel myself gently rubbed with that salt which must not be absent from the sacrifices of the Lord.* You flew towards me like one of the Seraphim all enkindled and a firebearer, and with the burning ember you took from the altar you sear the sin on my lips.* The more grave was my fault, the more charming was your chiding. Truly I am meeting in you a person other than I used to suppose. Now at last you have given me some taste of your prudence, for indeed the wise man is known by his patience.* Your patience I admire and respect. You gloss over insults; you restore your opponent to favor; you parry his thrusts; you reward one who has no merits or rather only demerits.

Your gifts are gifts pleasing to me, pleasing because of their author, pleasing because of their value. They are both a reminder to me of yourself and a likeness of myself. Gifts of a wise man cannot but be eloquent.* For what are you hinting to me by the crozier, except that I should be upright and firm, that I should not be characterized by the flexibility and fragility of the reed? In the words of the prophet: 'The Egyptian cane is a broken reed, on which will be pierced the hands of anyone who leans upon

Seneca, Epp. Mor. *81.1.*

Ibid. *81:2*

Ibid. *81:1*

1 P 4:8

Lv 2:13

Is 6:6

Pr 19:11

Seneca, Epp. Mor. *79:7; Ovid* Ars Amatoria, *3:656.*

it.'* Such a reed you have found me, and your hands could have been bloodied on the barbs of my broken reed, except that your hands are tough enough to blunt these hostile barbs. Blessed hands, for they know not how to crush the broken reed but rather how to strengthen it,[5] nor how to extinguish the smoking flax.* 'They shall be confounded', says Isaiah, 'the flax-workers, the combers and weavers' of subtleties.* Therefore I have been covered with confusion, for beneath the wool of your simplicity I have woven the flax of insincerity. Perhaps for the bruise of my duplicity you have sent me twin chalices. Weight varying from weight, and measure from measure are an abomination.* 'Woe to him who gives a drink to his friend, pouring in his own gall and making him drunk, to behold his nakedness! He will be filled with shame instead of glory.'*

3. What purpose do these paragraphs serve, my brother, except to commend your gentleness and to condemn my unfairness? But because it is a long journey to run through each of your headings individually, I am sending you a concise and summary answer.* I spoke unwisely and like one of the foolish virgins.† I acknowledge my sin; forgive me! When requested you will not deny the pardon which you are offering me freely. I might make excuses, or in acknowledging the charge minimize its enormity, or lay upon another the responsibility for the sin, or over the head of the striker brandish the iron sword with which I was wounded. Yet I refrain for I have turned rather to entreaty and supplications. In the process of mending these rents, I am unwilling to tear open again any cloak, however patched, and to protect my flank I am unwilling to wound another's.

On one point, however, I do not remain silent. Your house of mail has not been well linked; of the scales mutually supportive, each does not cling stoutly to his fellow, and too easily does the breath not of peace but of dissension blow through them.* To the other charges: that I procrastinated, that I resisted at length, that I am acting belatedly, that I said you would be a burden to me, I answer

2 Ch 18:21;
Is 36:6

Is 42:3; Mt 12:20

Is 19:9

Pr 20:23

Hab 2:15-16

Rm 9:28;
Is 10:22-3.

†Mt 25:8

Jb 41:6-7

briefly. In conversation we make many statements rather to probe the view of another than to scuttle our own. Indeed, I shall speak frankly and from the feeling in my heart:[6] I have desired to do desire your company, but I have delayed that this might come about more readily, assuming that you would be more a consolation to me than a burden, perhaps because of the similarity of our characters and of our interests. Would that I could welcome you forever rather than for a time, as an abiding rather than a transient guest. Farewell.

NOTES ON EPISTLE 1

1.   Brother Richard, offended by remarks of Gilbert probably at a recent visit, wishes to remain on good terms and seems to have sent Gilbert a gift of a crozier, a woolen chasuble and two chalices. Gilbert wishes to leave the door open so that Richard can either stay in office or gracefully stay on with Gilbert. Brother Richard may be Richard of Fountains, the third of that name (1150-70) to whom G. refers in Epistle 4.

2.   BR: *desides;* Mab. and Migne: *inutiles.*

3.   BR: *nemo qui non refulciat;* Mag. and Migne: *suffulciat.*

4.   BR: *navigationem, iterato restaures;* Mab. and Migne: *navigatione.*

5.   Reading *consolidant* for *considerant,* with BR.

6.   BR: *Nam ut nude tecum loquar et ex cordis mei sententia;* so also Mab. but Migne reads *et.*

EPISTLE 2,
To Adam

Gilbert writes a vocation letter to Adam, otherwise unidentified, that he may recall his earlier resolution and embrace the religious state.[1]

1. Adam is invited to fulfil his promise and to lead the way for others. 2. The study of the liberal arts is preparatory to the awesome study of wisdom. 3. Adam is invited to advance from worldly science to the pursuit of divine wisdom, to fill the cells of his capacious honeycomb with Cistercian teaching that he may become a Cistercian teacher. 4. The subtleties of Aristotle, for the new Adam, should yield to that silence which leads directly to the mind of Christ. 5. Not to mention the future, Adam should come to enjoy the present in the first-fruits of an eternal harvest.

HOW MUCH I LONG for you, my dear Adam, in the heart of Christ Jesus,* would that you understood personally, for my words to you are an inadequate explanation. Long ago I desired to explain, but something akin to hopelessness checked my intention. At present, however, my desire has matured and ripened[2] more fully than ever; it has burst into a longing for your entrance into religion. My earlier expectation, modest enough, was conceived from your words; I had been a little too unresponsive and

Ph 1:8

93

was writing with a reluctant hand,[3] because I feared
(let me admit this despite you) that your words had
escaped you through some slight and passing impulse.
But however your words were spoken, whether they
slipped out through an overeager and prompt affection or were pronounced after wise deliberation, I can
hope for nothing but good from you in the light of
the good example given at home. May our good
example here likewise bestir you or rather jog your
memory. Seizing the wings of a dove, may you fly
ahead of me by some lucky shortcut to this place of
peace, although you have made a late start.* How
wide a window will you open for the emulation of
others, soon to become an example for others yourself and to interject a text of our own, how wide a
door will you open upon the road to virtue.*
I seem to hear this verse of the Canticle being sung
about you: 'draw us after you; we shall run in the
fragrance of your perfumes.'*

2. Happy obviously and doubly happy will you
be, if you make your entrance an occasion of salvation for others, if you attract towards life and truth
those who run after you now*—in vanity, I was
sorely tempted to add, but shied away lest I offend a
sensitive affection still maturing in Christ. Not that I
disparage erudition in the arts, a ready memory in liberal studies and a clear understanding, for on these
depends the integrity of knowledge. For skill in the
arts is valuable provided one uses them rightly,* that
is, as a step and foothold where one does not stop
and rest, but on which one must rely[4] to rise to higher
and holier and more interior mysteries of wisdom, to
those hidden and pleasant retreats and to the very
light inaccessible which God inhabits.*

Of all the arts, this last I would call the art, the
law, the norm, the form, and the principle, the
universal, uniform, invariable exemplar. As we cannot
advance beyond it, so we ought not to rest this side of
it. In comparison with this wisdom, all other wisdom,
whatever its nature or its quantity, is not only vain if
it falls short of this, but is iniquitous if it does not
direct itself to this wisdom, if it so allures and entices

Seneca, Epp. Mor.
27:10; 72:12;
perhaps 109:8.

1 Co 16:9

Sg 1:3

Seneca, Epp. Mor.
15:10. See
de Lubac, Exégèse,
1:575, n. 3.

1 Tm 1:18. See
Lam 178, n. 47.

1 Tm 6:16

to itself our dedication that in itself it delays and
deludes our enjoyment, so that our mind, satisfied,[5]
acquiesces in this limitation, tolerating a rebuff that
prevents its rise to greater heights, trying to batten
on banality and still-life banquets, that it may never
hunger for and never taste how 'sweet is the Lord'.*   *Ps 33:9*

For what but the Lord is sweet?[6] The tenuous and
ambiguous knowledge of natures and principles, scarcely reached through long detours and winding curves,
delights you to excess, has stolen your attention and
allured your love to itself. How much more then should
creative Wisdom herself attract you, for through her
all these realities are fashioned that they may exist &
brought into the light that they may be recognized?
Will the winning of Wisdom not coax you to court her
much more earnestly? Will Wisdom not pour her sweetness with greater charm into the senses she has enlightened, as she awakens with novel affections an insatiable yearning for herself? Indeed she says: 'those who
eat me, will still hunger, . . . for my spirit is sweeter
than honey.'*   *Si 24:29, 27*

3. You have some large cells, my friend, for stor-
ing this very honey; I mean a keen and trained intel-
lect, a knowledge of many and subtle subjects. These
I would consider as the cells of a honeycomb, ample
but still empty. Come then to be saturated, that your
cells may be filled, that they may overflow, run over
and be spilled upon us, who will rightly praise you in
the words of the Canticle: 'a dripping honeycomb are
your lips.'* O would that some day I might listen to   *Sg 4:11*
you discoursing in the house of the Lord, explaining
the mystic and mysterious meanings of the texts, cup-
ping and delicately sharing with us some drops of the
majesty, the eternity, the immensity, the simplicity of
the divine Essence! There nothing is minimal, because
this Essence is simple; nothing multiple, because this
Essence is without measure; but the whole is infinite,
neither by succession in time nor by extension of
mass in space, but by essential force and power. Now
everywhere this Essence exists entire, just as it exists
entire in itself, for in nothing else is its entire power,
truth, will, either expended or expressed. Where there

Qo 1:8

may be some grounds for distinguishing, and in relation to ourselves some distinguishable meanings in
words, still the reality is unique and indivisible. All is
full of wonder, worthy of worship and gratifying to
explore. Then as Scripture says: 'the eye is not satisfied with seeing, nor the ear filled with hearing.'*

On a subject of this kind, willingly would I listen
to you in the chair of prophecy. When as an avid
searcher you had plunged into the vast depth of this
sea, happily would I see you spray the sweet dew of
life-giving Wisdom upon those who are not meant for
this more fruitful search. But when you had directed
your attention to the divine blessings, then willingly
would I listen to you explain more in depth and
develop at greater length your views on pardon, on
grace and on glory, on what the Lord has given,
restored or added, and on all he endured for us and
conferred upon us. I would listen to you review for
us the preceding sufferings in Christ and the glories

1 P 1:11

to come,* the endurance of trials, the anticipation of
rewards, the elements of faith, the laws of morality,
the individual steps of renewal and the stages of
progress towards perfection. Here obviously is an
abundance of material and an inviting occupation.
Nowhere else can any man of talent, however zealous
and however learned, employ himself more pro-
lifically, more fruitfully.

4. My words are meant precisely to prevent your
excusing yourself on the score of devotion to empty
literature, lest you follow a shadow only to be
deprived of the light, lest distorted by the subtleties
of Aristotle you find fault with our silence and our
simplicity.[7] Yet in silence and in simplicity especially is the occasion granted us, 'in contemplating
face to face the glory of the Lord, to be transformed
into the same image from splendor to splendor as it

2 Co 3:18

were by the Spirit of the Lord'.* Does our silence
seem to you inactive and artless, wherein the activity
described for you above is our preoccupation? wherein is taught and practised the art of advancing
towards God as it were in a straight line, and of
transforming[8] and changing oneself into the new

man, into the new Adam, and of reaching right up to
the mind of Christ, 'in whom are hidden all the
treasures of the wisdom of God'?* Here the veins   *Col 2:3*
of metal are unfailing, I assure you, and gleaming
almost at one's fingertips, believe me, if one but
prefer to dig in the depths rather than to be a
beggar outside.

5. I am not reviewing for you the divine blessings
conferred upon you, the graces of the Lord and your
ingratitude, or rather the poor recompense you make
for the best of gifts. I am not recalling the baleful
enticements of the world, towards which one rushes
in hot haste, so that we turn to the Lord not our faces
but our backs.[9] In my remarks, as far as possible, I
am extenuating the circumstances. Nor am I recount-
ing the troubles meant for our healing in the present
life. I am not referring to the punishments to come,
nor am I setting before you the glory to come; I am
not putting far off into the future your fear or your
expectation. I insist on picturing only the present,
not the future, reward, the first-fruits not the full
harvest.[10] It is not within my power to express the
reality in words; nor is it right that the sublimity of
so great a topic be compressed within the narrow
range of my lips.

Do but desire to make the test for yourself and
you will discover that the statutes of the Lord are the
theme of our songs even in this place of pilgrimage,[11]
and that the harvests to be at the end of the world are
planted in these pristine joys. Do not delay the
mellow fruit for another year.* Do not resist the   *Ps 125:6,*
grace which comes freely to meet you. Woe to me if   *adapted.*
you thrust from you the grace I found in your company. Follow with a gay and agile step where the first
charms of grace entice you. You asked me to send a
messenger to you; may you be found just where I left
you, at the very gates, believe me, and almost at the
threshold, on the point of abandoning the life of the
world. If in anything you think I can assist you as a
friend,[12] I shall expend myself without reserve, for I
am wholly in your debt. I am awaiting your reply in
person rather than in writing. Farewell.

NOTES ON EPISTLE 2

1.   In a significant letter G. tries to attract an able young cleric to the study of Wisdom in the contemplative life. Contrast Roger of Byland's letter to G., 'The Milk of Babes', and see Jean Leclercq, 'Lettres de vocation à la vie monastique', *SAn* 37 (1955) 169-97.

2.   B: *increbruit;* R. Mab. and Migne *increbuit.*

3.   BR: *pigrior aliquantulum fueram et tardante scripsi dextera, veritus etc.,* omitted by Mab. and Migne.

4.   BR: *quo nitendum sit;* Mab. and Migne: *quo utendum sit.*

5.   BR: *contentus;* Mab. and Migne: *contritus.*

6.   The reading of the text: *dulcis* or *dulce,* does not alter the meaning.

7.   Seneca, *ibid.* 88. The liberal arts which are only propaideutic to moral philosophy in Seneca, in G. are propaideutic to divine wisdom. G. conflates into one sentence what is plundered from several paragraphs in Seneca: *Tota rerum natura umbra est aut inanis aut fallax* (88:46). *Haec omnia in illum supervacuum studiorum liberalium gregem coice* (88:45). *Illi non praeferunt lumen, per quod acies derigatur ad verum* (88:45). *Audi, quantum mali faciat nimia subtilitas et quam infesta veritati sit* (88:43). See Lam 176, n. 40.

8.   BR: *transfundendi;* Mab. and Migne: *transmutandi.*

9.   The sense requires not a comma but a semi-colon after *faciem.*

10.   BR: *pingere,* not the emendation *pignore.*

11.   Ps 118:54, adapted, reading *dulcia* for *dubia* with BR and Mab.

12.   Ac 10:24, *necessarius,* as frequently, in the sense of a close friend.

EPISTLE 3,
To Brother William

Gilbert tries to dissuade William from his perilous advance towards the court and recommends a different spiritual advance.[1] 1. What a religious should request; how a monastic prelate should act. 2. Business at court is an obstacle to the piety of a religious. 3. One should be at home to the Lord in the paradise of pleasure. 4. Better to sacrifice familiarity than to imperil humility. 5. What are the steps of formation? 6. As a pious rival, emulate the journey of Abraham without growing faint. To beloved Brother William, Brother Gilbert sends greetings in the Lord.

OUR MOST WELCOME BROTHER R...[2] greatly cheered us up by his own arrival and, after giving us news of your good health, inspired us with deeper joy by conveying your respectful greetings and relaying your request for the assistance of our prayers. Would that my strength were more than usually equal to that task; I would acquit myself with a generosity to match your decision to spare us in other matters! I have heard you say frequently enough, repeating words full of significance,[3] that you insist on my pouring prayers for you more earnestly and that I should have no other anxiety than that. Well spoken, Brother, and as becomes a man of virtue. But why? Is there any other request which any one ought to make more readily or which a monk can make more licitly?

99

RB 33:5. See
Lam 17, n. 68.

I blush[4] at the impudence of some, who though 'they should expect all the necessities of life from the father of a monastery',* by begging assistance from all sources, procure for themselves some fine and rare hides, garish outfits, imported cloaks and other items too numerous to mention, devices of vanity provocative of pleasure for the nostrils, the eyes, and the palate. Contrary to the Rule, you may observe those who ought to be sparing in what is allowed for use wantonly squandering it on ostentation. That this blemish is wholly absent from your character, your plea for prayers, so often repeated, is proof enough and purifies the widespread pallor of this leprosy.[5]

Herein I am harsh and inhuman, they say, even though in other respects I am a handsome fellow, but in this role my appearance has been made blacker than lumps of coal,[6] because I have learned to disburse only what I have been accustomed to request. Let them rail at me to their hearts' content. Let them construe their graft as my greed. From their softness let them forge a greater austerity on my anvil. I have indeed 'set my face as the hardest flint', and though their mallet be smashed, I hope that 'I shall not be broken'.* Let me be branded as a poor sharer, as too tenacious. I would readily allow myself to be discolored with this blemish, provided those hounds, or rather those delicate little whelps, do not devour the bread of children, provided I do not make[7] the tatters of the poor into the superfluous fineries of others, provided I do not seek to acquire an empty fame and false favors for myself from the roaring belly of a brother.

Is 50:7

2. Now omitting myself for a moment to return to you, let me say that something should be requested from us: prayers you have sought, but for good measure I resort to exhortation, for I am zealous for you with a zeal from God.* Yet I have anxieties: lest your affections be corrupted and fall from that simplicity which is in Christ;* lest prayers for you be poured out fruitlessly, for on your own you are dashing towards a fall; lest you pray ineffectually to be rescued, when you are wittingly hastening into a

2 Co 11:2

2 Co 11:3

trap.* You are about to set out for the court, I hear.   *Pr 7:23*
You are about to set out for a place where you sus-
pect you will be detained. You are going to renew
old acquaintances with the Duke, to resurrect longings already buried or rather long dormant. Like the
ostrich in the parable, you are about to raise on high
wings long packed and folded,[8] now that you have
the occasion.* Both the stork and the swallow[9]   *Jb 39:18*
know the day of migration, when the wind begins to
blow warmer.*   *Jr 8:7*

I am saying to you frankly what others perhaps
are speaking of you behind your back. You are going
to the court and I do not know whether you have
been summoned. However, what do you intend to do
there? Will you share with the Duke the care of your
soul? Will you cool your overheated heart in an
audience with him? Yes perhaps, yes, but with that
chill of which Matthew writes: 'The charity of many
will grow cold.'* Hear the prophet in Scripture railing   *Mt 24:12*
against the like: 'What can I do with you, Ephraim?
What can I do with you, Judah? Your piety is like a
morning cloud, like the dew that early passes away.'*   *Ho 6:4*
Piety of a morning indeed, or better of a moment, for
though they have scarcely begun in the spirit, they
soon come to an end in the flesh.* The Bridegroom in   *Ga 3:3*
the Canticle complains that he had endured many
such persons: 'For my head is wet with dew and my
locks with the moisture of the night.'* By lofty living   *Sg 5:2*
they rise as high as the Lord's head, but linger on the
outside of his locks, busy with externals alien to the
breath he draws deep within; thus they become insen-
sitive with no taste for the things of God. Then the
Lord, not finding in such men whereon to lay his
head, if he finds someone[10] else within, asks that
the door be opened to himself.

3. Would that you also might tarry within, that
whenever Jesus knocks at your gate, you might straightway welcome him into the guestroom of your heart
and glory in exclaiming: 'my secret belongs to me!
my secret is all mine!'* In turn you will entertain   *Is 24:16*
that welcome word of praise: 'You are a garden
enclosed, sister, my bride, a garden enclosed, a

Sg 4:12

fountain sealed',* sealed, yes, with the seal of light
and with joy of heart, with the seal of the sevenfold
Spirit, which none but he alone can unseal, who
alone enters the east gate closed to strangers according to the word of the prophet: foreigners shall not

Ezk 44:9

pass through Jerusalem any longer.* Enclosed in such
a paradise of pleasure, or rather, you yourself like an
irrigated field and like a fountain in gardens where
waters never fail, will grow deaf to the call of
strangers. If worldly ambition should vex you, if an
opportunity for dignities should beckon you, if that
flattering bore, some hope of honors, should invite
you, you shall answer immediately in the words of the
bride: 'I have shed my robe; am I to don it again? I

Sg 5:3

have bathed my feet; am I then to soil them?'*

4. Of course, Brother, you see the reason why I
speak in words foreshortened like shadows, as I hide
rather than reveal the substance;[11] I am well aware
that I am addressing a wise man. You see, I repeat,
the kernel of my advice. I would recall you from this
perilous progress. I would mow down the occasions of
a speedy fall with the sickle of my warning. According to the precept of the prophet, for you I am making level a path full of stumbling blocks, removing

Is 62:10

boulders from the road.* For you my solicitude is
great; great is the confidence I place in you. Otherwise I would prefer to relax my close ties with you
for a while, rather than suppress in silence what I believe concerns your salvation. I would rather sacrifice
our familiarity than imperil the humility still tender
and growing within you. You were running well;*

Ga 5:7

beware lest fascination with trifles hide your real

Ws 4:12

good.* Though your conscience may remain un-
harmed, beware lest even your reputation be called
into question. You were running well, I may say; but
now whither do you hasten so quickly? You were
running well! But what if you do not finish the
race? Though you ought to be perfected in a short

Ws 4:13

time,* do you wish to complete a long career only
to hear Paul duly reproach you:[12] 'Have you suf-

Ga 3:4

fered so much in vain—if indeed it be in vain?'*

5. Would that I could be near you now. With my

living voice, would that I could, as it were, seize you
with a firm grip and lead you with Abraham into the
land of Canaan, that is into formation. 'They who
trust in the Lord will reform their strength.'*   Good   *Is 40:31*
is the reform which the same prophet mentions:
'There shall be five cities in the land of Egypt speaking the language of Canaan; one shall be called the
city of the Sun.'* It is obviously good to be led from   *Is 19:18*
the land of Egypt into the light, and after the palace
of Pharoah to be dedicated to the city of the Sun of
Justice. Good, I insist, is the formation where ob-
scurities are poured into the light and pluralities
joined into one. Scripturally, there is anxiety in multiplicity and but one thing is necessary.* Good is the   *Lk 10:41-2*
formation, when the bleariness of Leah and the an-
xiety of Martha are changed into Rachel's vision and
Mary's calm. This is why the cities which had once
belonged to Egypt, that is to darkness, are called the
cities of the Sun, and in place of the number five,
there is mention of only one.

The speaker in the psalm also knew that he had
been transformed: 'Bless the Lord, O my soul, and
forget not all his benefits; he pardons all your iniquities, he heals all your ills, he redeems your life
from destruction, he crowns you with kindness and
compassion.'* He speaks in the language of Canaan,   *Ps 102:2-4*
for he recalls so many transformations in himself:
from iniquity to atonement, from illness to con-
valescence, into eternity from the end of time; and
throughout each and every stage he expresses thanks
to its author. With testimonies of devoted steps forward, as if in a kind of language of transformation,
he cries with the psalmist: 'Now I have begun! This is
the reform of the right hand of the Most High!'* Yes,   *Ps 76:11*
what the prophet sowed, we may reap from the
apostle; what Isaiah hinted at, Paul proclaimed: 'You
were once darkness, but now light in the Lord.'* We   *Eph 5:8*
have heard of the transformation, but Paul alerts us
to the final stage: 'Walk then, as children of light.'*   Ibid.
He who walks in the day does not stumble.* Let   *Jn 11:9*
your light increase until that final day; and when you
have finished the course, you will seem to have just

begun. Hear how Paul himself continued to run and
to grow, not only from darkness to light, but from
light to light: 'with faces unveiled, reflecting as in a
mirror the glory of the Lord, we are transformed

2 Co 3:18   in his very image from glory to glory.'*

6. When you behold some who have renounced
the world, prosper in the world, do not let your feet

Ps 72:2   slip,* for while like blind men they stagger in broad
daylight, you may boast and say: I did not weary,
O Lord, in following your steps. 'For those who hope
in the Lord will reform their strength; they will fly
and not grow weary; they will walk and not grow

Is 40:31   faint.'* It would be a long journey, should I wish to
lead you through all the renewals of virtues, as through
different wayside inns of the land of Canaan. For in
the first place, a pious rival of the patriarch Abraham

Gn 12:6   must voyage to Shechem,* where on shoulders humbled and bowed, for Shechem means shoulders, he
must take up that lightest of burdens of Christ, since
'it is good for man to bear the yoke' of the Lord
'from his youth . . . . He will offer his cheek to the

Lm 3:27,30   striker; he will be sated with insults.'* Notice at once
in the word 'sated' not some slight resignation, as if
one tested with the tip of his tongue and spat out
what tasted bitter, but an insatiable hunger for suffering adversities.

Thus from Shechem, after blessed affliction and
Gn 20:1-18;   curative tribulation, having passed through Gerar,*
26:1-35.   when the wall of ancient hostilities has been demo-
Eph 2:14   lished,* then escaping from caves in the rock and
clefts in the cliffs in full flight at the call of the
Sg 2:14   beloved,* one emerges at the streams of Beersheba.
From Shechem, to repeat, that is from humiliation
and burden,[13] one may arrive at Beersheba, one may
come to the well of the Seven Lambs, or rather to the
Gn 22:30   fount of all graces,* 'for God gives his grace to the
Jm 4:6   humble'.* And because in another interpretation this
Gn 20, 21, and 26. is called the well of satiety,* according to the word
of Christ's invitation: 'Come to me, you who are
Mt 11:28   burdened, and I will refresh you',* after affliction
one may hasten to refreshment.[14] In drinking of this
sweetest water, tempted to a greater thirst, one may

experience in himself the truth of that word of
Wisdom: 'Those who eat me will still hunger; those
who drink me will still thirst.'* I am now opting for   *Si 24:29*
silence, since long ago perhaps, you began to weary of
my talkativeness. Farewell, and if you please, search
diligently for a copy of Jerome on Isaiah for me, so
that when I send for it, you may have it at hand.[15]

NOTES ON EPISTLE 3

1.   BR: *desiderantissimus;* Mab. and Migne: *desideratissimus.* Brother William, probably a Cistercian abbot, (Mikkers), and the Duke or Earl, *dux,* and his court have not been identified.

2.   It is tempting to suggest that R. was Roger of Byland.

3.   BR: *repetitisque verbis plenis significantia;* Mab. and Migne: *significantem.*

4.   BR: *erubesco;* Mab. and Migne: *erubesce.*

5.   Cf. Horace, *Satires* 1:6:65-69, for thought and words: *inspersos . . . naevos . . . avaritiam.*

6.   Though G. adapts Lm 4:8: *denigrata est super carbones facies eorum,* his meaning is clarified by a reminiscence of Persius, 5:107-8: *Quaeque sequenda forent quaeque evitanda uicissim, / illa prius creta, mox haec carbone notasti,* or better still, of Horace, *Satires* 2:3:246, . . . *Sani ut creta, an carbone notati?* In Treatise 7:1, G. quotes from this satire of Horace and Horace's line means just what G. intends: after the Greek manner of voting, Horace's critics cast into the ballot box, not chalk for acquittal but charcoal for condemnation of him as insane; G. is being blackballed.

7.   BR: *faciam;* Mab. and Migne: *faciant.*

8.   BR: *in altum alas erecturus;* Mab. and Migne: *evecturus.*

9.   On the ostrich, see S 14:6 and note; on the stork and the swallow, see Morson, 161, White, 117-8; on the whelp, see White, 61-67.

10.   BR: *quam;* Mab. and Migne: *quem.*

11.   BR: *rem magis comprimens quam promens;* Mab. and Migne: *premens.*

12.   BR: *ut iure tibi exprobetur;* Mab. and Migne, *ut iam . . .*

13.   BR: *onere;* Mab. and Migne: *oratione.*

14.   BR: *properet;* Mab. and Migne: *properat.*

15.   See Lam 180 n. 61.

EPISTLE 4,
To a Friend

In a brief letter Gilbert indicates that he cannot accede to a friend's request.

BY YOUR LEAVE I am replying, though your importunateness makes me recalcitrant; rather, the great insistence of those who use you as an intercessor somewhat lessens the value of your services to me. I am surprised that they did not also lure over us the Lord of Fountains, to overshadow me again with a cloud of imposing intercessors.*[1] To satisfy yourself with a brief response, however, the matter of your request I wished to decline rather by silence than by word. With deference then, and in my usual way, as in other matters which I have made no decision to perform, I am postponing rather than formulating an answer, until we can confer together shortly. Farewell.

NOTES ON EPISTLE 4

1.   G. slyly looks up expecting to see the Lord of Fountains in the lowering raincloud. Fountains was 'the Cistercian Abbey of St. Mary by the springs *(ad fontes)*, probably the best known of all monastic ruins', in England; see David Knowles and J. K. S. St. Joseph, *Monastic Sites from the Air,* 93-7. During Gilbert's abbacy, from shortly before 1150 (Mikkers, 35) to 1172, the Lord of Fountains was its 'fourth abbot, a native of York, precentor of Clairvaux, abbot of Vauclair, suffragan abbot of Fountains until the death of Archbishop Henry (Murdac) of York 14 Oct. 1153' and then Abbot Richard III, who died 31 May 1170. Gilbert is probably referring to this imposing figure who was succeeded by Abbot Robert, previously Abbot of Pipewell; see David Knowles, CN. L. Brooke, and Vera C. M. London, *The Heads of Religious Houses, England and Wales, 940-1216,* 132-3.

THE MILK OF BABES
ROGER [of Byland] SENDS TO
HIS MOST BELOVED G.[1]

*1-2. Roger of Byland sends Gilbert of Hoyland
a dispatch not from a temporal king but from
the eternal King. 3. His love for us is proven by
the paradoxes of his incarnate life and death.
4. He recalls those in quest of visible realities
to the quest of his invisible Reality. 5-7. He
rewards those who follow his liberating commands and likewise those who disregard his
word. 8-11. The risk of those who live in the
world is counteracted by those who live in
the Order. 12-16. The passionate love manifested by our heavenly King, especially in his
death and Resurrection, sheds a new light
on his will for us, the meaning of death,
self-will, carnal love, love of parents and love of
riches. 17-19. The stock objections against the
Order vanish in comparison with the harshness
of Hell or of martyrdom. 20-22. Consider the
reward of the heavenly King, and delay no
longer. Come!*

WRITING TO MY BELOVED, I have
not taken pains to fashion sparkling
circumlocutions or polished sentences
in the ornate style. Indeed, having
enlisted in the service of the Lord, I can not write
to you grandiloquently. Writing to one steeped in the
literature of a pagan. I should not attempt to present
the mysteries of divine law but to give some foretaste
of plain and simple truths, saying with the apostle:

1 Co 3:2   'I gave milk to drink, not solid food.'*

2. Now because no labor should seem hard and
no time long, whereby the glory of eternity is won,
Jb 38:3   'gird your loins like a man',* hasten to change your
soul's pursuit by preference from something even
Qo 2:3   carnal to something spiritual.* 'Brief are the days of
Jb 14:5   man',* and in our stormy times we see the young
swept away even more than the old. While then a
pliable and tender age contains within something
malleable and soft which can be easily shaped and
drawn to the will of another, scorn the desire for comfort, the lure of pleasure, the pomp of the world, the
responsibility for offspring.² Set your heart on real
wisdom, heavenly riches, immortal honors. Explore
with keen attention what the King of all ages advises:
'Come to me', he says, 'all you who labor and are
Mt 11:28   overburdened, and I will give you rest.'*

3. For the empire of an earthly king, believe me,
all are so prompt and so trained in the livery of
obedience, that they even long to hear his command.
But God himself, the inexpressible, eternal Majesty
and the incalculable Power summons us again and
again. He even sends us sacred dispatches and the
truly awesome letters of his commandments. Yet we
do not immediately welcome them with joy and
homage, nor do we consider as the highest blessing
the rule of so great and glorious a Power, especially
when not the advantage of the Commander but the
good of his subject prompts the summons.³ Now
what raises our minds more to higher thoughts, what
frees us more from despair of immortality, than the
fact that the eternal and immutable Reality, the
unconfined and unchangeable Word of God, should
Jn 1:14   become flesh for us and dwell among us?* What
could arouse us to divine love more than the fact that
the omnipotent and invariable Good, by whom all
things were created from nothing and becomingly
Ws 8:1   and beautifully arrayed,* that the one and only
supreme Good, whose greatness is without end and
Ps 146:5   whose wisdom is beyond counting,* determined to
become such a being as might experience the con-
finement of the womb, share the indignity of coming

to birth, endure the bonds of swaddling clothes, suffer the weakness of the cradle and, though he was the Word, ask with tears for nourishment and, though he was the Author of all time and space, be subject to growing up through the ages of man. By associating with us even in our flesh, he withdrew from us every alibi, he refuted all human sophistry. In fact, because devotees of pleasure perversely coveted the wealth of the people, he determined to be poor. They sighed for honors and power; he refused to be made a king. They thought children born of their flesh a great blessing; he scorned such marriage and progeny. They shrank from reproach; he endured reproaches of every kind. They thought insults insufferable, but what insult is greater than the condemnation of a just and innocent man? They abominated bodily pain; but he was scourged and mocked. They feared death; he was punished with death. They considered the cross the most ignominious form of death; he was crucified.

4. Hence his whole life on earth exemplified the right way for mankind, through the human form[4] he so graciously assumed. Indeed no sin can be committed, except when man covets what He despised and shuns what He endured.[5] When the rational soul, bound in the chains of death as a penalty for sin, was reduced to so weak a state* that it depended *Rm 11:12* upon suggestions from visible reality to reach invisible truth,* then in fact the omnipotent, eternal, *Heb 11:3* immense and invisible God, consented to become the visible food of a rational creature, not by the change of his own nature but by the assumption of ours, and he recalled souls from the quest for visible realities to the quest for his invisible Reality. Hence the soul found him in humility outside herself, whom in her pride she had abandoned within herself. By beginning to imitate his visible lowliness, the soul prepares to return to his invisible sublimity. Thus indeed man, though not yet equal to the angels,* could eat *Ps 77:25* the bread of angels, since the very bread of angels consented to be made equal to men.* *Heb 2:7, 9*

5. What then remains for us in this plan but to

keep his commandments with the full dedication of
our minds, for as his commandments confer eternal
life when observed,* so they confer eternal death
when despised. For among other things the Lord
says: 'Amen, amen, I say to you, if anyone will keep
my word, he will never taste death.' And again he
says: 'If you remain in me and in my word, you will
truly be my disciples, and you will know the truth
and the truth will make you free.'* O true liberty,
through which man passes from darkness to light,
from labor to rest, from punishment to delights!
Through this liberty, from grief man rises to joy,
from the earthly to the heavenly! Through this
liberty, from perpetual death man passes into everlasting life!*

6. So listen attentively, most beloved, and observe with what punishment the authority of Scripture threatens the avaricious, the wanton and other
wicked persons. To the avaricious: 'Do not lay up
for yourselves treasures on earth, where moth and
rust consume and where thieves break in and steal.
But lay up for yourselves treasures in heaven, where
neither moth nor rust consumes and where thieves do
not break in and steal. For where your treasure is,
there also will be your heart.'* To the wanton: 'He
who sows in his own flesh, from his flesh will reap
corruption; but he who sows in the Spirit, from the
Spirit will reap eternal life.'* To the proud: 'Whoever
exalts himself will be humbled, and whoever humbles
himself will be exalted.'* To the irascible: 'You have
received a blow; offer the other cheek.'* To those
who harbor hatred: 'Love your enemies; do good to
those who hate you.'* To the superstitious: 'The
kingdom of God is within you.' Seek not 'the things
that are seen, but the things that are unseen, for
the things that are seen are transient, but the things
that are unseen are eternal'.* To worldlings: 'Do not
love the world or the things of the world . . . for the
things which are in the world are the lust of the
flesh and the lust of the eyes and the pride of the
age.'* Finally Paul warns all: neither the avaricious,
nor thieves, neither the proud, nor adulterers, nor

Mt 19:17

Jn 8:51, 32.

Ga 5:13

Mt 6:19-21

Ga 6:8

Mt 23:12
Lk 6:29

Mt 5:44

Lk 17:21;
2 Co 4:18.

1 Jn 2:15-16

murderers, neither the covetous, nor the cursed, nor the perjured, neither the choleric, nor drunkards, nor detractors, neither fornicators, nor the wanton, nor homosexuals, 'will inherit the kingdom of God',* because 'perpetrators of such deeds' deserve death and likewise 'those who abet them'; for both perpetrators and abettors suffer the same penalty.*

1 Co 6:10

Rm 1:32

7. These are sons of death and darkness, boasting of temporal delights which for a moment sweeten their mouths but afterwards are found more bitter than gall. Indeed they spend their days amid good things and in a moment they descend into hell,* where 'will be weeping and gnashing of teeth',* 'where no order dwells but everlasting horror'.* There, is the gnawing of worms,* the racking of jailers,* the heat of flames,† unquenchable smoke,* fiery tears from the eyes, outer darkness without light,* punishment without end.† There, is neither honor nor respect for one's neighbor but continuous grief and lamentation. There, death is a yearning never granted. There, is no honor for king or elder. Neither does a master respect his servant, nor a daughter her mother, nor a son his father. There, every woe and indignity and stench and bitterness abounds. Who is such a man of iron that these torments do not move him? Who is so thick-skinned that such torments do not move and soften him? Do you hear these words chiselled in divine letters and still have no recourse to the help of Christ? Do you accept the words issuing from the lips of Truth and still not hasten to religious life?

Ps 54:16
Mt 8:12
Jb 10:22
Mk 9:48
*Mt 18:34.
†Lk 16:24.
*Is 34:10
*Mt 8:12
†Jude 7

8. Perhaps you will propose to me an objection common on everyone's lips: 'I can licitly remain in the world; I can be saved in the world. Indeed neither do all perish who are in the world, nor are all damned who do not enter religious life.' That is true indeed, nor do I deny it. But answer these questions. Who 'carries live coals in his bosom, without scorching his clothes?'* Who passes the lair of a lion, undaunted? Who sleeps beside a serpent, without anxiety? Who handles pitch and is not defiled by it?* But because the human mind is wont to be clever in

Pr 6:27

Si 13:1

Ps 140:4

finding an alibi for sin,* perhaps without speaking
your mind you still object: 'if I avoid those enormities you mentioned above, I shall be able to live
without anxiety'. Who, my dear brother, who avoids
those enormities? Pray tell me how many times a day
you kill your own soul! Certainly as often as you lie,
because 'a lying mouth kills the soul'.* Is it a trivial
sin to kill the soul of a man? Pray tell me how often
you make yourself liable to judgement or to the
council, how often you make yourself liable to the
Gehenna of fire! Certainly as often as you are 'angry
with your brother' or say 'racha' or 'fool' or utter a
word of indignation.*

Ws 1:11

Mt 5:22

9. For such a trivial or rather such a serious sin, is
it a trivial calamity for you to sentence yourself to
the flames of Gehenna? Pray tell me how often in
your life you have committed adultery! Certainly as
often as you looked 'at a woman lustfully', you have
committed adultery with her in your heart.* Is lust or
adultery not a criminal offense? Pray tell me how
often you commit murder! Certainly as often as you
hate your brother you are a murderer, because 'everyone who hates his brother is a murderer'.* And is not
murder considered among the greater enormities?
Pray tell me whether you incur the charge of
idolatry! Certainly as often as, goaded by greed, you
cling to some earthly substance more tenaciously
than you ought, you should know that you are
enslaved to the cult of idols and that your greed is
enslavement to idols.* And what is more criminal
than enslavement to idols?

Mt 5:28

1 Jo 3:15

Col 3:5

Do not flatter, do not congratulate yourself, most
beloved, for if you carefully examine each and every
sin, you will see that you are not entirely immune
from any one of them. To omit the rest, who has
become free from evil thoughts and idle words?
About thoughts the psalmist says: God scrutinizes
hearts and loins,* and 'you discern my thoughts
from afar',* and 'the Lord knows the thoughts of
men'.* About idle words, the Son of God says:
Amen, 'I tell you, on the day of judgment men will
render account for every idle word they utter'.*

Ps 7:10
Ps 138:3
Ps 93:11

Mt 12:36

O terrifying thunderbolt! If this is the lot of an idle word, what will be the fate of a harmful word? If this is the lot of the idle word, what will be our fate for the crimes we discussed?

10. For this reason, we in religious life rejoice in continuous silence, both keeping our tongues from evil and our lips from speaking guile.* For this reason, we lament our excesses and those of others, because 'blessed are they who mourn, for they shall be comforted',* and 'woe to you who laugh . . . for you shall . . . weep'.* For this reason, we are separated from association with worldlings, lest worldly or carnal charms corrupt us.* For this reason, by despising all things, as poor men we follow the poor Christ, to be devoted to Christ with a mind free from distraction. He himself testifies that 'no one can serve two masters',* and that whoever 'does not renounce all his possessions, cannot be my disciple'.* For this reason we labor, if indeed I may count my poor self in the list of laborers. We labor, yes, we fast, we watch, we pray, 'because narrow is the way which leads to life', and few enter that way; 'broad is the way and open, which leads to death'.*

Ps 33:14

Mt 5:5
Lk 6:25

1 Co 15:33

Mt 6:24
Lk 14:33

Mt 7:13

11. The road to death is pleasant, smooth, alluring, winding and broad, and along that road many make their way. Do not then, most beloved and great portion of my soul, do not with the many take to the open road, but with the few proceed along the narrow path.* Keep fresh in your memory the story of his life. He who is incalculably great above all things, amid all things condescended to become small. He who was fairest in form beyond the sons of men,* for the sons of men appeared a misshapen outcast. 'We saw him', says Isaiah, 'and there was no beauty nor comeliness in him. We considered him then as a leper and as one struck by God.' 'But he was wounded for our sins and crushed for our crimes.'* Certainly that head which all the dominations of heaven adore and before which all the angelic powers tremble was crowned with thorns.* His hands which wrought many wonders for us were pierced with nails for our redemption. To the

Mt 7:14

Ps 44:3

Is 53:2-5

Col 1:16

Saviour's mellifluous lips, through which his teaching
flowed, wicked hands thrust a cup of gall. He who
harmed no one was slain. He who cursed no one
endured obloquy and curses for us.

12. Open your eyes then, my beloved. Let God
give you understanding that you may see. See how
he chose a mother, from Whom is born the Creator
both of motherhood and of his own Mother. He wept
in his cradle, though he is the joy of the angels in
heaven. He was a man of sorrows, though sorrow and
grief fly before him.[6] He was fearful, though all
dreadful creatures fear him. He lacked possessions,
though he is the source of all possessions. He is moved
from place to place, though he is the immovable
Fullness. He fell asleep, though he is ever watchful
in the joy[7] of his Spirit. Hungry was 'the living
bread which comes down from heaven';* thirsty was
'the fountain of leaping water'.* Hungry was he,
thanks to whom no bird goes hungry;* thirsty
was he, who drenches and intoxicates the
soil.† Hungry was he, 'who gives food to all flesh';*
thirsty was he, the fountain of everlasting pleasure.* Now then stop in awe at this marvel, that his
growth increases with the passing of time, though he
always remains steadfast in the eternity of his Father,
though he always remains firm in the Majesty of his
Father. Marvel that he journeys from place to place,
although he is whole in every place and in himself
holds and possesses all creation. Marvel that the
Reviver of the dead at last lies dead, that the Resurrection of all persons is laid in a tomb, that he who
encloses all things, is enclosed in a tomb, that the
God of those above, is discovered among those below.

13. Certainly, after all the torments he bore for
us, he asks from us neither gold nor silver, nor
mantles nor priceless robes, nor bracelets, nor estates,
nor other possessions of that kind. He asks only that
we love him and for his sake keep our hearts and
bodies unsullied. 'You shall love the Lord, your God',
he says, 'with all your heart, with all your soul and
with all your mind,'* and unless we love, he
threatens us with eternal death.* 'If anyone loves

Jn 6:51
Jn 4:14
*Hymn of
St Ambrose
(Talbot 227, n. 9).
†Ps 64:10
*Ps 135:25

Ps 35:9

Mt 22:37
*Jude 7; 2 Th 1:9;
Mt 25:41.

me', he says, 'he will keep my word.'* Now you also, my beloved, how do you love him? He does not want to be loved in word alone but with a pure heart and with righteous deeds, because God is a reader not of words but of the heart.* How then are you keeping his word or his command,*[8] if you are pursuing not his will but your own? For you live as you wish; you go where you wish; you sleep when and as much as and as long as you wish; you eat and drink whatever and as much as and whenever you wish; you say what you please, with whom and wherever you please; you laugh and joke with whom you wish and whenever and as much as you wish. Finally, whatever is fragrant to your nostrils, harmonious to your ear, alluring to your touch, pleasing to your eye, enjoyable to your body, you welcome or pursue.

Jn 14:23

Pr 24:12
1 Jn 2:14

14. Come then, my beloved, come to fulfill not your will but the will of him who redeemed us with his precious blood.* For the Saviour of the world said: 'I came not to do my will but the will of Him who sent me.'* He did not wish to fulfill his own wishes, though always and truly perfect, but the wishes of another, and do you long to obey yourself? Never then, never let carnal love drive heavenly love away from you. Never let the fascination of the storm-tossed and pitiful world deceive you. Let no bodily charm seduce you, lest death enter your soul through your windows.* For what is beauty of the flesh? Does it not wither like grass scorched by summer's heat?* When death strikes and the last agony[9] seizes the limbs of the languishing, how much beauty remains in the body? Then you will realize the vanity of what was loved to distraction, when you have seen the whole body bloated and putrescent. Will you not avert your eyes then, lest the worms multiplying from the sores make you sick?*[10] Will you not mask your nostrils to avoid the stench? O where then will be the charm of wantonness and the banquets of merrymakers? Where then will be the flattering or coy words which used to tickle the ears of the company? Where the alluring banter which poured bitter-sweet into the ears of

1 P 1:19; Rv 5:9

Jn 6:38

Jr 9:21

Ps 101:12

Ex 16:20

Jos 9:13

Is 3:18

1 Jn 2:17

Jb 57:15

2 M 2:22-23.

*Mt 10:27, 35-37;
Mt 15:4-6;
Mt 19:29.

†Lk 9:59

Mt 10:37, 36

lovers? Where then the uninhibited and ribald laughter? Where then the joke and unbridled gaiety? Where then the subtlety of logic or of some other vain knowledge? Where then the syllogisms or proud sophistries? Where the gaudy costumes or the fancy shoes?*

15. Look, there is the end of carnal beauty and delight; there the finale of worldly charm.* This is the end of worldly pleasure. This is the goal of worldly gaiety. In truth, the world will pass away with its concupiscence.* Let nothing worldly divert your mind, my brother, let nothing distract you from the love of Christ. Let neither father nor mother, nor all the bonds of friendship prevent your coming to religious life. For if earthly parents are loved with great affection, because for a short time they shouldered[11] labors for us, should not the 'high and lofty'* God be more loved by us because he shouldered the cross for us? Yes, whatever devotion our parents showed us is his blessing, for before we were born into this world, by his providence he provided for us the parents by whose devotion we were cherished, and filled the breasts of our mothers with milk for our nourishment. So above all else, let us love our Redeemer and the One who fashioned with his own hands both ourselves and our parents, and to his good graces and not to our own powers let us attribute all the good which daily accrues to us.*

Scripture commands us to love our parents as our own flesh, if indeed they do not prevent our entering the service of Christ.* If they prevent us, we do not owe them burial.† Christ is to be loved above our parents, because parents do not grant us what Christ grants. He says in the Gospel: 'He who loves father or mother more than me, is not worthy of me; or he who loves' children or property 'more than me, is not worthy of me'. My son, if they should say: 'stay with us', do not agree, because 'a man's foes are those of his own household'.* Let no ambition for wealth delight you, because your fathers possessed churches by hereditary right. Listen to the psalmist: 'All who said: "for inheritance, let us possess the sanctuary of God", O my God, make them like whirling dust and like chaff before the face of the wind; as fire burns the forest and as flame consumes the mountains, so you will pursue them in your tempest, and you will terrify them in your anger.'* Do you see how the universal Church curses owners of this kind, as often as she sings this psalm?[12]

Ps 82:13-16

16. About refusing to seek riches,[13] I know not how many thousands of texts thunder. Listen to the Gospel about that rich man dressed in purple and at last buried in hell.* Listen also to the words of another rich man, when his fields had yielded abundant crops, 'Soul, you have ample goods laid up for many years', be merry, drink, feast! But the voice of God rebukes him: 'Fool, this night your soul is required of you; who then will own what you have amassed?'* With all your heart, then, shun riches. Those who wish to have riches neither seek them without effort nor find them without trouble, nor guard them without fretfulness, nor possess them without loving anxiety, nor lose them without grief.* 'And what does it profit a man, if he gains the whole world', 'but loses and forfeits himself?'† Just so, if eagerness for possessions attracts you, with carefree mind you may possess God, who possesses all his creation. In him keep whatever you desire to possess in holiness, because the Creator of all, whom none of his creatures can rival,[14] does not refuse to be possessed along with his creatures. But since no one possesses God but one who is possessed by God, by a holy life in religion you may first become the possession of God, that God may be your possession and portion.*

Lk 16:19-22

Lk 12:20

St. Aelred, Speculum Caritatis, 1:66 (Talbot 229, n. 6).
†*Mt 16:26; Lk 9:25.*

Ps 15:5

17. Here perhaps you will object: 'Harsh is the Order, many its labors, many its abstinences, much its endurance of cold, many its fasts, many the vigils there. Harsh there is the food and drink but harsher than both is the clothing.* Yet I am weak and delicate.* Because reared in the purple,† I cannot endure a life so hard or bear a regime so burdensome.' Oh, if only you knew how true is the saying: 'The kingdom of heaven suffers violence and the violent take it by storm',* how much violence you would do to

Talbot p. 219, n. 4
2 S 3:39.
†*Lm 4:5.*

Mt 11:12

yourself! For with violence, yes, with great violence
of the mind is God captured by the violent. Oh, if in
your mind's eye you should behold the torments of
the damned, how willingly you would endure the
light trials in this life, lest after this life you endure
eternal torments! Oh, do but consider the nature of
these evils: exclusion from the joy of divine contemplation; deprivation of the blessed company of all the
saints; exile from your heavenly fatherland; immer-
sion in everlasting fire with the devil and his angels,
where continual wailing, everlasting torment, supreme
grief and the pain of the senses rack souls without
respite and endlessly punish the bodies of the
damned. Consider the experience of fire in the
senses not because it illuminates but because it cruci-
fies;[15] the terrifying endurance of crackling and surging flames, your eyes blinded in the smarting gloom
of the smoking abyss; submersion in the depth of the
whirlpool of Gehenna, there to be gnawed forever
without respite by devouring maggots. These and
similar torments, I repeat, if you turn over alone
silently in your mind, I do not think this Order
should seem harsh to you, especially since blessed
Benedict arranges all things so discreetly, that neither
an old man should keep vigil, nor a young man keep
fast, nor should a weak man labor, nor in anything
should a healthy man overtax his strength.*

RB 48:24-5;
68: 2; 36.

18. Consider, moreover, with what loving kindness the divine Piety treats us in comparison with
those in the primitive Church. For we read that in
that tempest, for the love of Christ, not only youths
and old men but even very delicate maidens endured
punishments of all kinds. For some of them a great
sword with a sudden blow decapitated; others, the
wood of a cross framed; and others a saw with jagged
teeth slowly cut to pieces. Some were dashed to
pieces by the iron-shod hoofs[16] of wild horses;
others, mounted on wooden horses, were racked to
death. Some were incarcerated, others paid the penalty of exile. Some were exhausted by longlasting
hunger and thirst, others were weighed down by
heavy chains, while others were savagely beaten

until their bowels burst open. Some were torn limb from limb by the jaws of ravenous beasts, others were stung to death by the poisonous fangs of serpents, others in pathless ways were torn to shreds by the beaks of vultures, and others, exposed in the summer's heat, the sting of insects covered with sores. Some, left naked under the sky, froze to death in winter's frost; others, covered with earth, were buried alive; and some, flung from a height, were dashed to pieces. Some, lashed to treetops bowed to their roots, were torn asunder; others were torn limb from limb by mettlesome horses; and others, thrown into gorges, were swept away in the swirling waters. Some a raging fire consumed; others, not fire but acrid smoke suffocated; others, fiery hurdles or burning torches reduced to cinders and ashes; and others, not only glowing pitch or oil, but even boiling lead choked to death. Some were raised aloft on unbending cross-beams, others were pierced by the shafts of arrows, while others, attached to millstones, were drowned in the deep. Many a time also the divine Piety in its power snatched the elect from these tortures, so that their very torturers for the reward of martyrdom hastened exulting towards the palm.

19. Behold through what privations the holy martyrs of God merited the eternal kingdom. Not even the Son of God ascended to this kingdom without the anguishing torture of the cross. For this reason Truth in person says: 'If any man would come after me, let him deny himself, take up his cross and follow me.'* For this reason, permission was not *Mt 16:24* given to the disciple who wished to go bury his father.* For this reason, the poor of Christ are not *Mt 8:21-2* blessed with riches and Lazarus is preferred to the rich man in purple,* because narrow is the way *Lk 16:20-25* which leads to that life,* to which many are called *Mt 7:14* but few deserve to arrive among the elect.* For this *Mt 20:16* reason, without bloodshed, we in religious life endure serious and frequent privations, because it seems base and indecent for a soldier in comfort and ease to follow a King crowned with thorns, mocked,

pierced with a lance, covered with spittal and crimsoned with the blood of martyrdom. O the inestimable kindness of our eternal God! Though we who persevere in religious life do not feel the excruciating tortures of martyrdom, still he will grant us the rewards of martyrdom![17] So put an end to your delays. 'Perfect love casts out fear.* Take up the shield of faith, the breastplate of justice, the helmet of salvation and go forward to battle.* Modesty well guarded has its own martyrdom.

20. Consider the greatness of the promised reward, if indeed you can consider 'what no eye has seen, nor ear heard, nor the heart of man conceived'.* After the soul's departure, after the flesh's passing, after the embers and ashes, you must be renewed for a better state. With the elect you will be raised. Your body committed to earth must be lifted to heaven, and your mortality must put on immortality.* After this you are to be honored with the company of the angels. You will be welcomed into the eternal kingdom and remain forever with Christ. There you will fear no dissolution in time, once you are made secure in the glory of immortality and the splendor of incorruption. There all things which our first parent had corrupted by sin will be renewed in you for the better. You will enjoy understanding without error, memory without forgetfulness,* thought without distraction,†[18] charity without hypocrisy,** affection without offense,†† impassibility without weakness, salvation without sorrow, life without death, ease of movement without impediment, satiety without surfeit, and complete health without disease. Undoubtedly, so great is the beauty of justice there, so great the delight of eternal light that, were it not permitted to dwell there beyond the space of a single day, for this alone countless years of our life filled with delights would deserve to be despised. With neither feigned nor slight affection was it said: 'one day in your courts is better than thousands'.* Yet this text can also be understood in another sense, to mean 'thousands of days' in the changeableness of time, while 'one day' may be called the numberless-

Margin notes:

1 Jn 4:18

Eph 6:14-17

1 Co 2:9

1 Co 15:53-54

Aelred, Spec. Car., 1:9 (Talbot 229, n. 1).
†Na 1:11.
**Rm 12:9
††2 Co 6:3

Ps 83:11

ness of eternity.

21. Wherefore I pray and beseech you, most beloved, I pray and beseech you by the mercy of God, to despise everything base and perishable. In and above all things, 'remember your last end',* Always strive for those virtues of the soul wherewith one reaches the heights. For a virtue of your soul it is to safeguard the chastity of body and soul alike. A virtue of your soul it is to despise the vainglory of this world, to trample on all things of earth, to labor in the body for the love of him who redeemed you. A virtue of your soul it is to cherish humility and abominate pride. A virtue of your soul it is to check and repress anger and rage. A virtue of your soul it is to turn your back on all folly and to embrace divine wisdom. A virtue of your soul it is to suppress all love of the flesh and to lift your mind to Christ. A virtue of your soul it is to accompany whoever are good and to decline the companionship of the wicked, because 'evil associations corrupt good morals'.* Most truthfully was it said: 'with the elect you will be elect and with perverts perverted'.* Now the virtues I have mentioned, you will easily attain, if you check carnal desires under the vigorous regime of our Order. But if I should attempt to recount for you the virtue or holiness of our Order, believe me, day would fail me before my subject would.

Si 7:40

1 Co 15:53

Ps 17:27

22. So I bring your reading to an end, but never shall I bring my love to an end. Of this I warn you last, though of this I should have advised you first. Farewell, and above all, love Mary, the holy Mother of God, the Mother of Mercy.* Amen.

Antiphon, Salve Regina.

NOTES TO THE MILK OF BABES

1.   See 'A Letter of Roger, Abbot of Byland', introduction and Latin text of C. H. Talbot, in ASOC 7 (1951) 218-231. Talbot thinks the author of the letter is abbot Roger of Byland, the friend of St Bernard, St Aelred and Serlo of Savigny. 'Roger was one of the twelve monks who, in 1134, set out with their abbot Gerald from the Savigniac abbey of Furness to establish a house at Calder, and who, when that foundation was destroyed by the Scots and the community returned to take shelter at Furness, was turned adrift and forced to seek hospitality in Yorkshire. The community found a patron in Roger de Mowbray and by 1140, it was established on a firm basis at Hood. On the death of [abbot] Gerald two years later, Roger was elected abbot and continued to rule Byland for the next fifty-four years.' Probably this should read for the next fifty-one years, 1142-1193, for Roger resigned some three years before his death in 1196. Roger had much earlier confided his intention of resigning to Gilbert of Hoyland, whose answers are contained in Treatise 7 above. Roger's letter, an invitation to follow the Cistercian vocation, might well be compared with Gilbert's letter to Adam above, with St Bernard's Epp. 105, 106, 107, 108, 109, and with Petrus de Roya's 'inter epistolas S. Bernardi, CDXCII'. (Talbot, 218, nn. 3, 4) From the letter we learn much about Roger's attitude towards and understanding of the young, and much about G. whom Edmond Mikkers says is almost certainly Gilbert of Hoyland (272, n. 93).

I have checked Talbot's edition against a microfilm of the manuscript. Pembroke College, Cambridge, MS 154, ff. 169v-172v, and wish to thank 'The Master and Fellows of Pembroke College' and the College Librarian, R. C. Trebilcock, for the opportunity to consult the manuscript. My paragraphs vary slightly from Talbot's; the paragraphs have been numbered for convenient reference. The relationship between Roger and Gilbert has been considered in the introduction to the first volume of this work. In the first sentence the MS reads *elimare;* Talbot reads *eliminare.* For the rhetorical style of the first paragraph, see L. E. Marshall, 'Phalarae Poetae and the Prophet's New Words in the Anticlaudianus of Alan of Lille', *Florilegium* (1979) p. 255, p. 278, n. 35. Cambridge MS 154, from the late twelfth century, comes from Buildwas Abbey.

2.   MS *posteritatis crimen;* T. *prosperitatis crimen.*

3.   MS *quaeritur;* T. *quaerit.*

4.   MS *per hominem quem suscipere dignatus est.*

5.   Much of ¶¶3-4 ('In fact . . . endured.') is taken from Augustine, *De vera religione* 16.31.

6.   MS *Doluit quo aufugit dolor et gemitus.*

7.   MS *felicitate;* T. *securitate.*

8.   MS *custodis.*

9.   MS *dolor extremus.*

10.   MS *ne uermes scaturientes a sanie [facie?] nauseum provocent?*

11.   MS *sustinuere.*

12.   MS *recipit, reciuit* (?)

13. MS *De devitiis autem non appetendem (appetendis)*.
14. MS *equare*.
15. *nec sentire in illo ignem quod illuminat, sentire quod cruciat*.
16. Reading *armata* for MS *armato*.
17. MS *martirii tamen largiturus est donatiuum*.
18. MS *peruagatione*.

MASTER GILBERT, ABBOT, IN MS BODLEY 87
BODLEIAN LIBRARY, OXFORD

Master Gilbert, Abbot, is the author of a prologue and two sermons on St Matthew, in MS *Bodley 87, in the Bodleian Library, Oxford; he may be the author of other pieces in the same manuscript.*[1] *Jean Leclercq in 1953, Henri de Lubac in 1959, and Edmund Mikkers in 1963, drew attention to this Gilbert of Bodley 87.*[2] *In order of appearance the following authors contributed to* MS *Bodley 87: Peter Comestor, Bernard of Clairvaux, Aelred of Rievaulx, Achard of St Victor, Hugh of St Victor, Hildebert Cenomanensis, Master Gilbert, Abbot, Jean de Cornouailles, and Stephen Langton.*[3] *The authors of other pieces in the* MS, *I have not yet been able to identify; some of these will be considered later.*

From the titles to the prologue and the two sermons, probably in the same hand as that of the MS, *we can conclude that the author of these pieces was* Master Gilbert, Abbot. *In the summary catalogue of 1922, Madan and Craster added Gilbert of Hoyland. Jean Lelcercq in 1953, and Henri De Lubac in 1959, suggested as author, Gilbert of Hoyland, Gilbert of Stanford, or some other, not named. Finally Edmund Mikkers in 1963, although misled by the catalogue descriptions, suggested that the title of the prologue and the style of the first sermon suggest the authorship of Gilbert of Hoyland; he added, however, that the second sermon, thanks to the words of the title:* 'a magistro G. editus', *suggested a different author.*[4]

In the prologue, Master Gilbert, Abbot, in a light and friendly style reminiscent of Gilbert of Hoyland, acknowledges the receipt of a friend's commentary on Matthew and his request to Gilbert for comment and complementary notes. Deprecating his own ability, Gilbert consents to glean where his friend harvested, to fish with a line where his friend fished with a net, because Scripture is such a rich source of living nourishment. Many reasons prompt this printing of the Latin and the English versions side by side. Here some errors in the transcription of the Prologus *in* MS *15 (1953) 102-3, are corrected; here apparently is the first transcription of Gilbert's two Sermons on Matthew. The text follows the spelling of the Vulgate* Biblia Sacra *(Rome: Desclée, 1927) and of Lewis and Short,* Latin Dictionary *(Oxford: Clarendon, 1879, impression 1955).*

I. INCIPIT PROLOGUS GILEBERTI ABBATIS
SUPER EVANGELIUM SECUNDUM MATTHAEUM.

L USISTI UTILITER *ubertimque in ista jam pridem materia, et nunc supervacuos me jubes in ea labores instaurare. Quidni supervacuos? Verba haec a te sufficienter vindemiata sunt, et adhuc tenues, si qui residui sunt, me vis recolligere racemos.* Ero ergo juxta prophetam, 'sicut congregans in messe'* quod restiterit, et quasi spicas colligens,* si tamen colligens et non magis quaerens, sicut apud eundem prophetam in continenti legitur: 'Et erit', inquit, 'sicut quaerens spicas in valle.'* Quid enim est quod aut memoriam tuam fugerit aut non ingenium penetraverit? Quid est quod aut disputationis tuae copiae possit adjici vel cultius dici? Et praeripuisti quae dicerem et quae dicta sunt a te ne exspectes ut ego accuratius dicam.*

2. *Instas tamen et non raros racemos sicut cum finita vindemia,* sed ubertatem plenam deposcis uvarum. Nosti enim quod sacrae verba Scripturae, cum semel et bis vindemiata fuerint, ac si gravida sacris iterum soleant influere sensibus, et quasi prius tacta non essent, ubertim et inebriantem effundant expressa liquorem. Res ista nostrae facultatis non est, ◆ post veterum et modernorum studia, de pertractata materia novos et plenos sensus eruere. Spiritus ad oboedientiam promptus est, sed infirma* ad exsequendum scientia. Si ergo per noctem laborans nihil cepero, tibi imputa, in cujus imperio coactus quidem sermonis rete laxabo.* Si nihil cepero, tibi inquam imputa, qui totum extraxisti in sagena tua. Et quidem an aliquid sim capturus ignoro, unum autem scio quod in hoc me Jesus capit et claudit sermonem.*[5]

Dt 24:21
Is 17:5
Lv 19:9

Is 17:5

Is 24:13

◆ f. 90r

Mt 26:41

Lk 5:5

I. THE BEGINNING OF ABBOT GILBERT'S PROLOGUE ON THE GOSPEL ACCORDING TO MATTHEW

FOR A GOOD WHILE you have spent useful and abundant time on your commentary, and now you order me to take up a task you have made superfluous. Why superfluous? Having harvested the words of scripture like clusters of grapes, you wish me to gather up the sparse remains like dry stalks, if there be any to gather.* So according to the prophet, I shall be like one 'gleaning after the harvest'* whatever remains, and like one gathering kernels. Perhaps my task is not so much gleaning as searching,* as we read in the next words of this prophet: 'and he will be like one searching for kernels of corn in the valley.'* Now do tell me this. What has escaped your memory? What has not been lodged in your brain? What could be added to your ample exposition? What could be expressed in a finer style? You have anticipated any commentary of mine and please do not expect my commentary to be more refined than yours.

2. None the less you are importunate. You demand not the sparse gleanings after a harvest* but a full vintage from rich grapes. Yet as you know personally, even when the words of sacred Scripture have provided a first and a second vintage, because they are laden with sacred mysteries they are wont to well up again with fresh meaning, and as if they had not been touched before, they pour from the winepress an abundance of heady wine. The business you request is not within my power,♦ namely to elicit new and full meanings on passages already thoroughly treated after the studies of both ancients and moderns. The spirit is ready to obey but the mind is weak in execution. If then I toil through the night and catch nothing,* you may thank yourself, for subject to your bidding I shall let down the net of my sermon.* If I catch nothing, yes, you may thank yourself, for you caught the whole school in your seine. Though I do not know whether I shall catch even one fish, I do know one thing, that in this task Jesus both catches me and brings my talk to a close.[5]

SERMO DE EODEM INCIPIT SECUNDUM MATTHAEUM

THE BEGINNING OF A SERMON ON THE SAME
ACCORDING TO MATTHEW

1. The paradox in Jesus of peace vs. the sword. 2. The peace of God vs. the peace of the world. 3. The Apostles' thoughts of peace must be disciplined. 4–5. We must lift our longing for peace from earth to heaven. 6–7. Jesus fights peace with peace for his peace is a sword. 8. Against carnal peace, Jesus unsheathes a sword. 9–10. Peace with that strong one, the devil, is destroyed by the stronger Jesus, who releases his Church. 11. Where your love is, there is your peace! 12–13. Send fire and the sword, not of fear but of love! 14–16. The sword cuts the bonds of carnal affection, if they conflict with God's love. 17. The complementary interpretations of history and mystery. 18–22. The prodigal son compared with religious and monks. 23–24. From Jesus derive all the rights of carnal and spiritual kinship, and to him all should be returned. 25–26. Lay down your life and take up your cross, as did Christ the Protomartyr, Stephen the proto-martyr, and our own protomartyr.

[Throughout this section from Bodley 87, the paragraphs have been enumerated and summarized by the translator for the convenience of readers.]

II. SERMO DE EODEM INCIPIT
SECUNDUM MATTHAEUM[6]

1.' *IN ILLO TEMPORE dixit Jesus discipulis suis, nolite arbitrari quia venerim pacem mittere in terram', et reliqua.* Rem contra prophetarum proponit oracula et quod prius ipse mandavit et remandavit, jam demandare videtur.*[7] 'Nolite', inquit, 'arbitrari quia venerim pacem mittere in terram; non veni pacem mittere sed gladium.'*[8] Difficilis ad credulitatem res proponitur et quae nisi ipso Jesu auctore persuaderi non queat. Quis enim de Jesu aliud arbitretur? Quis non istud arbitretur? Quis non arbitretur Jesum venisse in opus reconciliationis et pacis? Apostolus se dicit pro Christo reconciliationis officio fungi,* quod ipse sit pax nostra qui fecit utraque unum.† Nonne et angelus in ipso ejus exortu pacem hominibus bonae voluntatis annuntiat,‡ et propheta in diebus ejus abundantiam pacis pollicetur?* 'Pacis ejus', inquit alius, 'non erit finis.'† Apostolus, propheta, et angelus pollicentur pacem, pacem super pacem in Jesu, et quomodo ipse dicit: non est pax?* Ergo confundas nos, Domine, ab expectatione nostra,* qui sustinuimus pacem et non venit. Propheta dicit, pax, pax, et tu dicis, non est pax.* Quod oracula de te perhibent, tu nos arbitrari prohibes: 'Nolite arbitrari quia veni pacem mittere in terram.' Et quidem pacem in Scripturam* non mittis, sed magis pugnam et deceptionem testimoniorum. Habemus de tua pace adversus te quasi 'quamdam nubem testium'* et tu dicis 'non veni pacem mittere in terram'. Et domestica verba quae procedunt de ore vestro*, ipsa adversus te testantur: 'Pacem', inquis, 'do vobis, pacem relinquo vobis.'*

2. Nonne haec sibi parum constare videntur, pacem non mittere et pacem relinquere? Quid sibi vult diversitatis hujus ratio: cum vadis, pacem dimittis; cum venis, pacem non mittis? Quid hic eligam*

*2 Co 5:18
†Eph 2:14
‡Lk 2:14

†Is 9:7

Jr 6:14, 8:11
Ps 118:116

Ez 13:16

sic MS

Heb 12:1

sic MS
Jn 14:27

THE BEGINNING OF A SERMON ON THE SAME
ACCORDING TO MATTHEW[6]

A T THAT TIME Jesus said to his disciples: Do not think that I have come to send peace upon earth', and so forth.* Jesus proposes something which contradicts the oracles of the prophets. What he himself previously commanded and recommended, he now seems to countermand:*[7] 'Do not think that I have come to send peace upon earth', he says, 'I have come to send not peace but the sword.'*[8] Something is proposed which is difficult to believe, and had Jesus not been its author, the proposal could not be accepted. For who would think of Jesus bringing anything but peace? Who would think that? Who would not think that Jesus had come for the work of reconciliation and peace? The apostle says that he was performing the ministry of reconciliation for Christ,* because Christ is our peace, for he made both [Jews and Gentiles] one nation.* At his birth did not the angel also announce 'peace to men of good will'?* And did not the prophet promise an abundance of peace in his day?* 'Of his peace', says another prophet, 'there will be no end.'* The apostle and the prophet and the angel promise peace, peace upon peace in Jesus, and how is it that Jesus says, 'there is no peace'?* Therefore you may disappoint us of our hopes, Lord, for we awaited peace and it did not come. The prophet says, 'peace, peace', and you say, 'there is no peace'. What the oracles ascribe to you, you forbid us to think of: 'Do not think that I have come to send peace upon earth.' In fact, throughout the Scriptures, you do not send peace, but rather quarrels and conflicting evidence. Concerning your peace, we hold over you, as it were, 'a cloud of witnesses',* yet you say: 'I have not come to send peace upon earth.' Your familiar words, which proceed from your own lips, bear witness against you: 'Peace I give you', your very words, 'Peace I leave you.'*

2. Do not these statements seem far from consistent: 'not to send peace' and again 'to leave peace'? What is the meaning of and the reason for this discrepancy? When you go, you send down peace; when you come, you do not send peace.* Which alternative I should prefer here, I do not

MS cupiditatem

Jn 14:27

♦ f. 90v

Ph 4:8

MS pre libero?

ignoro. Coartor quidem e duobus cupiditate hominis magis pacem penes te invenire et gratiam. An forte quia utrumque vitantis oraculum est, non optantis alterum eligere sed utrumque tenere? Et si alterum optabile est ut scilicet pacem relinqueres, alterum necessarium est ut pacem prius tollas, pacem illam quam signasti dicens 'non quomodo mundus dat, ego do vobis'. Est ergo pacis et pacis distinctio. Sed captioso ut sic dicam et ancipiti sermone, stuporem nobis et admirationem incurrere voluit et velut quemdam pigrae mentis excutere torporem, talia proponens quae et a prophetarum veritate, prima quidem facie, desciscant et humanae jura violent pietatis. Nam sermones quanto magis repugnantiam quamdam et inclementiam praeferre videntur in littera, eo nos ad perscrutandos congruos aliquos sed reconditos sensus in ipsis invitant.*

3. ♦ 'Nolite', inquit, 'arbitrari quia venerim pacem mittere in terram.' Cur istud sic dissuadet nisi quia videt vota eorem in hanc libenter reclinata partem et ad spem pacis prompte currentia? Cur, inquam, discipulos ab hoc arbitratu dissuadet, nisi quia videt eos et scripturarum in hoc ipsum informatos testimoniis et propriis animatos conjecturis? Etenim si oraculis non crederent, poterant operibus credere, operi pietatis. Pacis poterant spem parturire. 'Nolite', inquit 'arbitrari.' Durum est vobis et impossibile videtur de me durum aliquid, inhumanum aliquid, austerum aliquid arbitrari. Ideo quae amabilia sunt, quae placentia sunt, quae pacis, libenter arbitramini. *

4. Sed 'nolite arbitrari quia veni pacem mittere in terram'. Veni quidem pacem mittere, sed non veni in terram mittere, sed magis in terram et coelum. Veni enim pacificare non terrena terrenis, sed pacificare quae in terra sunt et quae in coelo. Pax ista non mittitur in terram, non in terram intendit, non dirigitur in terrena, sed trahit ad coelum. Illo nos minat, nam inde emanat. Mirabiliter blanditur et illectat per ubera pacis hujus et defloratae primitiae non tedium important sed ardentiore desiderio trahunt illuc ubi plena pax est et si quid potest dici plus pace.*

know. Of the two alternatives, I am constrained to choose by preference the longing of mankind to find peace and grace with you. Or am I constrained perhaps, because this is characteristic of one who would avoid both of the oracles and prefer not to choose one of the two but rather to cling to both? Now if one alternative is desirable, namely that you should leave peace, the other is necessary, namely that you should first take away peace, the peace you underscored by saying: 'not as the world gives, do I give you' peace.* So there is a distinction between one peace and another. But with his captious and ambiguous statement, so to speak, he wished to jolt us with wonder and amazement and to startle us from the stupor of indolent minds, by making statements which at first blush part company with the truth of the prophets and do violence to the rights of human loyalty. For the more his sayings literally seem to present some contradiction and unkindness, the more they invite us to search in them for some suitable though recondite meanings.

3. ♦ 'Do not think that I have come to send peace upon earth.' Why is he so intent on discouraging the thought of peace, if not because he notices that his disciples' longings readily veer towards peace and rush readily toward the hope of peace? Why does he discourage the disciples from this thought of peace, I ask, if not because he notices that they have been both trained by the witness of Scripture and inspired by their own conjectures to expect peace. Indeed, had they disbelieved the oracles, they could have believed his works, his work of salvation. They could have given birth to the hope of peace. Yet he says: 'Do not think!' It is hard for you and it seems impossible to think anything harsh of me, anything inhuman, anything austere. Hence you are quick to think of what is lovable, what is pleasant, what is characteristic of peace.*

4. But 'do not think that I have come to send peace upon earth.' I have come to send peace indeed. I have come to send peace, not upon earth, but upon earth and heaven. For I came not to reconcile things of earth with things of earth, but to reconcile what things are on earth and what things are in heaven. Your peace, Lord, is not sent upon earth, is not aimed at earth, is not guided towards earthly things, but draws towards heaven. To heaven it drives us, for from heaven it derives. In a marvellous way, it woos and allures through the breasts of this very peace. Its first fruits do not imply tedium in the harvesting, but with a keener desire attract towards heaven, where full peace exists with whatever reality may surpass our word for peace.

5. *Ubi pax est et id ipsum, id est pax et identitas,*
ibi veritas est et varietas non est. Veritas est in genera-
tione et non est vicissitudo interpolatione. 'In pace',
Ps 4:9   *inquit, 'in idipsum dormiam et requiescam.'* Illuc*
currunt et contendunt vota nostra sed requiescunt
illic ubi est pax et id ipsum, ubi est et pacata com-
munio et quod amplius est unio plena, ubi nec
contrarietas aliqua est, nec privati amoris in partem
Ps 67:14   *alteram avara contractio. 'Si dormiatis',* inquit*
psalmus, 'inter medios cleros', pacis et identitatis
illius volens depingere naturam, ubi de privato nullus
privatim exsultat sed dormit et delectatur et requies-
cit in communi. Quasi enim medium se inter dif-
ferentes sortes indifferentis gloriae collocat, qui vel
nil singulariter sibi optat, vel singulariter amat in se.
MS Non   *Nonne* tibi bene collocari videtur in medio et nullam*
plus reductus in partem, aequaliter et aliorum bona
sibi praesumens et sua illis impertiens? Magna pax
hujus et habens plus aliquid pace, et quamvis plenam
unitatem exprimere non queat, aemula tamen est
unitatis.

6. *Forte dicitis mihi: quo se proripit disputatio*
tua? quo sermo prolabitur? Quid tibi et paci illi?
Utinam totum, utinam multum, nunc autem modi-
cum est. Sed quid est? Sed tamen modicum pacis
hujus omnem exsuperat sensum. Etenim massae dul-
†MS deliberatione *cedo in delibatione† sentitur.* Bona quidam delibatio,*
*Rm 11:16   *gustus cujus omnem sensum exsuperat. Pax enim*
Ph 4:7   *Dei 'exsuperat omnem sensum',* non tantum scientis*
peritiam sed etiam experientiam sentientis. Quid
enim potest hac pace sentiri dulcius? Pax ista omnem
exsuperat affectum, et exsuperat et absorbet. Nihil
illi commune cum terrenis affectibus. Ideo dicit:
'non veni pacem mittere in terram'.

7. *Non potest illi terrena pax conferri nec potest*
MS illam   *illa* terrae. Non modo pax Dei exsuperat eam quam*
mundus dat pacem, sed absorbet atque abscidit, et
quasi gladius quidem separat animum ab his quibus
♦ f. 91r   *periculose inhaeret terrenis affectibus. Affectus ♦ af-*
fectum superat et pax absorbet. Videtis quo modo
Jesus pace adversus pugnat? Pax ejus et pax est et
gladius. Non mittitur in terram quasi pax sed quasi

5. Where peace exists and the self same, that is, peace and identity, there truth exists and change does not exist. Truth exists in generation and does not change through alteration. 'In peace in the self same', says the psalmist, 'I shall sleep and take my rest.' Our yearnings run and hasten heavenwards, but there they rest where peace and the self same exist, where undisturbed communion and, what is greater, complete union exists, where neither contradiction exists nor the covetous hoarding of selfish love for a single partner. 'If you sleep in the midst of the chosen',* says the psalmist, wishing to portray the nature of that peace and identity, when no one exults in private over private possessions but sleeps and takes his delight and his rest in common. Indeed, one who desires nothing for himself in a singular way, and loves nothing in himself in a singular way, places himself in the middle, as it were, amid different shares of undifferentiated glory. One who indiscriminately accepts for himself the goods of others and shares his own with them, does he not appear to you to be well placed in the midst and not drawn further away into some faction? His peace is great, indeed something greater than human peace, and although it cannot express full unity, still it does emulate that unity.

6. Perhaps you are wondering: 'where is your discussion leading? Where is your sermon veering? What have you in common with his peace? 'I wish my all were in common! I wish much of me were in common! But what I have in common is only a touch!' But what is that?' 'Even a touch of his peace surpasses all understanding, just as the sweetness of the whole batch of bread is tasted in the first crust.'* Good indeed is the crust, when its taste surpasses all understanding. The peace of God indeed 'surpasses all understanding',* not only the skill of one who has knowledge but also the experience of one who has sensitivity. What understanding can be sweeter than this peace? Your peace surpasses all affections, yes, surpasses and consumes. Your peace has nothing in common with earthly affections. Hence he says: 'I have not come to send peace upon earth.'

7. Earthly peace cannot be compared with your peace, nor can yours be compared with earthly peace. Not only does the peace of God surpass the peace which the world gives, but rather his peace consumes and cuts away earthly peace, and like a sword separates the spirit from these earthly affections to which the spirit clings to its peril. One affection ♦ surpasses another and one peace consumes another. Do you see how Jesus fights peace with peace? His peace is both peace and a sword. He is not sent upon earth as peace but as a sword, because his

gladius, quia pax hujus in terrenum et carnalem amorem incidit, non, sed succidit et absorbet eum. Non est illi pax cum affectu et pace carnali, nec communicat illi sed consumit illam. 'Non veni pacem mittere in terram sed gladium.' Ac si diceret: 'non veni pacem mittere' sed pacem tollere.

8. *Quid enim hoc, Domine Jesu? Cur non sufficit quod pacem non mittis nisi et gladium mittas? Pacem quam mundus amat non mittis. Cur illam adimis? Pax, fratres, pax carnis, inimica est Deo, non est paci Dei subjecta nec enim potest. Non potest subjici sed potest absumi. Non potest adhaerere paci Dei sed potest exhauriri ab ea. Qui in hac pace carnis sunt, qui non obluctantur, qui percusserunt foedus cum carne et cum mundo pacem, qui in hac inquam pace carnis sunt, hi Deo placere non possunt, quia nec Deus illis. Ideo pacem illam non bonam, pacem adversam paci suae, illam pacem non dimittit cum suam mittit, sed gladium educit adversus eam. Tenax enim est pax illa carnalis et violenti affectus co-*

MS *choérens*

haerens* glutino. Sed bonum non est. Idcirco gladio opus est ut possit pax prava dirumpi. Et si violenta est et vehemens ejus affectio, vehementior superveniens dividet illam et exhauriet. 'Cum fortis armatus custodit atrium suum, in pace sunt omnia quae possidet. Si autem fortior' supervenerit, 'universa arma' in quibus

Lc 11:21-3

confidebat, diripiet 'et spolia ejus distribuet'.*9

9. *Magna quidem et munita pax expressa est in eo quod ait, 'cum fortis armatus custodit atrium suum, in pace sunt ea quae possidet', sed fortior superveniens quia desuper veniens dissipavit pacem illam, coarctavit terminos fortis, exturbavit eum extra atrium quod in pace possidebat. Principem mundi ejecit*

Jn 12:31

foras.* Nonne tibi videtur iste fortis quasi in atrio locatus, cum in alicujus animo libere commoratur,

Cf. Bodley 87, f. 136r on Lk 11:21

cum evagatur spatiose, cum non certo coarctatur limite captivum eum tenens ad ipsius voluntatem, cum nemo pravos et indisciplinatos vel cogitatus vel actus compescit, nemo redarguit, cum non temptat qui tenetur captivitatis jugum excutere, non reluctari nec de libertatis suae statu controversiam movere, nonne in pace sunt ea quae fortis armatus possidet?

*Jr 3:3

peace cuts through earthly and carnal love, not only cuts through but also cuts down and consumes. He makes no peace with carnal peace and affection. He does not dally with this peace, he destroys it. 'I have not come to send peace upon earth but a sword', he said, as if he were to say, 'I have not come to send peace' but to destroy peace.

8.   Now why is this, Lord Jesus? Why is it not enough to say that you do not send peace unless you also send a sword? You do not send the peace which the world loves. But why do you destroy the world's peace? Peace, brethren, the peace of the flesh, is the enemy of God. That peace is not and cannot be subject to the peace of God. Though it cannot be made subject, it can be annihilated. Though it cannot embrace the peace of God, it can be throttled by the peace of God. They who dwell in this peace of the flesh, who do not struggle against it, who have made a pact with the flesh and peace with the world, they, in short, who coexist with this peace of the flesh, cannot please God for he cannot please them. Hence that peace without goodness, that peace opposed to his peace, that peace he does not send down when he sends his own peace, but against that peace he unsheathes a sword. Carnal peace is tenacious and stuck with the glue of passionate affection. But it is no blessing. Hence a sword is needed to cleave asunder that base peace. If in that peace there is a violent and passionate affection, an even more violent passion overtaking it will sheer it asunder and exhaust it. 'When a strong man, fully armed, guards his own palace, his goods are in peace. But if a stronger man' should overtake him, he will plunder 'all the armour' in which he trusted and 'auction off the spoils'.*[9]

9.   Some great and fortified peace was meant by what the Lord said: 'when a strong man, fully armed, guards his own palace, his goods are in peace', but a stronger man, overtaking him because coming from above, shattered that peace, limited the boundaries of the strong man, routed him from the palace which he was occupying in peace. The prince of this world, the Lord cast out.* Does not that prince seem to you like a strong man residing in a palace, when in someone's spirit he dwells undisturbed, when he wanders at large, when he is not confined within a fixed limit but keeps the spirit bound to his will? When no one restrains and no one checks his base and undisciplined thoughts or actions, when the captive makes no effort to cast off the yoke of captivity, nor to fight back, not to initiate an inquiry into the state of his freedom, is it not true that 'those goods are kept in peace, which the strong man fully armed possesses'? The one for whom the face of the harlot has been so made up that she knows not how to blush,* the one who dreads no

†Jr 8:12
‡Pr 1:25

Cui facta est frons meretricis ut erubescere nesciat,†
qui increpationes non veretur,‡ penes illum ille fortis
non in angulo latitat sed in animo palam versatur et in
pace. Illi qui possidet pax est, non ei qui possidetur;
species pacis est sed veritas servitutis.

Is 28:15

   10. *Percussit 'foedus cum morte et cum inferno'*
pacem. Quomodo non dicetur inisse pactum cum*
morte, qui pacem tenet cum stimulo mortis? 'Stimulus

1 Co 15:56

enim mortis peccatum est.' Durum tibi videtur*
contra stimulum hunc calcitrare sed durius erit serae
et infructuosae paenitentiae stimulum tolerare, sti-
mulum inquam serae paenitentiae et sempiternae
punitionis. Quae enim pax cum igne devorante et cum
ardoribus sempiternis? Videte quam iniqua pax cum
peccato de qua tales fructus proveniunt! 'Justitia',

Ps 84:11

inquit psalmus, 'et pax osculatae sunt', non pax et*
iniquitas. Veni, Jesu bone, mitte gladium, iniquam
hanc cautionem rescinde. Non stet foedus cum morte,

♦ f. 91v

nec pax cum peccato. ♦ Veni, domine, in gladio in*
quo datum est tibi juxta apocalypsium pacem tollere

Rv 1:16
Gn 3:15
†Lc 10:9

de terra, inimicitias quas pollicitus es pone inter*
mulierem et serpentem. Superiorem se illa agnoscat.*
Ambulet super serpentem et scorpionem.† Ille humi
repat; illa se erigat. Conterat et conculcet in terra
caput ejus. Et si ipsa conculcata aliquamdiu in terra
fuerat, de cetero calcet terram, dat enim Dominus

Is 42:5

'spiritum calcantibus eam'. Sublimis incedat, ne sit*
similis trahentium super terram atque serpentium, ne
gradiatur pectore et ventre, nec adhaereat pavi-

Ps 43:25

mento, nec conglutinetur in terra venter ejus. Non*
dicat mihi: adhaerere terrae bonum est et congluti-

Is 41:7

nari ei; ubi adhaesio est et glutinium, ibi amor. *

   11. *Ubi amor, ibi pax. Ideo pacem hanc amoris*
terreni abscidere volens, dicit Scriptura: 'nolite dili-

1 Jn 2:15

gere mundum, neque ea quae in mundo sunt', quia*
'omne quod in mundo est, concupiscentia carnis
est et concupiscentia oculorum et superbia vitae'. *

1 Jn 2:16

Flamma haec triplex difficile extinguitur. Flamma
concupiscentia est; fomes ejus quidquid in mundo;*

Si 9:9

ingens flamma et magnus fomes, flatus autem ser-
pentis succendens eam. Veni, Domine Jesu, 'veni*

Dt 8:15

ignem mittere in terram' qui illum ignem extinguat,

rebukes,* then in that soul, the strong man does not skulk in a corner but struts in that spirit openly and at peace. Peace belongs to the one who possesses, not to the one possessed; the latter possesses the appearance of peace but the reality of enslavement.

10. He made 'a convenant with death and peace with Sheol'.* How will one not be said to have struck a treaty with death, who keeps peace with the goad of death? For sin is the goad of death.* To you it seems hard to kick against the goad but it will be harder to endure the goad of a late and unfruitful repentance, I mean the goad of a late repentance and of everlasting punishment. For what peace is found with devouring fire and undying flames? See how iniquitous is peace with sin, from which such fruits derive. 'Justice and peace have kissed each other',* says the psalmist, not peace and injustice. Come, Good Jesus, send the sword, rescind this writ of iniquity. Spare neither the treaty with death nor peace with sin. ♦ Come, Lord, in the sword in which it is granted you, according to the Apocalypse, to expel peace from the earth.* Place between the woman and the serpent the enmities you promised.* Let her acknowledge her superiority. Let her tread upon the serpent and the scorpion.* Let him creep upon the ground; let her rise to her full height. Let her grind his head in the earth beneath her heel. And if for a time on earth she had been trodden under foot, in future let her tread the earth, for the Lord gives 'spirit to those who tread the earth'.* Let her advance with head held high. Let her not resemble those who drag themselves along and creep upon the ground. Let her not go upon her breast and her belly. Let her not cling to the hard ground; let not her belly be glued to the ground.* Let her not say to me; it is a blessing to cling to the earth and to be glued to the ground; where your embrace is and your bonding, there is your love.*

11. Where your love is, there is your peace. Desirous, then, of cutting off this peace of earthly love, Scripture says: 'do not love the world or things in the world', . . . for 'all that is in the world is the lust of the flesh and the lust of the eyes and the pride of life'. With difficulty is this triple flame extinguished. The flame is lust;* its tinder is anything whatever in the world; mighty is the flame and abundant the tinder, but the serpent's bellows fan the flame.* Come, Lord Jesus, come 'to send fire upon the earth', which can extinguish, which can consume that fire. That fire consumes to our ruin; your fire consumes for our salvation. Send fire, O Lord, and a sword. Let your fire ignite

qui absumat. Ignis ille ad perditionem devorat; tuus
ad salvationem. Mitte, Domine, ignem et gladium.
Ignis succendat; gladius succidat. Denique, gladius
tuus flammeus est,* ad aperiendam viam ligni vitae,†
cuncta temptamenta vel intercidens, ne continuata et
aequaliter vehementia sint, vel succendens et com-
burens, ut omnino non sint. O felicem animam in qua
ignis hujus scintillae quasi in arundineto discurrit,* in
qua facilem et aptam ad succendendum inveniunt
materiam et omni terreni amoris viriditate dessica-
tam, quae velut arundinea fragilis sit ante faciem
devorantis flammae tuae, ut ignis Spiritus leniter in
illa pertranseat et non subsistat aliquo retardatus
obstaculo.*

12. Emitte, Domine, ignem de coelo in ossibus
meis.* Superior inferiorem consumat. Mitte concupiscentiam spiritus adversus concupiscentiam carnis;
adversa sit, sed superior sit. Non sit inter illas aequa
congressio,* oportet enim hanc crescere et illam
minui.* Sed diu desaeviit sola concupiscentia carnis.
Intercide jam, Domine, flammam ignis ejus.† Intercide concupiscentiam carnis; spiritualis intercedat.
Intercide eam. Non audeo dicere ut plene succidas,
non enim venisti ad hanc* succisionem facere sed
separationem. Bona quidem separatio, ubi consensus
a concupiscentia carnali dividitur,* spiritualis enim
concupiscentiae dulcis violentia, quasi gladius acutus
et limatus intercurrens, consensum a carnali* concupiscentia diducit et abstrahit, et suae facit parti
favere. Dulcescit multo amplius concupiscentia spiritus, ideoque mentis propositum de quo conflictus
omnis est a carnali separat et illam temperat, immi-
nuens et dividens aestum ejus super terram* ut et
remissior sit et rarius veniens.

13. Acutus quidem timor est. Sicut dicit psalmus:
'confige timore tuo carnes meas',* sed ego in gladio
quem Dominus in terram mittit, non timorem sed
amorem intelligo, eo quod apostolus dicit: 'spiritum
servitutis' non accepisse nos 'iterum in timore, sed
. . . spiritum adoptionis filiorum'.* Et Dominus se
dicit ignem mittere in terram in quo Spiritum et
caritatem accepimus. Timor igneus non est, etsi

*Gn 3:24
†Pr 3:18

Ws 3:7

Ps 102:16

Jr 20:9

Jdt 7:9
Jn 3:30
Ps 28:7

MS hunc

1 Co 7:5

MS carna

Jb 38:24

Ps 118:120

Rm 8:5

and your sword excise. Your sword is aflame,* as Scripture says, to clear the path of the tree of life,* either cutting through all temptations lest they be equally incessant and violent, or igniting and burning until they are no more. O happy soul, in which the flame from this spark seems to race through the stubble,* in which they discover kindling ready and apt for burning, with the green wood of earthly love dried out! O happy soul, which resembles a fragile reed facing your devouring flame, so that the fire of the Spirit may gently pass through and not come to a stop, delayed by some obstacle.*

12. Send forth fire from heaven, O Lord, within my bones. Let your superior fire consume the inferior. Send concupiscence of the spirit to oppose concupiscence of the flesh; let it be opposed but superior. Between them let there be no equal contest,* for what is of the spirit must increase and what is of the flesh must decrease.* But for too long concupiscence of the flesh has raged unopposed. At last, O Lord, cut off the flame of its fire.* Cut off the concupiscence of the flesh; let the spiritual intervene. Cut off concupiscence of the flesh. I do not dare suggest that you cut it down completely, for you have come to complete not the severance but the separation. Good indeed is the separation, when consent is divorced from carnal concupiscence,* for the sweet violence of spiritual concupiscence, intervening like a sharp and polished sword, sunders and withdraws consent from carnal concupiscence and leads consent to favor the spiritual side. Concupiscence of the spirit becomes much more attractive; therefore it separates the resolution of the mind, the basis of every battle, from carnal concupiscence; it chastens that concupiscence, lessening and dividing its surge upon earth,* that it may be calmer and more infrequent.

13. Fear is indeed sharp. As the psalmist says: 'pierce my flesh with your fear.'* But in the sword which the Lord sends upon earth, I understand not fear but love, because the apostle says that 'we have not received a second time the spirit of slavery in fear, but . . . the spirit of adoption as sons'.* The Lord says he sends fire upon earth, in which we understand the Spirit and perfect love. Fear is not fiery, although it is sharp, but love is both sharp and fiery. ◆ Therefore even the bride in the Song of Songs confesses both that she has been

144 Bodleian 87: Sermon

acutus est; amor et acutus et igneus. ◆ Ideo et sponsa in Canticis Canticorum et vulneratam caritate se fatetur,* et animam ejus liquefactam alloquio dilecti.† Timor restringit, liquefacit amor. Ille mortificat, amor vivificat. 'Vivus est' enim amor Dei 'et efficax et penetrabilior omni gladio ancipiti, pertingens usque ad divisionem animae et spiritus'.* Et si pertingit hic gladius ad divisionem animae et spiritus, quomodo non multo magis carnis et spiritus? Si tamen aliqua est distinctio inter carnem et animam cum opponuntur spiritui, quid tamen non est loci hujus disserere. Id enim magis urget quod suscepimus spiritualis dilectionis edocere virtutem et quod illae, scilicet carnalis et animalis, non praevalent adversus eam.

14. Gladius iste acutus est, artissima vincula necessitudinis carnalis dirumpit. Quae artior necessitudo quam inter patrem et filium, matrem et filiam?[10] Quae dabit aut religiosiora* iura dilectionis aut dulciora? Quo propensior affectus, eo plus afferens impedimenti adversus negotia fidei et caritatem Dei. Magna obligatio et religionis praeferens speciem.* Sed audi quid ipse Jesus prosequatur in evangelio, qui non venit 'pacem mittere sed gladium'. 'Veni', inquit 'separare hominem adversus patrem suum et filiam adversus matrem suam et nurum adversus socrum suam'.* Et in sequentibus nec ut se ipsum diligat liberum esse sinit homini sed vult ut tollat crucem suam et sequatur ipsum.* Triplicem mihi videtur hic separationem† inducere et sub trina distinctione omnes commemorare personas in quas dilectionis solemus affectu moveri. Item* illas quae primo loco sibi necessitudinis iure colligatae sunt, ut pater et filius, secundo quae mediantibus aliis, ut socrus et nurus, tertio eas quae tam sibi aliquo vinculo adunatae sunt quam unae in se, ut cum vult hominem perdere animam suam propter se* et odio habere eam in hoc mundo,† hoc est, ut succincte dicam, et cognationis et affinitatis et identitatis, si sic dici potest, rescindit affectus, totum ad se trahere volens a quo totum est, a quo sicut et a patre omnis hac in terra paternitas nominatur.* Et si nominatur

Sg 2:5
†Sg 5:6

Heb 4:12

MS religiosora

MS 15 (1958) 102, n. 13

Mt 10:35, Lk 12:53
Mt 16:24, Mc 8:34, Lk 9:23
†Lk 12:51
MS Idem

Mt 10:39
†Jn 12:25

Eph 3:15

◆ f. 92r

wounded by charity,* and that her soul has melted at the word of her Beloved.* Fear congeals but love melts. Fear brings death but love gives life. The love of God is 'living and active, sharper than any two-edged sword, piercing to the division of soul and spirit'.* If this sword pierces 'to the division of soul and spirit', why not much more to the division of flesh and spirit? Now if there is any distinction between flesh and soul when they are opposed to spirit, still this is not the place to discuss what the distinction is. We have undertaken something more urgent: to explain thoroughly the virtue of spiritual love and that carnal and animal loves do not prevail against spiritual love.

14. The sword of the Lord is sharp; it severs the closest bonds of kinship. What bond of kinship is closer than that between father and son, between mother and daughter?[10] What confers more sacred or more tender claims of love? The more natural the affection, the greater the impediment it poses to the practice of the faith and to the love of God. Relationship is a serious obligation and gives the appearance of a sacred bond.* Hear how Jesus himself, who did not come 'to send peace but the sword', continues in this Gospel: 'I came to set a man against his father and a daughter against her mother and a daughter-in-law against her mother-in-law'.* In a later verse he does not leave anyone free for self-love but wants each to take up the cross and follow him.* Here he seems to me to introduce a threefold separation* and under a triple distinction seems to recall all the persons towards whom we are wont to be moved by affectionate love. Likewise he recalls first the persons who are joined together by the rights of kinship, father and son for example, secondly those who are joined together through intermediaries, mother-in-law and daughter-in-law for example, and thirdly those who are not so much united to each other by some bond but unified in themselves, for example when Christ wishes someone to lose his own soul for Christ's sake,* and to holds his soul in hatred in this world.* This means in a nutshell, that he cuts off the affections of kinship and affinity and identity (if one may so express it) because he desires to restore everything to him from whom everything comes, from whom as from a father all fatherhood on this earth derives its name.* Now if fatherhood derives its name from the Father, what is denominated and derivative ought not to lay down the law for its originator, nor should there be a stronger

ab eo, non debet originali denominata et derivata praescribere nec validior esse nexus aemulae et imitatricis quam principalis et propriae. Ideo inter patrem et filium separationem immittit pro fide, ne carnalis affectionis nexu adhaereat alter alteri contra fidem.

15. Non dirumpit vincula pietatis quae colligavit sed religionis impedimenta dissolvit. Dum enim vicissim consolationem sibi aut impendunt aut excipiunt, pigrius ad fidei religionem moventur, sed non penitus desistunt. Copula naturae in culpa non est, sed in causa. Affectiones dulces gignuntur ex ea et amor mutuosus* quasi quodam naturae debito et indissolubili jure offensiones in alterutram partem praecavens et deferens reverentiam. Sed praecepti auctoritas juris hujus, siquidem esse videtur, nexum solvit, et caritas diffusa in cordibus per Spiritum sanctum* aestuantis affectionis et in contrarium nitentis revincit ardorem flamma scientiore. Ergo et in eadem persona immissa est pugna inter carnem et spiritum et inter conjunctas naturae lege personas, dum studiis pro fide et contra fidem contrariis nituntur. Nec tam foedera in vitio sunt, quam necessitùdinis vinculo foederatae sibi invicem personae.

16. ◆ Denique et necessitudines in senario sunt, et juxta Lucam* in quinario personae, ut illas a culpa numeri perfectio vindicet† et numerus ad carnalium sensuum animalitatem pertinens istas incuset. 'Animalis enim homo non percipit quae sunt Spiritus Dei.'* Ideo impugnat illos qui cum prius animales essent, iam spirituales effecti sunt et ab illa in qua prius concorditer vixerant sensualitate divisi.* Putas autem mysterio vacare quod hi qui velut vitae praeferunt novitatem sicut filius, sicut filia, sicut nurus, ad senarii pertingunt medium cum e contrario vetustati* adhuc adhaerentes, id est pater et mater, citra subsistant nec possunt ex aequo cum illis ad perfecti numeri pertingere mensuram? Pulchra quidem mysteria adumbrantur* in istis, sed nobis liberum non est cuncta ex otio persequi sicut et illud quod de socru et nuru interserit. Plus ad mysterii videtur spectare secretum quam ad cohaerentiam et seriem litterae.

MS sic

Rm 5:5

◆f. 92v
*Mt 10:35,
Lk 12:52.
†MS vendicet

1 Co 2:14

1 Co 15:44-5

Heb 8:13

G. favors this
word. Cf. T 4.2.

link with a portrait or an imitation than with the original and the real person. Hence for the faith Christ interposes a separation between father and son, lest through the link of natural affection one should cling to the other contrary to the faith.

15. The bonds of devotion which Christ fashioned, he does not break, but he does remove impediments to religious life. For as long as relatives now give and now receive mutual consolation, they are less readily moved to a commitment of faith, although they do not entirely renege. Natural ties are not to blame but they are responsible. Tender affections are born of these ties, and love, derived as it were from some natural obligation and indestructible claim, tries to deflect attacks against either relative but to admit acts of deference. But the authority of a divine precept dissolves the link of natural ties, if it seems to exist, and 'love poured into our hearts by the holy Spirit',* with a wiser flame dampens the raging heat of contrary affections. Hence conflict has been sent between the flesh and the spirit even in the same person and between persons joined by the natural law, while they struggle with opposing interests, those for the faith and those against the faith. The point is not so much that alliances are faulty, as that persons are mutually allied by the bond of kinship.

16. ♦ In Matthew, kindred are divided into sixes,* in Luke persons are divided into fives,* so that the perfect number redeems Matthew's sixes from guilt but a number equivalent to the perception of the carnal senses leaves Luke's groups of five subject to reproach. For 'the sensual man does not perceive what things belong to the Spirit of God'.* Hence Paul assails those who, although previously they had been sensual, have now become spiritual and been divided from the sensuality in which they had once lived harmoniously.* But in your opinion, is it devoid of mystery that the young who prefer newness of life, the son and the daughter and the daughter-in-law, total one half of the number six, while on the contrary the elders who still cling to the old life,* namely the father and mother, fall short of and cannot equal their share of the perfect number? Beautiful mysteries indeed lurk in the shadows* of these symbols, but we are not free to explore all these points at leisure, for example the point he interposes about the daughter-in-law and her mother-in-law. This seems to relate more to the hiddenness of mystery than to a literal connection and sequence. What new truth is contained in the separation between a mother-in-law and

Quid enim novi continet separatio illa inter socrum et
nurum? Quando affectu concordi sibi confoederan-
tur? Omnes enim socrus oderunt nurus.* Zelo moveri
solent ad invicem et Dominus eas cum patre et filio,
cum matre et filia connumerat, quae personae pio
sibi conglutinantur affectu. An Dominus in eis non
ad consuetudinis vitia sed ad jura respexit necessitudinis? Fere ita est, nam etsi inter illas adsit usus
zelandi causa subest tamen amandi.

    17. Sic sentiat qui voluerit; mihi Christus in his
verbis mysteria loquitur. Nec sibi repugnant historia
et mysteria, series enim litterae sacramenta non
evacuat. Quocumque volueris intellectum verte; intellige hoc proprie et singulariter in personis; intellige in
populis; socrum synagogam accipe, nurum primi-
tivam de gentibus ecclesiam quae synagogae filiis,
apostolorum choro, nupsit. Quocumque rem vertas,
separationis non mutatur ratio, sed inter carnem et
spiritum conflictus vertitur et veteribus nova repugnant. Ubique Christus separationem immittit et quasi
ancipiti gladio hinc inde et hereditarium veritate
rescindit errorem et paternum caritate Dei resecat
affectum. Quod si patres carnis nostrae non reveremur
adversus caritatem Dei, illos patres a quibus et genera-
tionis initia et naturae substantiam ducimus, quanto
magis ille deserendus est qui magister erroris, qui in
cathedra pestilentiae sedit?* Est et ille non bonus
pater, quem Salomon senem et stultum vocat,† de
quo Dominus Judaeis improperat quod de patre
diabolo essent.* Hic est Ille 'incentor malorum'† qui
suggestione prava concupiscentiam carnalem, quae in
membris nostris est, corrumpit et adulterat, ut illa cum
conceperit pariat peccatum.* Hujus patris omnis est
in nobis exterminanda generatio, plantatio extir-
panda, parvuli quos genuit cogitatus allidendi ad
petram,* Christum.

    18. Bonum est si degenerem hanc generationem
deleas, si non genueris in reliquis ejus, si signa ejus
non resideant in te, si separaveris vilem hanc generationem a pretiosa. Quasi os Domini eris, 'si separaveris pretiosum a vili'.* Ideo contende, repugna et
gladio quem Dominus misit in terram abscide obsta-

Mi 7:6

Ps 1:1
†Qo 4:13

*Jn 8:44
†2 M 4:1

Ja 1:15

Ps 136:9

Jr 15:19

her daughter-in-law? When do they become allied in harmonious affection? All mothers-in-law and daughters-in-law hate each other.* They are wont to share the emotion of mutual jealousy. So the Lord enumerates them with father and son, with mother and daughter, although the latter persons are bonded together by devout affection. Or in these in-laws, was the Lord paying attention not to their usual bad habits but to the rights of kinship? That is close to the truth, for although the habit of jealousy occurs between them, still there remains an underlying reason for mutual love.

17. Anyone who so wishes may adopt this opinion; but in my view Christ is presenting mysteries in these words. History and mystery are not at odds, for the sequence of the literal sense does not exclude hidden meanings. Turn your attention wherever you wish; understand this point properly and singularly about the persons; understand it about the peoples; interpret the mother-in-law as the synagogue, the daughter-in-law as the primitive church of the gentiles which was married to the sons of the synagogue, the chorus of apostles. Wherever you turn this topic, the reason for separation does not change: a conflict arises between the flesh and the spirit, and the new is at odds with the old. On all sides Christ introduces separation. On left hand and right, as if with a two-edged sword, with truth he prunes the heritage of error and with the perfect love of God he lops off paternal affection. But if we do not revere the fathers of our flesh contrary to the perfect love of God, those fathers from whom we derive the first steps of our generation and the substance of our nature, how much more should he be abandoned who is the master of error and who 'sits on the throne of pestilence'?* Nor is he a good father, whom Solomon calls old and stupid,* and thanks to whom the Lord excoriates the Jews for being sons of their father, the devil.* He is that 'prompter of misery'* who by his depraved suggestion corrupts and adulterates the carnal concupiscence which is in our bodies which after conceiving, may beget sin.* In us, everything begotten of this father must be exiled, every plant uprooted, the brain children he has generated must be dashed against the rock, Christ.*

18. It is good if you destroy this degenerate generation, if you beget no offspring from his descendants, if you harbor in yourself no characteristic of his, if you separate a worthless breed from a priceless. 'You will be as the mouth of the Lord, if you separate what is precious from what is worthless.'* Hasten then and do battle; with the sword the Lord has sent upon earth, cut down the obstacles; do not cease

cula, ne cesses donec movearis et promovearis a generatione quae est in malo et a malo in generationem* sine malo. A tali ◆ patre te vult dividi Jesus. Hanc ille separationem mittit; nam est quae non est per Jesum nec illam ipse mittit. Si quis se a patre spirituali non dico loco sed vel affectu et animo disjunxerit, si consilia sua in ipso non maneant, si furetur illi conscientiam suam propriaeque voluntatis occultos panes libenter edat et aquam bibit furtivam, non talem separationem docet Jesus, qui venit non suam sed Patris voluntatem facere,* non Paulus, qui dicit: 'obedite et subjacete propositis vestris; ipsi enim invigilant quasi rationem reddituri pro animabus vestris.'*

19. Junior ille filius vide quam inutiliter se a patre fratreque diviserit, quomodo viae suae fructus comederit consiliisque suis saturatus sit, qui non potuit siliquis saturari. 'Da mihi', inquit, 'portionem substantiae quae me contingit.'* Nescivit subesse, nescivit coesse, subjectionem consortiumque declinans, et ideo in obligationem declinavit. 'Da mihi', inquit, 'portionem, quae me contingit.' Portionem separatam petit, qui totum in communi melius possideret. Dividi sibi voluit substantiam, ideo dispersit, dedit meretricibus.* Qui enim non colligit cum patre, mecum dispergit.† Accepit portionem, recessit a patre; et patrem et partem quam acceperat amisit, denique et se ipsum propterea, et in se ipso reversus dicit.* Tot mala invexit divisio mala. Videte, fratres, ne sit in aliquo vestrum cor malum singularitatis, discedendi a consortio fratrum, a spiritualis patris custodia. Videte ne quis vestrum qui communem estis professi vitam* in hoc ipsum incidat separationis et proprietatis exemplum. Ne dicat: 'da mihi portionem quae me contingit.' Et si ille adulescentior istud inutiliter dixit, forte licenter dixit. Vobis autem dicere non licet: 'da mihi portionem quae me contingit', quia nec particulariter possidere licet.

20. Utinam tamen imitemur adolescentioris hujus modestiam. Improbum quidem quod dividere voluit,

MS generatione
Ex 17:16
◆ f. 93r

Jn 4:34

Heb 13:17

Lk 15:17

*Ps 111:9,
2 Co 9:9
†Lk 11:23

Lk 15:17

MS 15 (1953)
102, n. 13

until you are moved and promoted from a generation which exists in evil and from evil to a generation without evil.* From such a father ♦ Jesus wants you to be divided. He sends this separation, for another separation exists which does not exist through Jesus and which he does not send. If anyone should withdraw himself from his spiritual father, I do not mean geographically but in affection and in spirit, if he does not keep his spiritual counsels, if he steals his own conscience from him, if he freely battens on the hidden loaves and drinks the stolen waters of his own will, such a separation Jesus does not teach, for he came not to do his own but his Father's will;* nor does Paul teach this, for he said: 'obey your leaders and be subject to them, for they are keeping watch over your souls, as men who will have to give account.'*

19. See how unprofitably that younger son cut himself off from his father and his brother, how he consumed his profits along his way and was glutted with his own counsels, although he could not be glutted with the husks of swine. 'Give me the share of property', he said, 'which falls to me'.* He knew not how to be subordinate, he knew not how to coexist, for he shunned both subordination and common life and therefore he fell under an obligation. 'Give me the share of property', he said, 'which falls to me.' He seeks a separate share, when he might more profitably possess the whole property in common. He wanted the substance to be divided for himself, and therefore 'he distributed, he gave'* to wantons. 'He who does not gather' with the father, 'scatters' with me.* He received his share. He withdrew from his father. He lost both his father and the share he received, and therefore, according to Luke, he lost even himself, for 'returning to himself, he said'.* An evil division brought on so much evil! Beware, brethren, lest in any of you there exist the evil heartedness of singularity, of withdrawing from the community of your brothers and the watchfulness of your spiritual father. Beware lest any of you who have made profession of the common life,* fall into this very pattern of withdrawal and private property. Let no one say: 'give me the share of property which falls to me.' If the younger brother made that statement unprofitably, perhaps he made it licitly. But it is not licit for you to say: 'give me the share which falls to me', because it is illicit for you to possess private property.

20. Now would that we might imitate the unassuming conduct of this younger son. It was shameful that he wanted to divide the pro-

sed modestum quod nisi a patre non voluit. Non clam tollit, non surripit, nec subducit, sed dicit: 'Da mihi'. Nobis autem ducere non licet, quia nec dicere licet: 'Da mihi portionem.' Quomodo dicere poterit: 'Da mihi portionem', quia et nuditatem professus est et communitatem. Non tamen in re pecuniaria haec ratio tantum vertitur. Qui singulari quadam reverentia prae ceteris tractari vult, suo degere iure ubi nemini permittitur ipsum sui esse iuris, qui illud sibi pro meritis postulat, nonne tibi videtur is portionem quae ipsum contingit quasi de excellentiae suae rogare jure? Quidam ne hoc quidem contenti sunt, sed hanc arbitrantur partem suam et quasi de jure debitam, si etiam alii eorum committantur arbitrio et curae deputentur. Is ergo quasi dicere videtur: 'Da mihi portionem, quae me contingit', qui tale aliquid et sibi deberi judicat, et dari desiderat et differi submurmurat.

21. *Sed jam revocemus sermonem qui quodam modo cum adolescentiore isto peregre profectus est, nec inutiliter tamen, nec in remotam a materia et longinquam nimis regionem. Quaenam enim causa magis efficit ut privatim ditescere velint qui proprietatibus renuntiaverunt, quam quod cognationis et carnis*

nondum affectibus valedixerunt? ♦ Ideo venit Dominus haec vincula dirumpere, solvere pacem, separare hominem adversus patrem suum, et filiam adversus matrem suam. Alioquin quibus haec vincula dirupta non sunt, non possunt sacrificare hostiam laudis, nec

vota reddere.* Non nos revocant affectus isti a fidei confessione, nec enim persecutionis modo tempora sunt, nec debent a nuditate vel excipienda vel exsolvenda professione. Multum eis ad resistendum inest obstaculi. Efficacior nulla pestis ad nocendem quam domesticus inimicus. Ideo Dominus quasi rationem reddens separationis quam facere venit, subjecit:

'Inimici hominis, domestici ejus.'*[11] Quam malae amicitiae quae inimicitias veras protexunt! Suspectae mihi sunt domesticae affectiones istae quae tanta damna important. Quaeres quae damna? 'Qui amat', inquit, 'patrem aut matrem plus quam me, non est me dignus; et qui amat filium aut filiam plus quam me,

non est me dignus.'* Quam commutationem accipiet

perty, but deferential that he wanted no one but his father to divide it. He takes his share openly; he does not steal or embezzle, but says: 'give me my share'. For us, however, it is illicit to take, because it is illicit to say 'give me my share'. How can anyone say 'give me my share', when by profession he has stripped himself and shares everything in common. Not only in monetary matters does this way of proceeding prevail. Anyone who wishes to be treated above others with some special respect, to carry on in his own right though no one else is permitted to live on his own responsibility, anyone who demands this for himself in return for his services, in your opinion does he not seem to ask as if by right of his superiority 'the share which falls' to him? Some are not content even with this. They consider this share their own and their due by right, as it were, even if others are entrusted to their guidance and assigned to their care. So this character seems to quote Scripture: 'give me the share of property which falls to me', for he concludes that something of the kind is his due, desires it to be given to him, and grumbles at the delay.

21. Now at last let us recall our sermon, which somehow has set out with the younger son into a far country, though not unprofitably, nor for a country too removed and too distant from our center of concern. What motive is more effective in making individuals, who have renounced their possessions, desire to be enriched privately, than the fact that they have failed to say farewell to affections for their kin and their own flesh? ♦ Hence the Lord arrives to break their bonds, to rupture the peace, to oppose a son to his father and a daughter to her mother. Otherwise, those for whom these bonds are not broken cannot offer a sacrifice of thanksgiving or pay their vows of praise.* These affections do not beckon us from our confession of faith, for these are not now times of persecution, nor should they be times of exemption from stark poverty and of dispensation from profession. Poverty and profession have a good store of ammunition for resistance. No pest is more able to cause harm than an enemy within the gates.* Hence in putting his finger on the reason for the separation which he came to make, the Lord concludes: 'a man's foes are those of his household.'*[11] How evil are those friendships which conceal real enmities! To me those familiar affections are suspect which open the door to such serious disasters! Will you ask what disasters? 'One who loves father or mother more than me', he says, 'is not worthy of me; and one who loves son or daughter more than me, is not worthy of me.'* What exchange will a man receive for his God? With what gain has he compensated for such a loss? Not on such terms did Paul know how to make an exchange, counting 'all things as

*Mt 26:26
†MS sic

Ph 3:8

Mt 10:37

Sg 2:4

Ps 118:91

1 Co 13:8

Ps 118:91

♦ f. 94r

homo pro Deo suo? Quo lucro tale detrimentum compensabat?† Non sic Paulus commutare novit, 'omnia detrimentum' arbitrans 'ut Christum' lucrifaceret.**

22. *Exosae plane sunt et inimicae hujusmodi amicitiae, quae divini nobis amoris gratiam invident, quae nos discipulatu ipsius reddunt indignos. 'Qui amat patrem aut matrem plus quam me, non est me dignus.'* Cernis quidem necessitudinis jura; non sunt in vitio sed amor nimius: 'Qui amat', inquit, 'plus quam me.' Naturales quidem et honestae sunt in his gradibus occasiones amoris, sed quae erat usu exercitata amandi; 'ordinate', inquit, 'in me caritatem'.* In patrio et filiali affectu honesta occasio sed non aequa collatio, si Domino Jesu plus diligantur. Origo bona sed ordo non bonus. Sub divino debet cognationis amor ordinari non superordinari, servire non superare. 'Ordinatione tua', Domine, 'perseverat dies'; 'Omnia serviunt tibi'* utique quae ordinata sunt, quia subordinata sunt. 'Ordinatione' Domini 'perserverat dies' caritatis Dei quae non excidit,* dies dilectionis. Et bene dies dilectionis, quem qui non diligit in tenebris manet. Quomodo enim diligit qui male diligit? Odium valet inordinata dilectio. 'Ordinatione ejus perserverat dies.'* Noli tu carnalis dilectionis noctem superordinare. Cognationis affectum Dominus non exterminat sed ordinat; non proscribit illum sed divinus amor praescribit illi. Denique non ait: 'qui amat patrem aut matrem' . . . 'non est me dignus' sed 'qui plus amat'.*

23. *Fratres, etsi Domini est modesta locutio, non tamen haec modesta aequatio. Injusta collatio, si aequales affectu, qui meritis non coaequantur. Et quidem cumulatoria in Jesu erga nos merita, quis infitiabitur fidelis? Sed quo ad invicem dilectionis obligamur jure, totum ab illo profluxit. Omnia enim necessitudinis jura ab ipso sunt nobis, non ab ipsis nobis. Carnalis cognationis jura ipse instituit, spiritualis ipse instaurat. Jesus ipse mihi secundum verbum suum et pater et mater et frater est. Audeo autem et cum Paulo dicere quia et filius est: 'filioli', inquit, 'quos ♦ iterum parturio, donec formetur Christus in*

refuse, in order to win Christ'.

22. Friendships of this kind are obviously loathesome and hostile, for they begrudge us the grace of divine love by rendering us unworthy of his discipleship. 'One who loves father or mother more than me, is nor worthy of me.'* Indeed you notice what is at fault: not the rights of kinship, but rather excessive love: 'one who loves' a parent 'more than me.' Within these degrees of kinship there are natural and honest occasions for love, but what has been practised in the commerce of love, says the Lord, 'set in order in me as perfect love'.* In the affection of father and son is an honest occasion, though the comparison is unequal if they are loved more than the Lord Jesus. The origin is good but the order is not good. Love of kin should be subordinate to and not overrule divine love;* it should be a servant and not a superior. 'By your ordination', O Lord, 'the day abides, . . . all things are your servants',* yes, all things in due order because they are subordinate. 'Through your ordination', O Lord, 'the day abides', the day of God's 'charity which does not fail',* his day of perfect love. This day is well named 'the day of dilection', for he who does not love the day, abides in darkness. How does he love at all, who loves evilly? Inordinate love is no better than hatred. 'By his ordination the day abides.'* Do not grant a higher order to a night of carnal delight. The Lord does not banish the affection of kinship but sets it in order. Divine love does not proscribe, but does prescribe for, such affection. Our text does not say: 'who loves father or mother . . . is not worthy of me', but 'who loves [another] more than me'.

23. Though the expression of the Lord is moderate, brethren, its extent is not moderate. The comparison is unjust, if they are equal in affection who are not coequal in merits. Who among the faithful will deny that Jesus' merits towards us are cumulative? But the bond of love by which we are obliged to one another, derived entirely from him. For all the rights of kinship belong to us, thanks to him and not to ourselves. He instituted the rights of kinship in the flesh; he initiated the rights of spiritual kinship. According to his own admission, he is in person my father and mother and brother. But with Paul I make bold to say even that he is my son: 'little children', says Paul, 'with whom ♦again I am in labor, until Christ be formed in you.'* He himself begets, is himself in labor, shares the same nature and himself is born of us. All

Ga 4:19

vobis.' Ipse gignit, ipse parturit, ipse connascitur, ipse nascitur ex nobis. Omnes naturales necessitudines ab ipso sunt. Spirituales etiam instaurantur in ipso, ut nemo adversus eum dilectionis merito glorietur, nemo de aequalitate concertet. Tot in te mihi sunt, Jesu bone, amoris merita, tot insunt amoris irritamenta, et quem assimilabo tibi, quem comparabo? In meritis amoris debitum; in irritamentis desiderium. Ibi amandi necessitas est; hic voluptas. Ibi obligor, hic allicior. Illic justum est meritis*

MS iocundum

referre gratiam; hic jucundum gloria frui. Quis gratiam et gloriam dabit sicut Dominus? Quis nisi Dominus Jesus? Et ideo quis diligendus sicut Dominus Jesus? Si ejus amori alium aequare vis, non illum aequas sed istum evacuas. Totum dedit te tibi, totum dedit se tibi, et tu dimidiare et quasi partiri te vis, partiri animum, partiri amorem, et dare ei portionem quae ipsum contingit! Atque utinam des quod ipsum contingit, id est non portionem sed totum!*

24. *Non se dividat amor tuus ad fontis instar, cujus hic inde rivi in diversa nituntur. Totus in illum fluat, totus inundet ut cum illo plenus fuerit; in ipsa quae sub ipso sunt redundet et refluat. Ipsum amet propter ipsum, cetera propter ipsum quidem sed tamen post ipsum. Non potest dici alius et alius amor, quo ipsum amplexaris et quo ipsum in suis non magis quam alius rivus in destinatum locum currens et in humiliora recurrens. Omnes affectus nostri in ipsum quasi receptaculum magnum et quasi flumina in mare decurrant et inde dulciores redundent. Ita fluentem in ipsum non repellit ipse nec dicit: 'non est me dignus'; 'Et qui non accipit crucem suam et*

Mt 10:38

sequitur me, non est me dignus'. Advertis quomodo tres gradus facit, dum ter dicit: 'non est me dignus'. Primo superiores personas ponit de quibus sumus, secundo inferiores quae de nobis sunt, tertio quae nos ipsi sumus, et in hac triplici distinctione quasi una sententiae clausula est dum aequaliter infitetur: 'non est me dignus.' Sed non una videtur causa ex qua talem promulgat sententiam. In duobus primis gradibus dicit: quia qui plus amat, non est me dignus; in hoc ultimo videtur innuere quare nisi quis se ipsum*

natural kinships derive from him. Spiritual kinships are also initiated in him, that no one can boast over him on the score of love, and no one vie with him on the score of equality. In you, good Jesus, so many merits of love are mine! In you are so many incentives to love! Whom shall I liken to you? Whom shall I compare with you? In your merits is my debt of love. In your incentives is my desire to love. There is the obligation of loving, but here its delight. There I am under obligation, here I am wooed. There it is just to feel gratitude for your merits, but here it is delightful to enjoy your glory. Who like the Lord will give grace and glory? Who but the Lord Jesus? Therefore who should be loved as the Lord Jesus? If you wish to make any other love equal to his love, you do not make that other love equal but you nullify his love. He gave you your all. He gave you his all. And do you wish to be halved and shared? Your spirit shared? Your love shared? And do you wish to give him 'the share which falls to him'? O that you would give him the share of love which falls to himself, that is, not a portion but your undivided love.

24. Let not your love be divided like a fountain whose rivulets hasten to run hither and thither in different directions. Let it flow wholly towards him, wholly inundate him that it may be filled with him. Let it stream over and flow back upon what lies below him. Let your love love him for himself, and all things else for him indeed, but after him. The love with which you embrace him, and the love with which you embrace him in his own people can no more be distinguished into two loves than the one river which runs along its usual bed and runs back upon lower ground. As rivers run down to the sea and thence flow back even fresher, so let all our affections ebb and flow into him as into a vast reservoir. One who so flows into him he does not reject, for he does not say: 'he is not worthy of me', nor to him does he say: 'he who does not take up his cross and follow me, is not worthy of me'.* You notice how he makes three steps, while he says the same thing three times: 'he is not worthy of me.' On the first step he places the older generation to whom we owe our existence, on the second step the younger generation descended from us, and on the third our own generation. Despite this triple distinction, one clause of the sentence remains the same, for he equally disowns all three: 'he is not worthy of me.' But there does not seem to be only the one reason for him to proclaim the same clause. Of those on the first two steps he says: one who loves more, is not worthy of me; of those on the last step he seems to suggest that unless one hates oneself, such a one

oderit, non est ipso dignus. Nonne velut odii imago putatur se ipsum exponere injuriis, crucem imponere? In superioribus amorem temperat, hoc in gradu tollit. Ibi dicit: 'qui amat plus quam me'; hic dicit: 'qui amat vel se', non est me dignus. Modesta distinctio, eo quod major injuriarum in nos ipsos quam in necessarios nostros nobis est permissa licentia. Denique non dicit qui patri aut filio crucem non imponit, sed 'qui crucem suam non accipit, neque est me dignus.'

25. *Quid sibi vult haec intentatio? Cur dicit: 'non est me dignus'? Immo cur non magis dicit: inferno est dignus, morte est dignus, maledicto est dignus? Maledictus enim homo qui patrem deterio-*

Gn 9:24, Pr 30:17 *rem facit.* Cur ergo non poenam intentat, sed sollicitat de praemio? Sed quae major poena quam ipso carere? non inveniri dignus qui sit ex patre ejus?*

♦ f. 94v *Vide modestum et temperatum ♦ Domini sermonem. Non terret, non compellit, sed allicit. Sicut superiorem in affectu tuo tenere vult gradum, ita et gratuitum eum vult esse. Vide certamen, vide et praemium; non illud imponit tibi sed istud proponit. Si praemium amas adipiscendi, legem observa. Si dura crux, mercedis amor mitigat eam. Et Dominus acceptam te vult crucem tuam habere: 'qui', inquit, 'non accipit cru-*

Mt 10:38 *cem suam',* qui non acceptam, qui non gratam eam habet. Simon ille Cyrenaeus qui Jesu crucem in*

Mt 27:32 *angaria portavit,* non eam abjecit, non tamen accepit eam, sed imposita est ei. Tu accipe crucem, sequere Jesum. Nemo, inquit, tollit animam meam sed ego*

Jo 10:18 *pono eam.* Nemo tollit animam tibi invito, sed tu gratis pro Christo pone eam.*

26. *Immo etsi eam ponere sicut ipse non potes, exponere tamen eam potes. Protomartyr iste noster cujus nos hodie festam laeti recolimus, crucem suam*

MS festa *accepit, secutus est Jesum.[12] Exivit ad eum 'extra*

Heb 13:13 *castra, improperium ejus portans'.* O felicem virum, eo quod 'improperia improperantium tibi', bone Jesu, 'ceciderunt super' eum.* Exivit iste sanctus*

Rm 15:3 *extra castra sequens Jesum, extra castra corporis et extra castra urbis, nam et Dominus extra portam passus est. Et Protomartyrem Stephanum sicut scrip-*

Ac 7:58 *tum est, eruentes lapidabant.* Magnum insigne proto-*

is not worthy of him. Is it not considered a pattern of self-hatred to expose oneself to insults, to shoulder the cross? He chastens the love of those on the first steps, but he withdraws love from those on the last step. For the former he says: 'one who loves more than me'; for the latter: 'one who loves even himself', is not worthy of me. The distinction is slight in so far as a greater liberty is allowed us to inflict injury on ourselves than on our relatives. In the text he does not say: one who does not impose the cross on his father or son, but 'one who does not accept the cross, is unworthy of me'.

25. What is the meaning of this reproach? Why does he say, 'he is not worthy of me'? Why does he not rather say: he is worthy of sheol, or worthy of death, or worthy of a curse? Cursed indeed is the man who humiliates his father.* Why then does he not threaten a penalty, but rather tempt with a reward? Yet what punishment is greater than to be deprived of him? not to be found a child worthy of one's father? Notice the delicate and chastened ♦ remark of the Lord. He does not terrify. He does not compel. But he does woo. Just as he wishes to retain a higher level in your affections, so he wishes this to be gratuitous. Behold the conflict; behold also the reward; the penalty he does not impose on you, but the reward he proposes to you. If you love the reward for achievement, observe the law. If the cross is hard, the love of recompense softens it. The Lord also wants you to consider your cross welcome: 'one who does not welcome his cross', these are his words, 'who does not consider it welcome, who does not consider it pleasing'.* Simon of Cyrene, who carried the cross of Jesus under constraint, did not reject, did not welcome, but did shoulder the cross under compulsion.* Welcome your cross. Follow Jesus. 'No one takes my soul', he said, 'but I lay it down myself.'* No one takes your soul from you against your will, but do you lay it down for Christ gratuitously!

26. Yes, although you cannot lay down your soul as he did, still you can lay open your soul. Our famous protomartyr, whose feast we joyfully recall today, welcomed his cross, followed Jesus.[12] He went out 'to him outside the camp, bearing abuse for him'.* O lucky man, because 'the reproaches of those who reproached you', good Jesus, 'fell upon' him.* The great saint went out, 'outside the camp', following Jesus, 'outside the camp' of his body and 'outside the camp' of the city, for his Lord also suffered outside the gate'.* 'Now casting forth the protomartyr Stephen', according to Acts, 'they were stoning him.'* It is a great sign of a protomartyr that he has something in common with them, for he suffered outside the gate with the Lord and the

sic MS

martyris quod habet aliquid commune cum istis,* passus extra portam cum Domino et protomartyre Stephano.[13] *Ultro posuit animam pro Domino, sed vide quot animas in mercede jam sumpsit. Dedit animam suam et tot animas jam accepit in commutationem pro ea. 'Si posuerit', inquit propheta, 'animam suam', 'videbit semen longaevum.'* Et tu, beate protomartyr noster, posuisti in morte animam tuam pro Domino. Ecce jam vides semen longaevum, semen numerosum. 'Leva', patrone sancte, 'leva oculos in circuitu et vide. Omnes isti congregati . . . venerunt tibi.'* Quid reliquum est, nisi ut ores quantivis veniant ad te qui veniunt tibi. Te impetrante, qui persequuntur te laudibus, sequantur virtutibus, immo quem secutus es, Dominum Jesum, quia qui accipit crucem et sequitur eum, ipso invenitur dignus. Quod nobis precibus tuis ipse praestare dignetur, qui cum Patre et Spiritu sancto vivit et regnat, Deus, per omnia saecula saeculorum.*

Is 53:10

Is 60:4

protomartyr Stephen.[13] Of his own will he laid down his soul for his Lord, but see how many souls he has already raised up in reward. He gave his own soul and he has already welcomed so many souls in exchange for his own. 'If he lays down his soul', says the prophet, 'he shall behold a long-lived progeny'.* And you, our blessed protomartyr, have laid down your soul in death for your Lord. Behold, now you see a long-lived progeny, countless descendants. 'Lift up your eyes', holy patron, 'lift up your eyes round about and see. All these hosts . . . have come in your honor.'* What remains but for you to pray that as many as you wish may come to you, for they are coming in your honor. At your intercession, those who persevere in following you with praise may follow in virtues, no rather, may follow the one you followed, the Lord Jesus, because he who welcomes the cross and follows

Jesus, is found worthy of him. Now may the Lord himself

be willing to grant us this through your prayers,

for he lives and reigns with the Father

and the holy Spirit, God,

for ever and ever.

ITEM SERMO DE EODEM INCIPIT A MAGISTRO G. EDITUS

HERE LIKEWISE BEGINS A SERMON ON THE SAME MARTYR PREPARED BY MASTER GILBERT

1. May your numbers and keenness increase the honor of the saint and the number of your virtues, for consumate love is consumate justice. 2. As we ended so we begin with the text from Matthew, on finding one's life and taking one's cross. 3. Those who cling to God will be two in one spirit; those who cling to the dust will be two in one flesh. 4. How does the soul become a spirit? 5. Job speaks of the soul's elevation from the dust, Paul of its being stripped of its cloak. 6. It is only profitable to lose one's life for Christ's sake. 7. Peace is love outpoured; the sword is blood outpoured. 8. Bountiful strippings and elevations mean bountiful harvests and gleaning. 9. Adam was frightfully stripped and meanly clad. 10. The stripping of death means no more tears, no more stumbling. 11. Losing one's life for the Lord is emancipation. 12. No sword can separate us from Christ. 13. The impious shun separation from the tawdry world. 14. 'One who loses his soul for my sake will find it.' 15. Your persecutor is your benefactor, 16. One who welcomes you welcomes me; one who welcomes me welcomes my father. 17. Welcome the prophet, and welcome the righteous man.

III. ITEM SERMO DE EODEM MARTYRE
INCIPIT A MAGISTRO G. EDITUS

MS Hostium

1. **O**STIUM* MIHI *hodie sermonis apertum est, magnum et evidens, et auditores multi. Evidens ostium aviditas illorum, sed et ipsa solemnitas martyris quam* continuata laetitia diebus istis celebramus, nonne loquendi nobis occasionem praebeat, et ostium aperit sermonis?[14] Alacres quidem vos video in laudibus Sancti. Sancti sed incrementum praesumo, si modestae cujusdam exhortationis flatus ad alacritatis vestrae flammam accedat. Atque utinam tam simus alacres ad aemulandum, quam sumus ad laudandum. Et si dura propter mortis ◆ passionem aemulatio, sed 'fortis est ut mors dilectio'.* Numquid non fortior? Vehementior est fervor amoris quam horror mortis et terrendi mors caret effectu, ubi caritas urget.* Non est veritus mortem martyr iste noster sed per gladium transivit in gaudium. In libro Job legitur quod 'transibunt per gladium et consumentur stultitia'.* Iste vero transivit per gladium et consummatus est gloria. Quidni consummatus in gloria, qui consummatus est in justitia? Consummatus amor, consummata justitia est.* 'Nemo majorem caritatem habet quam ut animam suam ponat pro amico suo.'* Consummata est justitia, consummata est caritas, quodam animae suae dispendio Christum mereri. Consumpta* est martyris caro supliciis et ipse consummatus est justitia. Non fecit animam suam cariorem se, nec fecit eam cariorem Deo suo. Pro Christo tradidit in mortem animam suam et dignus ipso reputatus est.

◆ f. 95r
Sg 8:6

2 Co 5:14

Jn 36:12

Ws 15:3

Jn 15:13

MS consupta

2. Modo audistis in evangelio Deum dicentem: 'qui non accipit crucem suam et sequitur me, non est me dignus.'* Hic est enim incohandum, quia ibi heri terminatum est. Quo ergo, Domine, dignus est qui te non est dignus? Numquid vel se ipso dignus est? Qui

Mt 10:38

III. HERE LIKEWISE BEGINS A SERMON
ON THE SAME MARTYR
PREPARED BY MASTER GILBERT

TODAY A LARGE and obvious introduction opens for my sermon and the audience is large. The obvious opening is the keenness of this large audience. But should not this very solemnity of the martyr, which during these days we are celebrating with ceaseless joyfulness, also offer us an occasion to speak and to unbar the entrance of our sermon?* Indeed, I notice your alacrity in praising the saint. Now I take for granted the increasing importance of the saint, if the breath of a moderate exhortation may approach the flame of your own keenness. Would that we might be as keen to emulate the saint as we are to praise him. Now, if emulation is difficult, ♦ because of the suffering of his death, still 'love is as strong as death'.* Is it not really stronger? The fervor of love is more passionate than the horror of death, and death is robbed of its power to terrify, when 'perfect love drives us on'.* Our famous martyr did not fear death, but by the sword he passed over into joy. In the book of Job, we read that 'they will perish by the sword and be consummated in folly'.* But our saint perished by the sword and was consummated in glory. Why should he not be consummated in glory, who was consummated in justice? Consummate love is consummate justice: 'No one has greater love than to lay down one's life for one's friends.'* This is consummate justice, this is consummate love, to merit Christ at the cost of one's life. The martyr's flesh was consumed by torture and he was himself consummated in justice. He did not esteem his life dearer than himself. He did not esteem it dearer than his God. For Christ he offered his life to death and was esteemed worthy of Christ.

2.   You have just heard God saying in the Gospel: 'one who does not accept his cross and follow me, is not worthy of me.'* From this verse we should begin, because with this verse   yesterday we came to an end. Now of whom is he worthy, Lord, who is not worthy of you? He is not at all worthy of himself, is he? One who does not follow you,

te non sequitur, nec te consequitur, non te invenit. Quem ergo invenit? Numquid se ipsum? Nec Christum invenit nec se ipsum invenit. Aut si invenit se, audi quid Dominus ipse subjungit: 'qui invenit animam suam, perdet eam.'* Si talis est inventionis causa, non expedit invenire eam, neque expedit quaerere. Non ait: qui habet, sed qui invenit. Ergo habere licet, et invenire non licet? An forte alterum dicitur sed alterum non excluditur? Idem in utroque reatus, sed in verbo inventionis major expressio. Qui inventionem condemnat,* quaerendi studium latenter suggillare videtur. Quod quis invenire vult, quaerendi illud curam adhibet, sollicitudinem impendit. Ergo inventionem confutat, quaerendi redarguit vota, studia reprobat. Nec tamen hac in parte multum oporteat quaerendi impensam applicare curam, ubi facilitas adest inveniendi. 'Qui quaerit, invenit',* quia etiam qui non quaerit vix effugit. Tam facilis utinam cuique fuga animae suae sit, quam prompta* inventio.

3. *Quid dico invento? Adhaesio est. 'Adhaesit' inquit 'pavimento anima mea',* pavimento carnis suae, pavimento terreni corporis hujus. Queritur propheta invenisse se in pavimento animam suam, non quaerit invenire. Affectuose adhaeret anima suo pavimento. Ideo facile invenitur in illo. Ne quaesieris illic invenire eam. Non lucrum credideris neque inventionem sed perditionem sed illic inveneris. Et si affectus quidem de vitio corruptae originis carni adhaeret, neque adhaereat delectatio, non consensus, neque intentio mentis. Noli animalem invenire animam tuam; noli illam, ut sic dicam, animam invenire sed spiritum. Non pavimento adhaereat sed Deo, quoniam 'qui adhaeret Deo, unus spiritus est'.* Si autem adhaeserit carni, erunt jam duo in carne una.* Discedat a pavimento, elonget fugiens.† Maneat in quadam solitudine insuetae contemplationis, in singularitate divini amoris, non in multitudine sollicitudinum.*[15] *Profugiat et*

> *Geminum incommodum: non mereri Christum,*
> *non sibi manere. Qui invenit animam suam,*
> *perdet eam.*

Marginal notes:

- Mt 10:39
- MS condempnat
- Mt 7:8, Lk 10:11
- MS: promta
- Ps 118:25
- 1 Co 6:17
- *Gn 2:24, Mt 19:25, Eph 5:31 †Ps 72:27
- marginal note in same hand

or does not pursue you, does not find you. Whom then does he find? Does he find himself? He finds neither Christ nor himself But if he finds himself, hear what the Lord himself concludes: 'one who finds his life, will lose it.'* If such is the purpose of finding, it is expedient neither to find nor even to seek one's life. The Lord does not say: one who possesses, but one who finds. Is it licit therefore, to possess but not to find? Or perhaps 'finding' is mentioned, but 'possessing' is not excluded. The same offence is in both 'finding' and 'possessing', but 'finding' is the more expressive word. When he condemns 'finding', tacitly he seems to knock the wind out of our motives for seeking. Everyone is at pains and is full of anxiety to seek what he wishes to find; so the Lord discredits this 'finding', reproves our longings to seek, refutes our motives. On the other hand, however, there is not much need to devote intensive pains to seek, when such ease of discovery is present: 'One who seeks, finds.'* Because even one who does not seek, scarcely avoids finding. Would that for everyone an escape from life were as easy as its 'finding' is ready at hand.

3. Why do I say 'finding'? It is clinging. 'My soul clings to the dust', says the psalmist, to the dust of my flesh, to the dust of my body of clay. The prophet complains that he has found his soul in the dust; he is not seeking to find it. The soul clings affectionately to its dust. Hence it is easily found in the dust. Do not seek to find it there. Consider that neither a gain nor a 'find', but a loss, but there you will find her. And if after the distortion of our corrupt origin, some affection clings to our flesh, let no delight cling there, no consent, no fascination of the mind. Refuse to discover your animal soul. Refuse to discover her, if I may say so, as *anima,* but find her as *spiritus.* Let your spirit not cling to the dust but to God, because 'one who clings to God, is one spirit'.* If, however, it shall cling to the flesh, they shall be two in one flesh.* Let it depart from the dust, let it outdistance the dust in flight.* Let it dwell in some desert of unwonted contemplation, in the concentration of divine love, not in the diffusion of anxieties.[15] Let it take wing ♦ and hasten wholly to God; and be hidden in the hiding place of his face.*

A double trouble—not to deserve Christ
but to desert oneself. 'One who finds his life
will lose it.'

◆ f. 95v.
Ps 30:21

Ps 67:9
corrected in MS
from *liquescit*

Pr 31:10

Ps 10:2

Ps 118:81

Mt 22:40

1 Tm 1:5
Ph 3:20

Ps 118:25
*Jb 7:15
†2 Co 11:8

Col 3:9
1 Co 2:14

Gn 35

Ga 3:3

◆ *pergat tota in Deum, abscondatur in abscondito faciei* ejus.*

4. Quo modo inveniri poterit quae elongat a se, quae sic elongat a carne, quae sic elongat, sic fugit, sic absconditur? Quali putas absconditur in conflatorio, quali camino, qui absconditur in abdito illo faciei Domini? Caeli distillabunt a facie Domini?* Et quomodo non distillabit, non liquescet* anima illi abscondita? Animam quae sic latet, sic liquescit, quis inveniet? 'Procul et in ultimis finibus'* commoratio ejus, quia non est in carne sed in spiritu. Ideo non est illam invenire quasi animam, sed quasi spiritum. Anima tua transmigret in montem,* pavimentum deserat, non descendat de tecto, in montes fugiat, stipendium eligat, 'deficiat' juxta psalmum 'in salutare' Dei.* Quis dabit mihi sic liquescere et sic illaquearí? Liquescit qui deficit; illaqueatur qui stipenditur. Dulcis et tenax laqueus, nexus caritatis; ab hoc pendent lex et prophetae.* Triplex est laqueus caritatis: caritas 'de corde puro et conscientia bona et fide non ficta'. Qui suspenditur hoc funiculo in sublimibus est, in caelo conversatur cum Paulo.* Non jam adhaeret etsi aliquando cum propheta 'adhaesit pavimento anima'* ejus.

5. Suspensionem Job eligit animae suae,* Paulus exspoliationem.† Et forte idem est pavimentum et vestimentum. A pavimento suspendimur, vestimento exspoliamur. Spoliantes, inquit, vos veterem hominem,* carnalem hominem, animalem hominem qui 'non percipit quae sunt spiritus Dei'.* Hunc exspolia, hunc abjice, nec laeteris si quae prius abjecisti invenias iterum hujusmodi spolia multa, spolia vetusta.* Quam indecoram enim et quam abjectam rem facis, si vetustatem sordidam quam semel exuisti denuo resumas, si cum spiritu coeperis, nunc ut sic dicam, anima consumeris!* Sicut in carne non contemnatur superbia sed carnalitas, sic in anima non redarguitur ipsa, sed quaedam ejus animalitas, id est in carnis appetitus reclinatio prona, et arbitrii proprii voluntas. Qui talem eam invenit, quasi animam eam invenit, quasi suam eam invenit, quasi in pavimento eam invenit, id est non spiritum, non deum, non suspen-

4. How shall the soul be found which outdistances itself, which so outdistances its flesh, which so escapes and departs and is so hidden? In what kind of crucible, in what kind of furnace, in your opinion, is she hidden, when she is hidden in the recess of the face of the Lord? 'The heavens will drop down dew from the face of the Lord.'* And how will the soul hidden by him not melt and dissolve into a dew? Who shall find a soul which so hides, which so melts? Far off in the outermost bounds is her dwelling,* because she is not in the flesh but in the spirit. Hence it is possible to find her not as a soul but as a spirit. Let your soul migrate to the mountain, abandon the dust, not descend from the roof-top, flee to the mountains,* choose its reward, and, according to the psalm, 'let it languish for the salvation' of God.* Who will allow me to be so melted and so ensnared? The soul melts when it faints; it is ensnared when it is rewarded. A tender and tenacious snare is the bond of charity; on charity depend the Law and the Prophets.* Of three ply is the snare of charity: charity 'from a pure heart and a good conscience and unfeigned faith'.* One who climbs this rope, tumbles amid the stars, for with Paul his conversation is in heaven.* Although once upon a time his soul 'cleaved to the dust' with the prophet, now he so cleaves no longer.

5. Job prefers to speak of the elevation of his soul,* but Paul of the stripping of his soul.* Now perhaps 'dust' and a 'cloak' are the same thing. From the dust we are elevated, of our cloak we are stripped. 'Stripping yourselves of the old man', says Paul*, the carnal man, the unspiritual man, 'who does not perceive the things which belong to the spirit of God.'* Strip him, cast him away, do not rejoice if what you earlier cast away, you again discover as plentiful spoils, heirlooms as old as Rachel's.* What an ugly, what a base thing you do, if you again don the squalid cloak you once rejected, if when you have begun in the spirit, pardon my words, you are now devoured by the sensuous soul! Just as in the flesh one may censure not pride but lust, so in the soul one may not rebuke the soul [anima] but some animality in the soul, I mean its proneness to appetites of the flesh and its determination to have its own way. One who finds such a soul finds, as it were, an animal soul, finds a soul of its own, finds a soul in the dust; I mean that one finds not a spirit, not a god, not a soul stripped. A soul 'which clings to the Lord is one spirit'.* A soul which cleaves to itself is only a soul, only its own, only of the flesh. One 'who finds his own soul, will lose

1 Co 6:17

sam. Quae 'adhaeret domino unus spiritus est'.* Quae adhaeret sibi non nisi anima est, non nisi sua est, non nisi carnis. 'Qui invenit animam suam perdet' eam et qui 'perdiderit animam suam propter me inveniet

Mt 10:39

eam'.*

6. *Non simpliciter bona censetur perditio animae sed propter Deum sicut nec inventio universaliter mala sed contra Deum. Haec est enim generatio prava et*

Mt 12:39, 16:4

adultera,* quaerentium quae sua sunt non quae Domini, generatio quaerentium se non Deum, quaerentium in vano accipere et invenire animam suam, qui perditionem ejus putant, cum talis ut supra diximus non est, et ideo inventionem quamdam et quasi voti et studii adeptionem, cum talis est. Quomodo illud de psalmo dicitur: 'qui non accipit in

Ps 23:4

vano animam suam',* ita et hoc dictum intellige: 'qui invenit animam suam', ut accipias illud non de substantia ipsius dictum sed de modo quodam utendi ea. Alioquin quomodo accipit vel invenit eam quam non habere non potest, imo quae ipse* est. Denique si bona

sic MS

est et commendabilis perditio, ab opposito inventionem malam intelligere vales, ut hoc sit invenire eam quod non perdere eam, non suspendere a voluptate carnis, a voluntate propria, non eam elongare, eam a se, et transfundere in Deum, aut certe fundere eam pro Deo. Hunc enim praecipue sensum velle videtur

♦ f. 96r

♦ *sermo evangelicus.*

7. *Effusio illa amoris est, ista cruoris. Cur dicis, Domine, te gladium mittere et non magis gladios?*

Lk 22:38

'Ecce enim duo gladii hic.'* Unus persecutionis est, dilectionis alter. Unus tuus est, alter etsi contra te, per te tamen. Unus mentem transverberat ne carnalis sit; alter ipsam animae substantiam a carne separat, ut penitus in ea non sit. Ille gladius carnalitate spoliat; hic carne. Quis mihi dabit sic spoliari et sic suspendi? Suspensio enim et temporalis dilatio est, quod anima non conformatur carnalitati et quod ipsa non commoratur in carne. Non quod iterum ad carnalitatem redeat quamvis redibit ad carnem, sed quod in carne

MS incorruptibile

glorificata et spirituali incorruptibili voluptate patie-

1 Co 15:53,
MS immortale

tur. Oportet enim corruptibile hoc* induere incorruptelam, et mortale hoc . . . immortalitatem.* Bona

it, and one who 'has lost his own soul for me, will find it'.*

6. The loss of one's soul is not considered a good plain and simple but only for God's sake, just as its finding is not considered an evil invariably but only in opposition to God. This is indeed an 'evil and adulterous generation'.* They seek what pertains to themselves and not to God. They seek themselves and not God. In vain they seek to grasp and find their own soul, as if they considered it lost when its nature is not such as we described above, and therefore they consider it found and their longings and search rewarded, when it is of such a nature. Just as you interpret that verse of the Psalm: 'He who does not receive his soul in vain',* so interpret our verse as meant in the same way: 'one who finds his soul', that you may take it to refer not to the substance of the soul but to some distinct way of using the soul. Otherwise how does one grasp or find a soul which one cannot fail to possess already, or rather the very soul which one is in oneself! In our text, if the loss of the soul is good and commendable, on the contrary, you can interpret its finding as evil, so that to find the soul is the same as not to lose it, not to withdraw it from the pleasure of the flesh, from self will, not to take it on a journey far from itself, and to pour it out into God, or certainly to pour it out for God. This text of the Gospel seems to intend this meaning above all.

7. ♦ Peace is an outpouring of love, the sword an outpouring of blood. Why do you say, O Lord, that you send one sword and not many? 'Look, Lord, here are two swords.'* One is the sword of persecution, the other of love. One is yours, the other, although against you, is against you only in part. One pierces through the mind, lest it be carnal; the other separates the very substance of the soul from the flesh, that it may not wholly exist in the flesh. One sword strips us of carnality, the other of flesh. Who will help me to be so stripped, so elevated? This is both an elevation and a lapse of time, since the soul neither conforms to carnal life nor lingers in the flesh. Not that it may again be restored to carnal life, although it will return to flesh, but that it will experience in the flesh glorified and spiritualized an incorruptible pleasure. 'For this perishable nature must put on the imperishable, and this mortal nature must put on immortality.'* Good is this elevation to withhold the affection from carnal delight, until we enjoy

suspensio affectum a delectatione cohibere carnali,
donec indefectura delectatione in resuscitata carnis
fruamur substantia. Seminatur enim corpus infirmum,
resurget in virtute. Seminatur in corruptione, resurget
in gloria. Seminatur corpus animale resurget spiri-
tuale. *

1 Co 15:42-44

8. *Vides hic quasi quasdam expoliationes et sus-*
pensiones. Dum seminatur, exspoliatur, sed quia resur-
get, suspenditur. Quid vereris veste spoliari, quam sus-
pendis resumpturus eam? Vetustam suspendis, eandem
novam resumes. Suspendis animalem, spiritualem eam
resumpturus invenies. Ideo suspende animalitatem,
projice, fac jacturam ejus, noli servare sed seminare;
*ne parcas. 'Qui enim parce seminat, parce et metet.'**

2 Co 9:6

Sed quando metet? Forte in futuro. Futuri expectatio
longa. Laborantis agricolae spem defatigare et refrin-
gere potest. Ego autem dico hoc modo laborantem
agricolam etiam in presenti de fructus laboris percipere.
Nam et si longa spes, 'expectatio tamen justorum lae-

*Pr 10:28
⟨interlined⟩

titia'. Bonus ⟨vel ergo⟩ autem fructus, quia bonus*
gustus et in laetitia exspectantis et in benedictione
seminantis. An non in benedictionibus illum seminare
censes et non parce, qui animam pro Domino semi-
nat? Quomodo non prodigus seminator, qui nec ani-
mae parcit? Etsi prodigus videtur, providus est. 'Qui
enim seminat in benedictionibus, de benedictionibus

2 Co 9:6
Mt 10:39
1 Co 15:37

et metet.' Qui sic 'perdiderit animam suam propter*
me, inveniet eam'. Seminas cum perdis, metis cum*
invenis. Et si 'nudum granum' seminas, non nudum*
metis, non nudum invenis, sed Deus vestit illud atque
unumquodque granum palea sua. Nec paleae mentio-
nem ad sterilitatem levitatemque trahere nitaris, ego
enim et spiritualis et glorificati corporis tenuitatem
paleae volo verbo intelligi. Nudum ergo semina gran-
um, ut Deus vestiat illud.

9. *Male spoliatus gloria sua in paradiso Adam,*
male nudatus, deterius indutus. Foliis ficus primo
pudenda contexit, tunicis deinceps totus vestitus et
involutus pelliceis. Exspolia ergo hanc quae polluta
est carnis tunicam, veterem exue hominem. Alioquin
non vestietur granum quod seminas, nisi vetustate
nudaveris illud. Exspolia primo animam tuam carnali-

an imperishable pleasure in the revived substance of our flesh. For the body is sown in weakness and shall rise in strength. It is sown in corruption, it will rise in glory. It is sown an animal body, it will rise a spiritual body.*

8.   Here you see, as it were, several strippings and elevations. While the body is being sown, it is stripped, but because it will rise, it is elevated. Why do you fear to be stripped of your garment of flesh, though you will don again what you have put on a hanger? You hang up an old coat, but you will put it on again retailored. You hang up an animal body; at your reinvestiture you will find your body spiritual. So go hang up your animality, cast it off, jettison it, do not stow it away but sow it unsparingly. 'One who sows sparingly, will reap sparingly.'* Yet when will one reap? Perhaps in the future. Waiting for the future is tedious. It can weary and break the expectancy of the laborer in the fields. Yet I claim that even in expectancy the laborer in the fields even in the present receives the fruit of his labor. For even if waiting is tedious, still 'the expectation of the just is joyfulness'.* Good is the fruit then, because it tastes good both in the joy of anticipation and in the bounty of the sower. Do you not agree that he sows his seed in bounty and unsparingly, who sows his life for his Lord? How is the sower not prodigal, who spares not his own soul? Although he appears prodigal, he is provident. 'Yes, one who sows bountifully, will also reap bountifully.'* And one 'who loses his soul for my sake, will find it'.* You sow when you lose, you reap when you find. Now if you sow 'a bare kernel',* you neither reap it bare nor find it bare, but God clothes yours and every single kernel in its own sheath. Please do not attempt to turn into chaff and a jest the mention of the word 'sheath', for by that word I wish you to understand the delicacy of a body both spiritual and glorified. Sow then a bare kernel, that God may clothe it.

9.   Adam was frightfully despoiled of his glory in paradise, frightfully stripped and meanly clad. First with fig leaves he covered his loins until he was fully clad in tunics and wrapped in animal skins. So strip off this tunic of flesh which was polluted. Put off the old man.* Otherwise the kernel you sow will not be clad, unless you strip it of its old rags. First despoil your soul of its carnal ways and then, if need be, of its flesh. First pour out your soul into your God; afterwards it will

*tate, deinceps si necesse est carne. Effunde primo
animam tuam in Deum tuum; erit post hoc et facile et
dulce effundere illam pro eo.*

♦ f. 96v

MS interimt
MS morti

10.   *Si dulcis* ♦ *praesentia Domini, dulcis itaque
omnis occasio quae desideratae praesentiae moras
interimit.* Dura quidem mors, sed durior mora dilatae
visionis. Luctuosum plane mortis compendio vitae
hujus laboriosae et lubricae vel molestias evadere vel
insidias evitare. Etsi mors accelerata et immatura
videtur, non sunt immaturi fructus quos carpis de
morte. Cum erepta fuerit anima tua de morte, tunc et
oculi a lacrimis et pedes evellentur a lapsu, et a lapsu
et a laqueo, a lapsu infirmitatis domesticae et a laqueo
venenantium inimicorum, in quem laqueum originalis
ignorantiae incauta frequenter se caecitas involvit, et a
quo se non evellit a vitiata origine transducta infir-
mitas. Nonne ergo bonum accelerare compendium
mortis quae velut janua quaedam est et ingressus
regionis vivorum?*

Ps 114:9

11.   *'Placebo Domino in regione vivorum.'* Ibi
placebis ei cui te probasti. Ibi 'erit ut conplaceant
eloquia oris' tui 'et meditatio cordis' tui 'in conspectu'*

Ps 18:15

ejus 'semper'. Dixissem et opera complacitiora illic
sed unum erit ibi opus, exsultare in Domine et*

Ps 97:4

psallere.* 'Beati ergo mortui qui in Domino mori-

Rv 14:13

untur', sed beatiores videntur si commoriantur.
Durus exitus sed ingressus delectabilis. Immaturam
mortem gaudia praematura solentur. Quid tibi deperit,
si animam impendis? Solvis; quod si et nolis,
aliquando expensurus es; si Christo commoreris, et
remunerationis hora citior et mortis gloria major.
Mors communis; mors quam aut defectio aut casus
aut morbus affert, testis est mortalitatis; mors mar-
tyrum, mors ultronea, suscepta pro Domino, testis est
veritatis. Ibi carnem nostram Domino supplices com-
mendamus; hic carnem Domini tuendam constanter
suscipimus. Nonne gloriosa mors, quae patrona quodam modo et testis est veritatis? Desaeviat persecu-
toris gladius quantum potest. Tibi, Domine, servit.
Tuos temptamenta probatiores reddunt et alios eorum
exempla promptiores. Et hunc gladium tu, Domine,
mittis, quia toleras, quia dispensas, quia provocas.*

be easy and pleasant to pour out your soul for him.

10. ♦ If the presence of the Lord is pleasant, then pleasant is every chance of eliminating the postponement of his desired presence. Harsh indeed is death, but harsher is the delay of his postponed visit. Surely it is grievous to use death as a shortcut either to escape the annoyances or avoid the snares of this toilsome and elusive life. Although death seems precipitate or premature, the fruits one plucks from death are not immature. When your soul shall have been snatched from death, then your eyes will be relieved of tears and your feet from stumbling and from snares, the stumbling of one's own weakness and the snares of venomous foes. In these snares the unwary blindness of original ignorance frequently entangles itself and from these snares the weakness transmitted from our wounded origin does not disentangle itself. Is it not a good thing then, to hasten the shortcut of death which is like a door and an entrance into the realm of the living?

11. 'I shall please the Lord in the realm of the living.'* There you will please him for whose sake you proved yourself. There 'the words of your mouth and the meditation of your heart will be ever acceptable in his sight'.* I should have said that your works also would there be more pleasing, but there the sole work will be to exult and sing psalms in the Lord.* 'Blessed then are the dead who die in the Lord',* but they seem more blessed if they die with the Lord. Harsh is the exit, but the entrance is delightful. Let early joys be a comfort for a premature death. What do you really lose, if you spend your soul? You emancipate yourself. Yet even against your will, some day you must spend your soul. If you stay with Christ, even the hour of reward is quicker and death's glory greater. Death is common. Death brought on by weakness, accident, or illness, is a witness to our mortality. But the death of martyrs, voluntary death accepted for the Lord, is a witness to truth. Dying as suppliants we commend our own flesh to the Lord; dying as martyrs we resolutely undertake to protect the flesh of the Lord. Is that death not glorious, which is somehow the patron and witness of truth? Let the sword of the persecutor slash to his heart's content! It is your servant, O Lord! Assaults only render your people more tried and true and their example makes others more eager. You send this sword also, O Lord, because it strikes with your sufferance, your dispensation, your provocation. Indeed you provoked your adversary against yourself, you irked 'the prince of this world',* while you make his name

Provocasti enim adversarium adversus te, irritasti 'huius mundi principem',* dum nomen ejus, dum regnum irritum reddis. Tormenta ejus ducuntur in irritum et procax conatus idcirco amplius provocatur. Denique ad exemplum Goliath,* suo ipse mucrone conciditur et gladius quem adducit applicatur in ipsum.

12. 'Diligentibus enim Deum omnia cooperantur in bonum.'* Ideo sanctis commodus est gladius persecutionis quos praeoccupavit gladius affectionis. Cetera cooperantur in bonum, operatur immo est ipsum bonum. O felicem hominem cujus anima traditur in manus gladii hujus, per quem omnes hostiles quotquot intentantur gladii non modo operantur sed cooperantur. 'Quis nos', inquit apostolus, 'separabit a caritate Christi?'* Persecutio, an fames, an nuditas, an periculum, an gladius? Vides quot enumerat quasi gladios. Et homines invalidi et inefficaces reddentur adversus caritatem, et ipsa sibi majorem constantiam affirmit injuriis lacessita. Per hanc anima effundit se ipsam liquefacta in Deum. Per hanc cum causa sic exigit, se effundit gratulanter pro eo. Per hanc se non tantum semel a carne sed semper ♦ dissociat a carnalitate. Per hanc cotidie tollit crucem suam, circumfert mortificationem Jesu, pia crudelitate persequitur et perdit se ipsam.

13. Impii enim se perditos putant, si eos praetereat 'flos temporis',* non se coronant rosis antequam marcescant, si non sunt et vino infusi et unguentis perfusi, et omni luxu et levitate curiositatis effusi. Prudens vero ista transilit, ista perdit ne se perdat, ista aut fugit aut despicit aut nescit. Fugit ne teneatur quia illecebrosa sunt; despicit quia non tenentur, labilia enim sunt. Nescit, dum melioribus oblectamentis tenetur, quae vera et aeterna sunt.

14. 'Qui perdiderit animam suam propter me, invenient eam.'* Quidni inveniat quam commendat Christo? quam recondit in Christo? 'Mortui estis', inquit, 'estis* et vita vestra abscondita est cum Christo in Deo.'* Bona talis mors per quam vita sic perditur ut perpetuetur. Pone animam tuam pro Christo, sed prius repone eam in Christo. Apud* illum

Jn 12:31

1 S 17:15,
MS Goliae

Rm 8:28

Rm 8:35

♦ f. 97r

Ws 2:7

Mt 10:39

sic MS
Col 3:3

MS aput

and his kingdom null and void. His torments reach a dead end and so his brash attack is provoked even more. After the precedent of Goliath in Scripture, that prince is slain with his own sword and the sword he unsheathed is turned against himself.*

12. 'Yes, for those who love God, everything cooperates unto good.'* Hence for saints the sword of persecution is appropriate, because the sword of affection has first won them over. 'All things else cooperate unto good', but the sword operates, or rather is goodness itself. O happy man, whose soul is betrayed into the hands of this sword, for through it whatever foemen's swords are unsheathed not only operate but also cooperate. What sword 'shall separate us from the love of Christ?' says the apostle.* Shall persecution or famine or nakedness or peril or the sword? You see how many quasi-swords he enumerates? Men will be rendered weak and ineffective against perfect love, and such love, though wounded with insults and injuries, claims for itself a greater constancy. Through this love, the soul melting pours itself into God. Through this love, when circumstances demand, the soul pours itself out for him with thanksgiving. Through this love, the soul divorces itself not once only from the flesh ♦ but always from carnal ways. Through this love, it takes up its cross daily,* carries with it the death of Jesus,* prosecutes and loses itself in devout cruelty.

13. Yet the impious consider themselves lost, if the 'flower set on youth'* should pass them by, if they do not garland themselves with roses soon to wither, if they are not sotted with wine, scented with perfume, and distracted with all the luxury and levity of idle curiosity. The prudent soul vaults over such follies, destroys them lest he destroy himself. Such a soul shuns or despises or refuses to recognize them. He shuns them, lest he be caught, for they are seductive; he despises them, because they are not held fast, since they are slippery; he refuses to recognize them as long as he is captivated by better delights, which are real and everlasting.

14. 'One who loses his soul for my sake will find it.'* Why should one not find the soul one commends to Christ,* the soul one hides in Christ? 'For you have died', says Paul, 'and your life is hid with Christ in God.'* Good is such a death, through which life is so lost that it becomes everlasting. Lay down your soul for Christ, but first lay it by in Christ. In his keeping lay aside your will, your longings, your affec-

depone voluntatem tuam, vota tua, affectus tuos.
Animam tuam pone in manibus Christi et invenies
eam. Alioquin dormies somnum tuum et nil invenies

Ps 75:6

in manibus tuis.* Quod Christo committitur, cumu-
latis cum incrementis ipsa reconsignat. Nec enim
invenies solam animam tuam, cum illam in Christo
inveneris. Non est sola, non est vacua, quae invenitur
in Christo, quae invenitur plena Christo. Denique sic
invenies illam ut solum invenias Christum in ea,

1 Co 15:28

quoniam ipse erit 'omnia in omnibus'.*

15. Vide enim quanta unione in animabus sanctis
et in praesenti maneat, nam subjungit: 'qui vos

Mt 10:40

recipit, me recipit'.* Magna unitatis expressio, sed
differens ratio. 'Qui vos' inquit 'recipit', et 'me
recipit', quia velut una persona sumus. Qui me et
patrem, quia vere una substantia sumus. 'Qui vos
recipit, me recipit.' Magna in hoc unitatis cujusdam
designatio, et ideo magna exhortatio ad exhibendam
quos mittebat discipulis reverentiam. Ipsi ad sub-
eundam passionis tolerantiam* in superioribus refor-

2 Co 1:6

mantur, ad eorum susceptionem alii isto animantur in
loco. 'Qui' inquit 'perdiderit animam suam propter

Mt 10:39

me, inveniet eam.'* Et addit: 'Qui vos recipit, me
recipit', ac si dicat: vobis quidem utilis est pro me
persecutio suscepta, sed aliis commoda est vestri pro
me sancta receptio. Vobis prodest qui persequitur,
sibi qui recipit. 'Qui vos enim recipit, me recipit.' Ad
utrosque refertur ista receptio, ad officia caritatis et
verbi quod disseminabant credulitatem. Qui fidei
verbum pie complectitur, qui sanctitatis aemulatur
exempla, ille recipit vos, ille et me, propter me vos,
me per vos.

16. Vos quidem sermonis exercetis ministerium,
sed ego Dominus et Magister agnoscor, et vester Dominus et Patris Filius. Qui enim me recipit, recipit
eum qui me misit, hoc est et recognoscit in me
gratiam beneficientiae et non diffitetur veritatem
paternae substantiae. Ideo discipulorum receptionem
ad se refert et suam refundit in Patrem, ut intelligatur
in ipso et redemptionis auctoritas et majestatis
aequalitas, humanitatis dispensatio et Deitatis aeterna generatio. Non enim recipit Jesum, qui aut mys-

tions. Lay down your soul in the hands of Christ and you will find it. Otherwise you will sleep a sleep of your own and find nothing in your hands.* Because your soul is entrusted to Christ, it returns to its origin enriched with blessings. Nor will you find your soul alone, since you will find it in Christ. It is neither alone nor empty, since it is found in Christ, since it is found full of Christ. According to Paul, you will so find your soul, that you will find only Christ in it, since he will be 'all in all'.*

15. Now notice with how much unity he remains in holy souls even in the present time, for he adds: 'one who welcomes you, welcomes me.' Here is an important expression of unity, though the reason is different. 'One who welcomes you', he says, also 'welcomes me', because we are, as it were, one person. One who welcomes me, welcomes also my Father, because we really are one substance. 'One who welcomes you, welcomes me.' Herein is an important indication of unity of a special kind, and therefore an important exhortation to show reverence to the disciples whom he was sending out. In previous verses the apostles themselves are transformed in order to undergo endurance of the passion,* but in this passage others are being inspired to welcome his apostles. 'One who loses his soul for my sake', he says, 'will find it.'* And he adds: 'one who welcomes you, welcomes me', as if he were saying: persecution undergone for my sake is indeed useful for you, but the holy welcoming of yourselves for my sake is opportune for others. Your persecutor is your benefactor, your host is his own benefactor, 'for one who welcomes you, welcomes me'. That welcome refers to both groups, to the good offices of charity and to receptivity of the word which the apostles were sowing. One who devoutly embraces the word of faith, who emulates the examples of sanctity, such a one welcomes you, welcomes me also, you for my sake and me through you.

16. Of course, you exercise the ministry of the word, but I am acknowledged as Lord and Master, both your Lord and the Son of my Father, 'for one who welcomes me, welcomes him who sent me',* that is, he not only recognizes in me the grace of beneficence but also does not doubt the truth of my Father's substance. Hence the Son refers to himself the welcoming of his disciples and transfers to his Father the welcoming of himself, in order that one may recognize in the Son, not only his responsibility for the redemption and his equality in Majesty, but also the stewardship of his humanity and the eternal generation of his divinity. Indeed he does not welcome Jesus, who

sterium incarnationis diffitetur aut divinae genera-
tionis consubstantialitatem non credit. Non abjecta
doctorum receptio ◆ per quos vitae semina sparguntur
aeternae. 'Haec est' inquit 'vita aeterna ut credamus
te', scilicet 'verum Deum et quem misisti Jesum
Christum'.*

17. *Felix est cordis terra quae fidei suscipit grana*
istius et fideli quodam piae affectionis* fovet in
gremio. Felix plane qui utrosque hoc modo Christi
discipulos recipit, ut verbo illorum piam credulitatem
impendat et dignae honorificentiae circa illos clemen-
tiam servet. 'Qui enim recipit prophetam in nomine
prophetae, mercedem prophetae accipiet et qui reci-
pit justum in nomine justi, mercedem justi accipiet.'*
Videtis quomodo Dominus in ista distinctione et
justum prophetae subjungit? Vult enim et juste con-
versentur, qui justitiam annuntiant et a quibus veritas
exoritur; justitia quae de coelo* est prospiciatur in eis
ne coelestis divinaque doctrina conversatione degen-
eri offuscetur.

◆ f. 97v

Jn 17:3

MS afectionis

Mt 10:41

Ps 84:12

either doubts the mystery of his Incarnation or does not believe in the consubstantiality of his divine generation. Not wasted is the welcome of those doctors ✦ through whom the seeds of eternal life are sown. 'This is eternal life', he says, that we should believe you, namely 'the true God and Jesus Christ, whom you have sent.'*

17. Happy is the heartland which gathers up the kernels of this faith and cherishes them, so to speak, in the believing bosom of a devout affection. Clearly happy is one who welcomes both groups of Christ's disciples in such a way as to grant a devout receptivity to their word and to maintain towards them the graciousness their honor deserves. 'One who welcomes a prophet because he is a prophet shall receive a prophet's reward, and one who welcomes a righteous man because he is righteous shall receive the reward of the righteous.'* Do you notice how in that distinction the Lord adds the righteous man to the prophet? Indeed he wants those to live in righteousness, who proclaim righteousness and from whom truth originates. The righteousness which descends from heaven should be conspicuous in them, lest their heavenly and divine doctrine be obscured by their degenerate conduct.

NOTES TO MASTER GILBERT, ABBOT

1.   Thanks to the Keeper of Western Manuscripts at the Bodleian Library, Oxford, I have been able to work from a microfilm copy of MS Bodley 87. Its contents are listed in Bernard, *Catalogi Librorum Manuscriptorum Angliae et Hiberniae*, I: 1, pp. 91-92. The MS is described in Madan and Craster, *A Summary Catalogue of Western Manuscripts in the Bodleian Library at Oxford*, (Oxford, Clarendon, 1922) Vol. II, Part 1, p. 92, no. 1872. 675: 'In Latin, on parchment: written about A.D. 1200 in England: 8-7/8 x 6¼ in., ii + 187 leaves: with one miniature (fol. 27), illuminated borders and capitals, some fine, etc'. This miniature is reproduced in black and white on the jacket of this volume.

2.   Jean Leclercq, 'Ecrits monastiques sur la bible aux XIe–XIIIe siècles', MS 15 (1958) 95-106; Henri de Lubac, *Exégèse Médiéval*, I:126; Edmund Mikkers, 'De Vita et Operibus Gilberti de Hoylandia', *Cîteaux* 14 (1963) 33-43, 265-279, especially pp. 265-6, and 273-7.

3.   The identified authors are here listed in order of appearance, with the folio number of their incipits and the references to publication.

a) **Peter Comestor:**

Ir. PL 171:627B-631A, incorrectly attributed to Hildebert Cenomanensis: see Hauréau 1:155-6, 5:156; André Wilmart, 'Les Sermons de Hildebert', RB 47 (1935) 12-51, who does not claim this sermon for Hildebert.

4v. PL 171:665A-671D, incorrectly attributed to Hildebert, but correctly to Peter Comestor in **PL 177:769D-770D** and **198:1782**, Hauréau 1:157-8, and Schneyer, *Repertorium*, 107.

7v. PL 171:476A-481B, incorrectly attributed to Hildebert, but correctly to Peter Comestor in **PL 198:1764**; see Hauréau 1:160, 2:164.

12v. *Incipit sermo Petri Comestoris de confessione et profectu satisfactionis.* '*In umbra alarum . . . volabo, inquit, terrena deserens et caelestia appetens, et requiescam vera libertate aeternaque fruens beatitudine. Amen.* A later hand, in the margin, attributes this to Hugh of St Victor, but the next entry, 16v, confirms the authorship of Peter Comestor.

16v. PL 198:1813D-1817A, 'Item sermo *ejusdem Petri* incipit'; see Hauréau 1:138; Schneyer, *Repertorium*, Peter Comestor 52.

19r. PL 171:761A-765C, incorrectly attr. to Hildebert Cenomanensis, but corrected to Peter Comestor in **PL 198:1817B**, Hauréau 1:139, 2:170; the *judicet* and *judicare*, characteristic of Peter Comestor, in some sermons of Peter, have been sometimes altered by scribes or editors to suit their attribution to someone other than Peter Comestor.

22r. PL 199:1817B-1821A, *Peter Comestor*; Hauréau 1:139.

24v. PL 198:1821A-1824A, 'Sermo ejusdem', i.e. Peter Comestor; Hauréau 1:140.

58r. PL 198:1792C-1796C, *Peter Comestor*; Hauréau 1:144.

60v. PL 198:1796C-1800B, *Peter Comestor*; Hauréau 1:144.

63v. PL 171:538C-543C, incorrectly attr. to Hildebert Cenomansis, but corrected to Peter Comestor in **PL 198:1768A-1769D,** Hauréau 1:152, 2:165, 6:50; the ending is characteristic of Peter Comestor.

b) Bernard of Clairvaux:

11v. S. Bernardi Opera IV: 263-266: Sermones I, Nativitatis, J. Leclercq, H.M. Rochais, (Rome: Editiones Cistercienses, 1966). Hauréau, *Initia,* Appendix.

c) Aelred of Rievaulx:

35r. Sermones Inediti B. Aelredi Rievallensis, ed. C. H. Talbot, Series Scriptorum S. Ordinis Cisterciensis, Vol 1. (Rome, 1952) pp. 31-37.

d) Achard of St Victor:

38r. Achard de Saint-Victor, **Sermons inédits,** text latin avec introduction, notes et tables par Jean Chatillon, (Paris, Vrin: 1970) pp. 196-203. On **f. 39r,** *malus* is substituted for *pater mendacii* to conclude what is only the introduction of a much longer sermon. See Hauréau 1:27, f. 151, 3:57, f. 120; J. Chatillon, 'Sermons et Prédicateurs Victorins', *Archives d'histoire doctrinale et littéraire du Moyen âge,* 40 (1965) p. 33, no. 48, which does not mention MS Bodley 87.

e) Hugh of St Victor:

39r. PL 177:610C-613A; See Hauréau 3:318, f. 145; Jean Chatillon, 'Autour des Miscellanea attribués à Hugues de Saint-Victor', in RAM 25 (1949) 299-305; Roger Baron, 'Hugues de Saint-Victor, contribution à un nouvel examen de son oeuvre', *Traditio* 15 (1959) 223-297, Miscellanea on p. 290 ff; André Wilmart, 'Opuscules choisis de Hugues de Saint-Victor', RB 45 (1933) 242-248.

41r. PL 176:554D-556D, *Hugonis de S. Victore;* Hauréau 2:295, f. 71.

41v. PL 176:556C-559D, *Hugonis de S. Victore.*

42v. PL 176:559D-560C, *Hugonis de S. Victore;* Hauréau 2:295, f. 71; 'Nous en ignorons l'auteur'.

43v. PL 176:528D-531B, *Hugonis de S. Victore.*

48v. PL 176:527C-528A, *Hugonis de S. Victore.*

71v. PL 176:977A-979B, *Hugonis de S. Victore;* Hauréau 3:146, f. 52; Roger Baron, 'Hugues de Saint-Victor', *Traditio* 15:243.

72v. PL 176:979C-980D, *Hugonis de S. Victore;* Hauréau 3:146, f. 52; Baron, II:243; A. Wilmart, 'Opuscules choisis de Hugues de Saint-Victor', RB 43 (1933) 242-248.

73r. PL 176:980D-983B, *Hugonis de S. Victore.*

74v. PL 176:983B-988A, *Hugonis de S. Victore.*

76r. PL 177:1209-1210, *Hugonis de S. Victore;* Baron, 260; Wilmart, 'Opuscules Choisis', 242-248, esp. 245.

76v. PL 177:1209A-1222D, *Hugonis de S. Victore;* Baron, *Traditio* 15:260; A. Wilmart, RB 45:245.

97v. PL 176:836A-838D, *Hugonis de S. Victore;* Baron, *Traditio* 15:243; *The Didascalicon of Hugh of St. Victor, A Medieval Guide to the Arts,* trans. from the Latin with an intro. and notes by Jerome Taylor, (New York–London: Columbia U. Press, 1965) p. 225, n. 53.

98v. (Not in PL) Charles Henry Buttimer, ed., *Hugonis de Sancto Victore Didascalicon de studio legendi,* a critical text, Studies in Medieval and Renaissance Latin, X. (Washington: Catholic U. of America Press, 1959) pp. 134-135: Taylor, *The Didascalicon,* pp. 155-6, 226-8; R. Baron, *Traditio* 15:250-251.

99r. PL 175:405A-410C, *Hugonis de S. Victore;* Baron, *Traditio* 15: p. 276; Wilmart, RB 45: pp. 243, 246.

103r. PL 176:935A-D, *Hugonis de S. Victore;* Baron, *Traditio* 15:276.

103r. bis. John Baptist Schneyer, *Repertorium der Lateinischen Sermones des Mittelalters,* (Münster, 1959): *Hugonis de S. Victore,* 94.

104r. PL 176:15A-18B and **1005B-1006B,** *Hugonis de S. Victor* (etiam

PL 6:843, *S. Augustini*); Baron, *Traditio* 15 (1959) 280, 8; Wilmart, RB 45 (1933) 244, VII.

105r. PL 176:797A-798A, *Hugonis de S. Victore;* Baron, 249; Taylor 132-3; 221, nn. 36-39.

105v. PL 177:623AB. Appendix ad *Hugonis* opera dogmatica.

106v. Last 9 lines of passage in MS partly from **PL 176:525CD;** Wilmart, RB 43:243, II, who refers to **PL 176:525C,** line 8–**526B,** line 13.

107v. PL 177:289D-292A and **PL 177:820B-821A,** *Hugonis de S. Victore;* Baron, 280.

108v. PL 177:572A-574A, Appendix ad *Hugonis* opera dogmatica, miscellanea; Wilmart, RB 45 (1933) 248, no. XIII.

109v. PL 177:511B-512A, Appendix ad *Hugonis* opera dogmatica; Wilmart, RB 45:243, I.

110r. PL 175:422C-424D, *Hugonis de S. Victore;* Baron, 282, 9, 'Le Canticum ou Sermo pro Assumptione Virginis Mariae, est une oeuvre authentiquement Hugonienne'; Baron, 'La pensée mariale de Hugues de Saint-Victor', in RAM 31 (1955) 249-271, esp. 250-251, no. 12.

111r. PL 176:528A-D, 115A, *Hugonis de S. Victore;* Hauréau 6:26; Baron, *Traditio* 15:263.

111r. - bis. Schneyer, *Repertorium, Hugo* 122: Duo sunt equites.

111v. PL 177:504C-505B, Appendix ad *Hugonis* Opera Dogmatica, Miscellanea.

112r. PL 177:505C-506B, *Hugonis de S. Victore.*

112r. - bis. PL 176:993B-998A, *Hugonis de S. Victore;* Wilmart, RB 43:244, IX: Baron, *Traditio* 15:273, 4.

117r. PL 177:626C, Appendix ad *Hugonis* opera dogmatica.

f) **Hildebert Cenomanensis:**

55r. PL 171:947B-950D, *Hildeberti Cenomanensis;* Hauréau 2:312 and 5:253 André Wilmart, 'Les Sermons d'Hildebert', RB 47 (1935) 18, 32 III; Hauréau, *Incipits: David futura spiritu, Hildeberti.*

82v. PL 171:162B-168B, *Epistola Hildeberti Cenomanensis.*

85r. PL 171:183C-186A, *Epistola Hildeberti Cenomanensis.*

85v. PL 171:193B-197A, *Epistola Hildeberti Cenomanensis.*

87r. PL 171:197A-202D, *Epistola Hildeberti Cenomanensis.*

179v. PL 171:149B-153B, *Epistola Hildeberti Cenomanensis.*

181r. PL 171:156A-160C, *Epistola Hildeberti Cenomanensis.*

183r. PL 171:227A-228B, *Epistola Hildeberti Cenomanensis.*

183v. PL 171:225A-226D, *Epistola Hildeberti Cenomanensis.*

184r. PL 171:243A-244B, *Epistola Hildeberti Cenomanensis.*

g) **Master Gilbert, Abbot** (*Hoylandiae,* according to Madan and Craster) wrote a prologue beginning on **f. 89v,** and two sermons beginning on **ff. 90r** and **94v.** on St Matthew, and probably other pieces in this MS not yet firmly identified. The prologue and two sermons in Latin and English versions may be examined in this volume, pp. 129ff.

h) **Jean de Cornouailles: 106r.** PL 177:315A-318C, *Jean de Cornouailles;* Hauréau, 6:25, 38—*Hugonis de S. Victore,* but Baron, *Traditio* 15:265, *Jean de Cornouailles.*

i) **Stephen Langton: 150r.** *Incipit praefatio sequentis libri super Cantica Canticorum. In hoc libro sicut in ceteris, tria debent inquiri: utilitas, intentio et cui parti supponatur vitae. Utilitas est quies aeternae beatitudinis.* . . . **150v.** *Et signa nobis designantia cantica, id est jucunda et delectantia verba, quae verba sunt canticorum, id est, perfectorum qui sunt cantica Deo perfectorum dico in parte sic dicentium.* See Mgr G. Lacombe, 'Studies on the Commentaries of Cardinal Stephen Langton, Part I', and Beryl Smalley, 'Studies on the Commentaries of Cardinal Stephen Langton, Part II', and Mgr Lacombe and Beryl Smalley, 'Indices of Incipits, Indices of Manuscripts', and Alys L. Gregory,

'Indices of Rubrics of the principal Manuscripts of the Questiones of
Stephen Langton', in *Archives d'histoire doctrinale et littéraire du
Moyen âge*, 5 (1930) (Paris: Vrin, 1930); see especially pp. 140-144,
Oxford MS Bodley 87, with incipit at f. 150 and explicit, ad graviora
peccata perducat, at f. 179v (not at f. 185 as indicated in *Archives*,
p. 141).

150v. EXPOSITIO SUPER EUNDUM. *'Osculetur me.'* (Sg 1:1) Mgr Lacombe,
Archives, 5: pp. 140-144, discusses seven copies of this gloss of
Stephen Langton on the *Cantica Canticorum*, which he divides into
two groups representing two *reportationes*. 'This leads us to think that
the book was explained by Langton in one of his lecture courses at
Paris.' Mgr Lacombe gives an example of each type of this gloss and
subjoins the mss. which belong to each class. Some *errata* in transcrib-
ing from Oxford, MS Bodley 87, should be corrected here:
Title: Anonymous.
Inc.: *In hoc libro sicut in ceteris* f. 150
Expl.: *Ad graviora peccata perducant* f. 185. (should be 179v)
'Before attempting an explanation of the differences between these
two groups' of MSS, Mgr Lacombe reproduces 'a collation made of the
two Bodleian MSS. The choice of the passages to be collated was made
at random.' The first and third passages chosen from Bodley 87 should
be corrected to read as follows:

f. 150v. *Expositio super eundem. 'Osculetur me.' (Cant 1:1) Et intelligendum
est quod hoc dicunt amici de Vetere Testamento ad ipsam, non
audentes loqui ipsi sponso, et sic dicunt: O sponsa et O collectio, quae
es propinquior Deo. Ille de cujus adventu totiens locuti sunt mihi
Prophetae, precor et desidero ut per tuam intercessionem osculetur
me, id est, tangat me osculo oris sui, id est, dulcedine suae praesentiae,
id est, ipse praesens adveniat sumendo carnem ut facies ad faciem eum
videam. Osculetur me, dico non figurativo osculo sicut per* ◊ **(fol. 151r.)**
*Eliseum fecit, sed osculo oris sui, id est, visitatione sui praesentis. Per
Eliseum enim Deus osculatus est humanum genus figurative, qui Eliseus
misit puerum et baculum suum ad suscitandum quemdam puerum
mortuum, quem cum non posset suscitare per baculum vel per puerum
ipse Eliseus venit et membratim adaequavit se illi mortuo, ita quod os
ejus super os mortui et cetera membra fuerunt similiter adaequata,
sicque inspirationem suscitavit mortuum.*

f. 151v. *Oleum effusum est, (Cant. 1:2)*, is correctly transcribed.

f. 154v. *Ego flos campi. (Cant. 2:1). Vox sponsi ad sponsam: dixisti quia
lectulus meus est floridus et bene dixisti, quia ego per quem floridus
est, Deus, natura sum flos campi, ed est, intemeratae Virginis Filius,
quae est campus, id est, inarata et incorrupta terra et bonos flores
generans. . . .* **179v.** *ad graviora peccata perducat. EXPLICIT EXPO-
SITIO STEPHANI SUPER CANTICA CANTICORUM.*

185r. In a later hand is a partial list of contents in MS Bodley 87, which
includes Gilbert with three other authors who have the largest numbers
of contributions: *Hildeberti epistola*, 9; *Gilberti Abbatis sermones;
Petri Comestoris sermones; Hugonis a S. Victore sermones.*

4.   Leclercq, 'Ecrits monastiques' p. 102, n. 12; De Lubac, *Exégèse* I:126,
who refers to Leclercq; Mikkers, 'De Vita et Operibus p. 275. The text of the MS
shows both sermons to be by the same author.

5.   This prologue may introduce more than the two sermons on Mt 10:
34-41, which immediately follow it. The prologue may also have introduced
any or all of five other sermons on Matthew in Bodley 87, whose author(s)
remain unidentified:

f. 51v. *DE SANCTO ANDREA. 'Ambulans Jesus juxta mare', etc. (Mt 4:18)*

Attendite, fratres. Attentos vos lectio praesens desiderat. Vocatio piscatorum discutitur . . . . Ad quod nos perducat idem de quo in praesentiarum agimus Jesus Christus, Deus et Dominus noster, cui est cum eodem Patre et Spiritu sancto, honor et imperium et nunc et semper, per omnia saecula saeculorum.

f. 142r. *INCIPIT SERMO SECUNDUM MATTHAEUM. 'Nemo potest doubus dominis servire,' et cetera. (Mt 6:24) Si ad litteram respicimus, non solum duobus dominis verum etiam multis secundum diversas possessiones quandoque servitur . . . . Nos ergo, fratres mei, qui Christiano nomine censemur, qui speciali Deo servitio signamur, ad exemplum volucrum caeli et liliorum agri non cogitemus de crastino nec sollicitemur de aliquo, quatenus exuti pompa scilicet liberius Deo serviamus, ut ad eum in futuro perveniamus. Amen.* (This does not seem to be the sermon mentioned by Hauréau, 2:121 or 5:137, nor by Phyllis Barzillay Roberts, *Stephanus de Lingua-Tonante* (Toronto: PIMS, 1968.).

f. 145r. *SERMO DE MULIERE CHANANAEA SECUNDUM MATTHAEUM. 'Egressus Jesus secessit in partes Tyri et Sidonis. Et ecce mulier Chananaea de finibus illis egressa clamavit dicens: Miserere mei Domine, Fili David; filia mea male a daemonio vexatur,' et cetera.* (Mt 15: 21) *Quidquid DNJC in carne quam pro nobis suscepit fecit, nobis fecit, pro nobis fecit, in nobis fecit, . . . Sed ne fastidium audientibus generemus et ut etiam ipsi teneant quae dicta sunt, respiremus paulisper, et cetera quae sequuntur immo haec ipsa prolixius et perfectius exponenda ad alium sermonem differamus.*

f. 145v. *ITEM DE MULIERE CHANANAEA SERMO INCOHAT SECUNDUM MATTHAEUM. 'Egressus Jesus inde secessit in partes Tyri et Sidonis,' et cetera. (Mt 15:21) Tribus modis vel tribus causis, vel tribus profectibus, quidquid Deus nobis, vel pro nobis, vel in nobis, in carne operatus est vel locutus, est exsecutus, videlicet vel ad fidei roborationem vel morum correctionem, vel virtutum imitationem . . . . Nihil ibi deficit, nihil superfluit. Sed haec ad alium diem et alium sermonem exsequenda procrastinemus.*

146v. *SERMO DE EODUM INCIPIT SECUNDUM MATTHAEUM. 'Egressus Jesus inde, secessit in partes Tyri et Sidonis.' Primum quaeritur quare a Judaea egressus sit, cum non sit 'missus nisi ad oves quae perierunt domus Israel'. (Mt 15:21, 24) Numquid causa vagandi . . . Et quia nos easdem filias habemus, sanentur et ipsae a vero medico Jesu Christo, ut mundati ab omni labe peccati, digni inveniamur aeterna beatitudine et solatio cum Ipso. Amen.*

The **John Boston of Bury** who records that Gilbert of Hoyland wrote a book on Matthew, located at that time in the Cistercian monastery of New Minster, likewise recorded that Gilbert of Hoyland wrote a book entitled, *De casu diaboli,* located in the same monastery of New Westminster. Mikkers, 'De Vita et Operibus' p. 277, perhaps relying on Thomas Tanner, *Bibliotheca Britannico-Hibernica* p. 317, note b, says that *De casu diaboli,* attributed by other authors to Gilbert of Hoyland, is attributed by John Boston of Bury himself to abbot Gilbert Crispin of Westminster (circa 1100) and that Mikkers himself to that date (1963) had not found a copy. *Five sermons on Lk 11: 14-24,* in Bodley 87, may well be the missing text, *De casu diaboli,* and as attributable to Gilbert of Hoyland as to Gilbert Crispin: their incipits and explicits are as follows:

f. 131r. *SERMO SECUNDUM LUCAM. 'Erat Jesus ejiciens daemonium et illud erat mutum,' etc. (Lk 11:14) Quia singula verba hujus evangelicae lectionis nec hora permittit exponere, nec imperitia nostra sufficit,* *aliqua tamen excipere volumus, . . . Jam ergo exponere incohavimus, ne onerosa dicta, fratres, fastidiamus, executioni diem alterum aliumque sermonem statuamus.*

f. 132v. SERMO DE EODEM INCIPIT, SECUNDUM LUCAM. 'Erat Jesus ejiciens daemonium, et illud erat mutum.' *(Lc 11:14) Hoc in superiore sermone disputati, non humanitati ascripsimus . . . . Magnum miraculum, venerabile signum, de quo cetera quae sequuntur ad alium sermonem differamus, orantes ut idem miraculum operatur in nobis DNJC, qui cum Patre et Spiritu sancto est Deus benedictus in saecula.*

f. 134v. SERMO ITERUM DE EODEM INCIPIT: Cum ergo scribae et pharisaei. *Cum ergo scribae et pharisaei tantam Dei virtutem, qua daemonium expellitur, caecus illuminatur, commendare deberent, non glorificaverunt Deum . . . . Sed quia haec et difficultatem habent et mystice intellecta mysterium, et moraliter aedificationem, et nos sermonem protraximus, diem alterum executioni statuamus, orantes semper et satagentes ut diaboli regnum semper sit divisum a nobis non in nobis, et regnum Dei semper idem in nobis et non divisum a nobis.*

f. 136r. SERMO DE EODEM INCIPIT: Cum fortis armatus custodit atrium suum. *'Cum fortis armatus custodit atrium suum in pace sunt omnia quae possidet' et cetera. (Lc 11:21) Sicut in superiore sermone praediximus, in his verbis causa diutinae vexationis humani generi a diabolo continetur . . . . Claudendus est praesens sermo et quid diabolus egerit post expulsionem suam et qualiter arma fracta redintegraverit, vel nova cuderit, sequenti reponamus sermoni.*

f. 140r. ITEM SERMO DE EODEM. *'Cum immundus spiritus exierit ab homine' et cetera. (Lc 11:24) Jam tandem, donante Deo, ad id quod supra distulimus, duce textu evangelico et ordine praescripto pervenimus, videlicet quid diabolus expulsus a corde et corpore humano egerit . . . . Ut ergo novissima nostra meliora sint prioribus, non deteriora, omnem potestatem inimici in nobis extinguamus, et ipsum captivum, immo mortuum teneamus sine intermissione militantes Deo per Jesum Christum. Amen.*

Of the remaining pieces in MS Bodley 87, whose authors have not yet been identified, the incipits and explicits are as follows:

10v. SERMO DOMINICA TERTIA POST PASCHA. *'Obsecro vos tamquam advenas et peregrinos abstinere vos a carnalibus desideriis, felices qui se praesenti saeculo tamquam advenas peregrinos exhibent, immaculatos se custodientes ab eo neque enim hic habemus manentem [civitatem] sed futuram inquirimus'. (1 Pet 2:11, Heb 13:14) Peregrinus siquidem via regia incedit, . . . Nonne solito amplius solitae opus est insistere pugnae, ut magna quaedam victoria, regeneratio ad gloriam, nobis perveniat ad salutem.*

27v. INCIPIT SERMO PRIMUS LIBRI HUJUS. *Dulcia lectori cibaria exprimens ex sponsae Christi exsultatione: 'Dilectus meus misit manum suam per foramen et venter meus intremuit ad tactum ejus'. (Cant 5:4) Inter ea quae ad nostram doctrinam scripta sunt, specialem nobis ingerit dulcedinem doctrinae salutaris proposita nobis auctoritas sumpta de cantico amoris, cujus nimirum auctoritas . . .* **28r.** *cujus venter ad dilecti tactum intremuit, nimirum per admirationem in contemplatione Sponsi sui et in contemplatione caeli in visione gloriae Dei, cui honor et gloria per saeculorum saecula.* (A miniature at **27v** illuminates the text; a copy of this in black and white appears on the dust jacket of this volume).

28r. SERMO DE SANCTA TRINITATE INCOHAT. *Libera nos, justifica nos, salva nos, O beata Trinitas! Proficiente, dilectissimi, processu temporis, pia devotione fidelium animorum proficit in ecclesiis Dei cultus, crescit*

*religio, augetur numerus et honor indeficiens sanctarum solemnitatum
. . . . Laudemus in saecula nomen sanctum tuum cum angelis et arch-
angelis sine fine dicentes: Sanctus, sanctus, sanctus, Dominus Deus
exercituum, Tibi gloria et imperium per omnia saecula saeculorum.*

30r. *SERMO DE SANCTO LAURENTIO INCIPIT SIVE DE QUOLIBET ALIO
MARTYRE. 'Nisi granum frumenti cadens in terram mortuum fuerit,
ipsum solum manet. Si autem mortuum fuerit, multum fructum affert'.
(Joan 12:24) Variis ac diversis modis, dilectissimi, operariis suis sum-
mus Paterfamilias verbi sui praeparat refectionem. Alios namque pascit
manifestis, alios exercet obscuris. Aliquando loquitur nobis Dominus in
parabolis, aliquando palam loquitur et proverbium nullum dicit, sed
quid agere debeamus palam ostendit nobis . . . . Sic postremo fructifi-
cantes in Spiritu, gaudebimus de bonis Domini, satiabimurque cum
apparuerit gloria ejus, quia de Spiritu metemus vitam aeternam. Amen.*

31v. *SERMO DE EPISTOLA OCTAVIS PASCHAE. 'Omne quod natum est
ex Deo, vincit mundum', (1 Joan 5:4) Duo sunt consequentia hujus
capituli. Virtus enim ejus commendat, haec lectio comprobat veritatem. Virtus est eminens et evidens veritas . . . . 35r. Quantum vero ad
virtutes spectat et verba, verba inquit quae ego loquor vobis, ipsa testi-
monia perhibent de me. Et item: 'Si mihi non creditis, operibus
credite' (Joan 10:38).*

40r. *SERMO SUPER MARCUM PERUTILIS, DE QUOLIBET CONFESSORE
ATQUE PONTIFICE. 'Videte, vigilate et orate'. (Mc 13:33)* [Text is
illustrated in the lower margin with a watchdog.] *Quid videndum, aut
qualiter, quomodo vigilandum, quemadmodum denique orandum?
Veritas, magister in his, suadeat, prout ipse dederit, omnes pariter
audiamus . . . . 40v. Sed pro peccatis ut solvantur, pro virtutibus ut
tribuantur, quo his velut quodam vehiculo, ad aeterna et permanentia
veniamus gaudia. Amen.*

44v. *QUOT SUNT QUAE FACIUNT HOMINEM A VITIIS TEMPERARE?
Tria sunt quae faciunt hominem a vitiis temperare, id est aut metus
gehennae, sive praesentium legum, aut spes atque desiderium regni
caelorum, aut affectus ipsius boni, amorque virtutis.* [In same hand in
margin: *Hominem a vitiis*] *. . . Ideoque isdem vitiis monachum sub-
jacere certissimum est, quae in alio inclementi atque severitate inhu-
mana condemnat.*

46r. *DE MULTIS SCIENTIARUM GENERIBUS. Multa quidem scientiarum
sunt in hoc mundo genera; tanta siquidem earum quanta et artium
generibus disciplinarumque varietas est. Sed cum omnes aut omnino
inutiles sunt aut praesentis vitae commodis prosunt, nulla tamen est
quae non habeat proprium doctrinae suae ordinem atque rationem . . . .
47v. Unde sacramenta sunt ibi, non quod illi quae per mala opera sua
figurentur intelligerent, sed Deus eorum malitiam convertit in utilita-
tem, dum eorum facta mysteria aliorum fecit et per illa ista praesignavit.*

47r. *SERMO PERUTILIS. Pro statu atque mensura uniuscujusque mentis
scriptura divina ad diversos perfectionum gradus arbitrii nostri revocat
libertatem. Nec enim informis poterat . . . verus Dei Filius, qui peccatum
non fecit, nec inventus est dolus in ore ejus, habere non potuit.*

49r. *DE QUOLIBET MARTYRE. 'Beatus vir qui in sapientia morabitur'.
(Si 14:22) Ordo iste, fratres, ut videtur, artificialis est; si naturalis,
secundum dispensationem vitae doctrinalem loquor. Sic nempe pueri
ad socialem vitam aptant. Denique moribus informantur. Postremo ad
sapientiae gravitatem cohortantur vel corroborantur . . . . 49v. Quarum
prima instruit, secunda provehit, tertia perficit, in Christo Jesu Domino
nostro, cui honor et imperium per omnia saecula saeculorum.*

49v. *SERMO DE QUOLIBET CONFESSORE ATQUE ABBATE. 'Justum* *deduxit per vias rectas Deus et ostendit illi regnum Dei', etc. (Sap 10: 10) Breve verbum, fratres, sed consummatum, in quo nec verbi iota videtur otiosum, in quo littera sine officio, nec verbum aliquid sine sacramento . . . .* **50v.** *Ad quam cognitionem perducat nos idem ipse Jesus Christus, Deus et Dominus noster, qui tecum vivit et gloriatur nos per omnia saecula saeculorum.*

50v. *SERMO DE QUOLIBET CONFESSORE ET PONTIFICE.* 'Amavit eum Deus et ornavit eum' etc. *(Deut 10:15) Revolutis diebus anni, fratres carissimi, confessoris egregii dies solemnis occurrit, cui honor debitus et sermo solitus debetur, praesertim cum et vos petatis et nos necesse habemus modis omnibus vestris desideriis pro modulo nostro votisque concurrere . . . .* **51v.** *Tertia aeterna dei missio et caelestis repromissio, qua vos in perpetuum frui faciat, Jesus Christus, Deus et Dominus noster, cui est cum Patre et Spiritu sancto aequa potestas, honor et imperium, et nunc et semper et per omnia saecula saeculorum.*

52v. *SERMO IN PURIFICATIONE BEATAE VIRGINIS MARIAE.* 'Postquam impleti sunt dies purgationis Mariae', etc. *(Lc 2:22) Scriptura Dei gemina lingua loqui consuevit, una qua rei gestae veritatem denuntiat, altera qua nos ad eorum quae gesta sunt imitationem invitat . . . .* **55r.** *ut in divina contemplatione sustolli, et per virilem operationem in ea sanctus vocari mereatur et effici, largiente ipso qui vivit et regnat Deus per omnia saecula saeculorum.*

56v. *'IN CATHEDRA SENIORUM LAUDENT EUM'. (Ps 106:32) Communis debet esse laetitia totius gregis solemnitas sui boni pastoris, illius videlicet cui Deus curam et custodiam specialiter suae familiae commendavit dicens: 'Pasce oves meas'. (Joan 21:17) . . . . Quem denique paupertas non frangit, a gratiarum actione non retrahit, in temporalium desiderium non attendit, scit penuriam pati. Hunc ita institutum nec abundantia in superbia elevat.*

57v. *'AEGROTANTE ELISEA, IN INFIRMITATE QUA MORTUUS EST, descendit ad eum rex Israel et coepit coram eo flere'. (4 Reg 13:14). 'Cui dixit: aperi fenestram orientalem', (4 Reg 13:17) et 'affer arcum et sagittas', (13:16). Et supposuit manus suas manibus ejus et ait: 'Percute jaculo terram. Cumque percussisset' terram, (13:18) ait illi: 'si percussisses quinquies aut sexies, percussisses Syriam usque ad consummationem', (13:19). In his verbis nostrum subtiliter profectum indagare debemus. Per Eliseum igitur qui Dei mihi salus dicitur, designatur ille cui Pater ait: 'Dedi in lucem gentium, ut sis salus mea usque ad extremum terrae', (Is 49:6) . . . . Hoc magis agens percutit Syriam quae sublimis dicitur, usque ad consummationem, quia omnem superbiam saeculi a corde suo eliminat.* See Hauréau, 3:48, 4° (?).

65r. *IN NOMINE DOMINI, SERMO INCIPIT DE TRINITATE.* [A miniature has been removed, but the folios have been rewritten and the attractive miniature repeated.] *Credimus sanctam et ineffabilem Trinitatem unum Deum esse. Haec est, carissimi, fides nostra, credere in Patrem et Filium et Spiritum sanctum, unum Deum, unam substantiam, tres personas. Haec est, inquam, fides nostra, hoc fundamentum salvationis nostrae . . . . ab amaritudine in suavitatem, quam nobis conferre dignetur de qua locuti sumus sancta Trinitas, terna unitas, vivens et regnans per omnia saecula saeculorum.*

66r. *QUID SIT SPIRITU AMBULARE?* 'Spiritu ambulate et desideria carnis non perficietis', (Ga 5:16). *Praesens apostoli lectio expositione multum indiget, quia in superficie levis est et morum profectibus inservit . . . .* **68r.** *donec resurgentes in Christi gloria perpetua collectemur, in qua vivit et regnat cum Patre et Spiritu sancto per omnia saecula saeculorum.*

68r. *DE PUDORE, TIMORE, SPE ET AMORE. Quotiescumque in honorem cujuslibet sanctorum festivum satagimus diem recolere, interiori necesse est intuitu cordis secreta rimemur, si illius delectemur gaudio, si ad imitandum praeparemur, si dulcedinis qua ille nullo interveniente fastidio exsaturatur, nos vel odorem gustamus . . . .* **68v.** *timore coacti revocamur ad spem, quae quia non confunditur, perducit nos ad caritatem, de qua et in qua exsultant sancti Dei per saecula saeculorum.*

68v. *DE HIS QUI HABITANT IN DOMO DOMINI. 'Beati qui habitant in domo tua, Domine', (Ps 83:5). Per prophetam ostendit hic Spiritus sanctus beatos esse inhabitatores domus Dei et subnectit causam, quoniam in perpetuum Deum laudabunt. Sed quaerendum aestimo quae sit haec domus Dei, qua qui inhabitant beatificantur, eo quod in laude continue commorentur . . . . ut ipsum Deum et Dominum nostrum perpetuo laudemus, qui vivit et regnat per omnia saecula saeculorum. Amen.*

70v. *SERMO DE CIRCUMCISIONE DOMINI. Solemnitatem hujus diei compendiose satis nobis beatus indicat evangelista. Sic namque summam tangit historiae, ut in historicis verbis eis qui exercitatos secundum apostolum habent sensus, altum quid relinquit inquirendum. Vult etenim et hoc demonstrat ordine suae narrationis ut prolata verba subtiliter indagemus, indagata inveniamus, inventa ruminemus, ruminata degustemus, quatenus interioris medullae sapore praecepto et ipsi pro modulo de eisdem pascamur . . . . Sicut circumcidat circumcisione spirituali, qui cum Patre et Spiritu sancto vivit in gloria genitali per omnia saecula saeculorum.*

101r. *SERMO DE DIE PENTECOSTES. 'Erant omnes discipuli pariter congregati in eodum loco', (Ac 2:1). Completi sunt enim dies hi, quando veniunt ad quinquagesimum . . . . Unde et illi sancti in timore semper sunt, quia tam subtilis est superbia ut vix ipsi de se possint judicare an gloriantur in se.*

114r. *DE NUPTIIS IN CANA. 'Nuptiae factae sunt in Cana Galilaeae et erat mater Jesu ibi', (Jo 2:1-12). Haec qualiter ad sacramenta ecclesiae relata sunt a sanctis Patribus novimus . . . . id est omnis chorus sanctarum virtutum gratiae Dei subjiciantur jure, a qua et per quam omnis incohatus et crescit salutis profectus, ut 'qui gloriatur, in Domino glorietur'. Amen. (2 Co 10:17)* See Hauréau, 6:28, 3°, who quotes this text and incipit among several anonymous sermons from MS Paris Bib. Nat. 18096, fol. 31-36, and adds: *'Pas d'autre* copie', by which he means that he has not encountered these sermons elsewhere; he makes no attribution.

117r. *SERMO DOMINICA TERTIA POST PASCHA. Dixit Dominus Jesus discipulis suis: 'nisi ego abiero, paraclitus non veniet ad vos. Si autem abiero, mittam eum ad vos. Et cum venerit ille, arguet mundum de peccato et de justitia et de judicio', (Joan 16:7-8). Omnis humana sapientia, divinae comparata, stultitia, est, etiam si ad divinam sapientiam referatur . . . . ut nos digna dicere possimus et vos digne audire et nos pariter et vos ipsum paraclitum suscipere ipsoque refoveri, ipsoque doceri, ipsoque glorificari et beatificari, qui cum Patre et Filio est unus Deus in aeternum et in saecula saeculorum. Amen.*

119v. *ITEM SERMO DE EODEM. 'Nisi ego abiero, Paraclitus non veniet ad vos' et cetera. (Joan 16:7) In superiore sermone dubitavimus quomodo abeundum fuit Domino, ut Spiritum sanctum quem praesentem habuit daret, . . . nec animaliter cognoscamus, nec animaliter sapiamus, et veniat ad nos quo modo venturum promisit Spiritus sanctus, immo tota Trinitas, quae est Deus benedictus in saecula.*

122r. *SERMO DE EODEM. 'Cum autem venerit Paraclitus, ipse arguet* *mundum de peccato et de justitia et de judicio'. (Joan 16:8) Ad hoc quod superius promisimus, Deo donante, pervenimus, . . . Det Deus ita a nobis dicta observari, ut si merito arguet mundum de peccato et de judicio, ita corripiamur ut corrigamur, correpti et correcti a Spiritu sancto visitemur, confortemur et gratia donemur, eodem Spiritu purgente et beatificante, qui cum Patre et Filio est Deus benedictus in saecula. Amen.*

125r. *SERMO DE JOANNE BAPTISTA. Ascendit Judas ad tondendas oves in Thamna et ibat cum eo Hiras Odollamites, opilio gregis sui. Quod cum audisset Thamar, nurus sua, mutavit habitum suum et accepit theristrum et sedit in bivio et accepta arrhabone a Juda, baculo et anulo et armilla, concepit ab eo et peperit ei duos filios, Phares et Zara, (Gn 38:29-30) Quid haec ad Johannem Baptistam pertineat in explanatione liquebit . . . . et Deo nostro duos filios generabit, id est geminae caritatis opera ex se procreabit et in operum suorum messione vero Sponso suo in gratia et gloria copulabitur sine fine. Amen.*

6.   The title, *Sermo de eodem [martyre] incipit secundum Matthaeum,* presupposes a previous sermon on Stephen, probably on his feast day, 26 December 1171; the two sermons in hand would have followed immediately, on 27 and 28 December, apparently on Stephen, but actually in anticipation of the first anniversary of the murder of Thomas Becket. The text is not chosen from the Mass of St Stephen but from the Gospel of the Mass, *In virtutem,* for a martyr outside paschaltide. Though death by stoning, the fate of Stephen, might have provided rich material for the exegete, the speaker has chosen to speak of division by the sword, almost irrelevant to Stephen but most appropriate for Becket. The sword eloquently symbolized the new division between Henry and Becket, King and Archbishop, friend and friend, and even churchman and churchman. The sword would be the instrument of Becket's death. When Becket for their own safety had dismissed all his churchmen, a lone cleric and master, Edward Grim, remained as his cross-bearer; his loyalty was matched by the disloyalty of a subdeacon, Hugh Mauclerc of Horsea, who acted as abettor to the four knights bent on Becket's death. In attempting to divert the first blow of a sword, Edward Grim's arm was almost severed from his shoulder and the bones broken, but after the last blow Hugh Mauclerc 'placed his foot on the martyr's neck, and with the point of his sword drew the brains from the wound and scattered them on the pavement, and finally shouted out: "Let us go; the traitor is dead; he will rise no more".' John Morris, *The Life and Martyrdom of St. Thomas Becket,* 2nd ed. (London: Burns and Oates, 1885) p. 419. In the earliest extant painting, no more than 30 years after the event, and in all the early iconography of Becket, the swords of the knights are prominently displayed.

7.   In both Latin and English versions of the prologue and the sermons, the text has been divided into paragraphs and the paragraphs numbered for convenience. One notices many stylistic characteristics of the twelfth century and perhaps particularly of Gilbert of Hoyland: the alternation of singulars and plurals of address; the soliloquies, dialogues and colloquies; the frequent word play and secound play, e.g. even in the second sentence here: *Rem contra prophetarum proponit oracula et quod prius mandavit et remandavit, jam demandare videtur:* 'Jesus proposes something which contradicts the oracles of the prophets. What he himself previously *commanded* and *recommended,* he now seems to *countermand.*' The distinction and paradox of the two kinds of peace and of Jesus' bringing a sword for the world's peace and a peace of his own not of earth but of heaven, seem very much in the manner of Gilbert of Hoyland. Nor should one overlook the prominence of Scriptural quotations and the disguising of almost all other references.

8.   As in note 6, I shall continue to cite Fr John Morris' *Life,* which David Knowles in *Thomas Becket* (Stanford, 1971) p. 176, considered 'the best life of its kind' among 'modern works', an estimate confirmed by Dr William Urry:

'I get more and more respect for the work of Fr. J. Morris on St. Thomas Becket. He has accumulated far more fascinating detail than anyone else and with more accuracy, too'—(hereafter, Morris).

The morning after Becket's final joyful return to Canterbury, 'the King's officials came, accompanied by the chaplains of the three Bishops [excommunicated by Alexander III through Becket], to ask for absolution from the censure. "He had not come", they said, "in peace, but with fire and sword"',' (Morris, 382). Gilbert's text on peace and the sword, however disguised as a commentary on Matthew and adapted for the feast of St Stephen, aptly picks up the accusation of the bishops, reflects on both the actions and the martyrdom of Thomas Becket, though Thomas is not mentioned by name.

The period between the murder of Thomas and the reconciliation of Henry II and Alexander III at Avranches was perilous for any outspoken friend of Thomas Becket. Conditions in Canterbury and Kent at the time were treacherous. I am grateful to Dr William Urry of St Edmund's Hall, Oxford, for the following helpful notes in answer to my questions:

> The area was or had been under the domination of the Broc Family gang, headed by Rannulph de Broc who had managed to get possession of Saltwood Castle near Hythe which actually was a fief of Thomas Becket as Archbishop. Henry of Essex the Constable held it but lost it after his cowardice in action against the Welsh. It should have escheated to the Archbishop but in the crisis over Becket it went to the de Brocs. Rannulph's nephew occupied the Palace at Canterbury during the exile of Becket, and knowing the place showed the knights the way round on 29th December 1170.
>
> The Brocs were ravaging about in East Kent well after the murder right into 1171 and there was no knowing what they might do. Both Rannulph and Robert his nephew were deeply implicated in the murder. They had no wish to give up Saltwood. They were great royalists and Rannulph held Haughley (Hagenet) Castle in East Anglia in the revolt of 1173-4, though he was driven out by the rebels. They were both in royal service years later (*teste* Pipe Rolls). So there was the chance that anyone preaching pro Becket in 1171 might find himself in trouble. Admittedly the King was becoming penitent but he was far away in Normandy or Ireland.
>
> The prominence of St-Victor in the MS is intelligible. Becket knew the place and preached there. Christopher de Hamel (now of Sotheby's) says that the great Becket books once assigned to Pontigny, are much more likely to come from the St-Victor atelier.
>
> The *gladium* points to Becket very well, though topographical suggestions, such as *extra portam* don't apply so well. Becket was slain just *inside* the door.

9.   Later in this MS Bodley 87, ff. 131r-142r, a series of five sermons on these verses of Luke, 11:21-23, might well be entitled: *De casu diaboli,* a lost work of Gilbert of Hoyland by that title; see note 5 above.

10.   Compare Roger of Byland, 'The Milk of Babes', paragraph 15.

11.   We may remember not only the disloyalty of the subdeacon, Hugh Mauclerc of Horsea, but also of Robert de Broc, once a cleric (Morris, 414), the apostate monk, who had been solemnly excommunicated by Thomas Becket on Christmas Day, 1170, and who guided the four knights to their prey (Morris, 414) and made his way first to the Archbishop's room to 'guard' the latter's precious possessions (Morris, 421).

12.   Thomas' own presentiment of martyrdom was reinforced by many a warning. The day before he was snubbed by the young King Henry, 'a crazy woman named Matilda, amidst the general joy [of his return] called out

repeatedly, "Archbishop, beware the knife".' (Morris, 386) After his men had
been threatened by the sword, 'The Archbishop then made use of a gesture and a
phrase that he repeated later, "Here, here," said he, striking himself a light blow
on the neck, "the varlets (*garciones*) will find me" ' (Morris, 388). On Christmas
Eve and on Christmas Day, 1170, he celebrated Mass, and had 'preached a
beautiful sermon on the text which so much occupied his thoughts: "On earth
peace to men of good will". When he came to speak of the holy Fathers of the
Church of Canterbury, the confessors who were there, he said that they had one
Archbishop who was a martyr, St. Elphege and that "it was possible that they
might soon have another".' (Morris, 395) On Tuesday, 29 December, at dusk,
'When the Saint saw that the blow was coming, he joined his hands, and covered
his eyes with them, and bowing his head, said: "I commend myself to God, to
holy Mary, to Blessed Denys, and St. Elphege".' St Elphege (954–1012) after
spending his last six years as Archbishop of Canterbury, much of the time in
exile, had been felled with an axe.

    13.   If during Thomas Becket's exile, his people were 'living and partly
living', if they briefly exulted at his return to Canterbury, then as they heard the
news of his murder in his own Cathedral, their hearts stopped and time stood
still. In this context it is crucial, then, to understand the last paragraph of this
sermon and the first paragraph of the next. The subject is clearly *protomartyr iste
noster,* 'our famous (or if you will, infamous) protomartyr'. This is neither
St Elphege nor St Stephen but Thomas Becket. Later we must discover in exactly
what sense he was called by Gilbert '*our* famous protomartyr'.

    Some minor points may first be clarified. *Extra castra,* 'outside the camp',
and *extra civitatem,* 'outside the city' in Scripture were often terms of opprobrium, places for the leper, the adulteress, the blasphemer, the outcast, the scape-
goat. It will be remembered from Acts 7:58, that Stephen was to be stoned
extra civitatem, 'outside the city'. Avoiding the words *extra civitatem,* four times
Gilbert says of Thomas that he carried the opprobrium of the cross *extra castra,*
outside the camp: a) 'outside the camp' to meet Jesus in opprobrium; b) 'outside
the camp' to follow Jesus carrying his cross; c) 'outside the camp' of his own
body; and d) 'outside the camp' of the city, where Gilbert uses not *civitatis* but
urbis, again clearly distinguishing Thomas from Stephen. To be able to appeal to
the text of Hebrews 13:12–13, which has both *extra castra,* 'outside the camp',
and *extra portram,* 'outside the door', Gilbert adds once *extra portam,* outside
the door. Of course, we learnedly recall the allusion to Becket's insistence,
against his monks' advice, that the doors of the cathedral be unbarred, despite
the proximity of the threatening knights. Gilbert would have been aware of that
lively exchange and its result, but Gilbert's immediate purpose in using this text
was to show that Becket was a genuine protomartyr in following both Christ the
protomartyr and Stephen the protomartyr outside the doors and walls of camps
and civilization into the wilds and wastelands of the outcasts and the reprobates.
As Gilbert says, the characteristic which Thomas held in common with Christ and
Stephen was his bearing of abuse, his suffering of reproaches, his shouldering of
the cross to the shedding of blood. The symbol of the later Canterbury pilgrim
would be the phial of blood. Gilbert, without reference to Tertullian, seems to
allude to the shedding of blood as the seed of Christians, and offers as proof the
long-lived progeny, the countless descendants, all the hosts already assembling
in Thomas' honor. Nothing could stop the trek of the pilgrim people to the martyr's shrine. Canterbury would rival Jerusalem.

    Now why is Thomas Becket addressed by Master Gilbert, Abbot, as '*our
famous protomartyr*'? Jean Leclercq points out that the first sermon is addressed
to religious, that the author speaks of the entrance into religious life which
separates a person from his family (f. 92), of the common life professed by his
audience (f. 93), and cautions against the disease of being singular, of withdrawing from the company of one's brethren, and the care of one's spiritual father,

—*'pensée très cistercienne'*, MS 15 (1953) 102, n. 13. Gilbert's references to the great numbers present would suggest that the audience was not limited to Cistercians. It seems evident enough that a Cistercian is talking to Cistercians and their friends about a fellow Cistercian, on the anniversary of the latter's death.

What were the ties between Thomas Becket and the Cistercians? In 'Becket and the Cistercians', *The Canadian Catholic Historical Association*, 35 (1968) p. 16, Professor L. A. Desmond, of St. Paul's College, Winnipeg, writes that Becket

> returned to the cloister of Pontigny (Nov. 30, 1164). There, only forty miles from his spiritual overlord, he resided for the next two years. His sojourn in this house is remarkable for the mutual respect and love which it generated between hosts and guest. Thomas wholeheartedly adopted the harsh life of a White monk; Alexander sent him the Cistercian habit of thick and rough woolen cloth which he privately received from the hands of Abbot Guichard.

After Becket's murder, according to Fr Morris, p. 423, vigil was kept throughout the night,

> the monks saying in silence the commendation of his soul. Robert, the Prior of Merton, who, as his confessor, knew his austerities, showed the monks, who had no suspicion of anything of the kind, how he was vested. He put his hand into the Martyr's bosom, and pointed out that his cappa, as a canon regular, covered his cowl as a monk, and that under this was his hair-shirt. The sight turned their sorrow into spiritual joy; they knelt down, kissed his hands and feet, and called him, 'St. Thomas, God's holy and glorious Martyr.'

We may dwell a moment longer on the final step from martyr to proto-martyr. The surprising series of events followed in rapid succession. On Tuesday evening, 29 Dec. 1170, eight days after his fifty-second birthday, Thomas Becket was murdered at Canterbury. On the following feast of St Thomas the Apostle and Becket's birth date, 21 Dec. 1171, Canterbury Cathedral was reconciled after the desecration through Becket's murder. After the reconciliation, Bishop Bartholomew of Exeter preached the first sermon on the text: 'According to the multitude of my sorrows have thy consolations rejoiced my soul: *'Secundum multitudinem dolorum meorum in corde meo consolationes tuae laetificaverunt animam meam'*, Ps 93:19 (*Dictionary of National Biography*: 3:331: 'Bartholomew, Bishop of Exeter' by T.A. Archer). 'It is surprising', in the comment of Beryl Smalley, *The Becket Conflict and The Schools* (Oxford: Blackwell, 1973) p. 220, 'that Baldwin's friend Bishop Bartholomew of Exeter left no written sermon on the martyr', either then or later. 'He preached in the cathedral at Canterbury at the invitation of the prior and convent when it was reopened after the closure following on its desecration'.

The three sermons of Master Gilbert, Abbot [of Hoyland], apparently on St Stephen, but the second and third really on Thomas Becket, were delivered apparently 26-28 December 1171, and here Thomas Becket is called 'our Protomartyr'. On 22 May 1172, Henry II received the apostolic absolution from the legates of Alexander III at Avranches. In 1172, possibly on 25 May, the day of his commemoration in the Cistercian Menology, Gilbert of Hoyland died at L'Arrivour, in the Diocese of Troyes. On 21 February 1173, two years and less than two months after his death, Thomas Becket was canonized.

Again, Miss Smalley, *The Becket Conflict*, 222-4, calls attention to 'two sermons preached by Gervase' of Chichester, which 'have been preserved for us by a lucky chance in a sixteenth-century transcript made by a sub-dean of Chicester called Nicholas Hickett. His transcript is now in MS 14 of Westminster Abbey.' Both sermons were 'preached in the chapter of Chichester on the feast of

St. Thomas the martyr, December 29th, the earlier in 1172 anticipating the canonization, the later in 1173 on the first solemnity of St. Thomas Becket's feast-day.'

> The earlier sermon addresses priests on their duties on the text: *I am the good shepherd* (Io. X, 11). Thomas was both *a good shepherd,* who laid down his life for his sheep, and an *atoning sacrifice* (Num. v, 8), who expiated the sins of the English Church. He preferred a glorious passion to apostasy from the divine law. He defeated the forces of evil by choosing to die . . . . The sermon on his feast day elaborates the theme. Gervase describes the martyr's austerities as proved by the vermin found in his hairshirt. He draws the familiar parallel with the passion of Christ. Then he points to a contrast: Christ redeemed us from eternal bondage, St. Thomas from temporal. We give thanks to them both . . . . Gervase ends his sermon by calling upon his hearers to show themselves worthy of the sacrifice which St Thomas made on behalf of their order. He agreed with Robert of Crichlade, preaching in the same years, that St Thomas had saved the clergy by his resistance to secular oppression and by his martyrdom. It was a shared illusion (*The Becket Conflict,* 223-4).

14.   Lightheartedly, Gilbert plays on the *ostium,* the wide open door, of the church or cathedral, yes, with the many pilgrims streaming through, but also the opening of his sermon and the open door of his lips with the words streaming through to encourage not only praise of the protomartyr but also imitation of his virtues. The sermon comes hot on the heels of yesterday's sermon, and Gilbert takes the opportunity to ring the changes on *gladium,* 'the sword', and *gaudium,* 'joy' through the sword. Joyfulness and exultation replace the caution and timidity of the previous day. Gilbert does not stop to measure and explain the exact location where Becket was felled, however much we regret his omission. Thomas had insisted on opening the doors of the cathedral to all comers; still more, he had insisted on opening the door of the eternal cathedral on Mt Sion. Would that the evidence showed that these sermons were delivered at Canterbury, even in the protecting candlelight of some hospitable chapter house. At least the subtlety of burying them in a commentary on Matthew, under the guise of sermons on the protomartyr Stephen, has preserved them for our eyes.

APPENDIX:
A Letter to Gilbert of Hoyland from his translator

My Lord Abbot and dear Father Gilbert,

1. Poring over your folios for some seven years now, I have become familiar with the style of your *literarius sermo,* your use of sacred Scripture and your theology of the heart. Although your work has not been published completely or in a modern critical edition, I rashly accepted the invitation from mutual friends to present your writings in a modern English version. To solve some questions which bring the blush to my face, gladly would I visit you in the kingdom of thingdom in Hoyland or in the kingdom of the Saints in Joyland, if return transportation were cheap and guaranteed. But let me present these questions, my Lord, in the hope that with your usual finesse and charity you may inspire some answers.

2. A helpful Reader points out that Bodley MS 87, is a 'clear almost calligraphic English proto-gothic script written about 1200 AD.' In this MS, a prologue and two sermons are attributed to 'Master Gilbert abbot', who I think is my Lord Abbot, Gilbert of Hoyland. These three contributions appear in the distinguished company listed above (p. 127). In a later hand on the back cover, f. 187r, Master Gilbert is listed with the three authors who have contributed the largest number of pieces to this MS: Hildebert with nine epistles, Gilbert's sermons with those of Peter Comestor and Hugh of St Victor. Master Gilbert's three pieces are sandwiched between an Epistle of Hildebert and an excerpt from Hugh, both already published.

3. Now the first question I am asked by mutual friends, my Lord, is what type of Latin edition I have edited, on what principles, with what orthography, folio division, and capitalization. With its English version, this Latin edition, apparently the first, falls between a literal transcription and a modern critical edition. This text, as also *Mira Simplicitas* in Cistercian Fathers, Number 26, sees the light with current punctuation, capitalization, and paragraphing. The classical spelling follows the modern Vulgate edition of Scripture and *A Latin Dictionary* of Lewis and Short. For clarity, *e* is expanded to *ae* or *oe,* consonantal *i* and *u* are spelled *j* and *v*, *t* is preferred to *c* as *c* is to *k*. Undoubtedly I have been too considerate of myself and the general

reader with a classical background and too inconsiderate of the scholar who may or may not have access to a microfilm reproduction of the original manuscript. Although I intended to note the front and back, *r* and *v*, of every folio, I failed to split words to accommodate a folio. Pardon me, my Lord, and assign a penance for a scribe who is not error-free and self-consistent, *non enim sum 'fortis et in me ipso totus, teres, atque rotundus'* (Horace, *Satires* II, vii, 86).

4. What effort did I make to locate previous editions? The answer, my Lord, may resemble a litany of thanksgiving, a good tonic for humility. Over the past seven years I spent hours with Cistercian literature, including the volumes of *incipits*, of Hauréau for example, Schneyer, Stegmüller, and the periodical literature. Keen to advance their work, the editors of Cistercian Publications were very helpful. After her publication of a first *Guide to Cistercian Scholarship*, Dr E. Rozanne Elder shared her knowledge of bibliography and work in progress. Dean Lawrence Desmond shared information on Gilbert from his burgeoning bibliography on Cistercianism. Fr Jean Leclercq promptly answered all oral and written queries. Frs Bede Lackner and Louis J. Lekai shared their knowledge and enthusiasm. In search of answers to outstanding questions, in August 1979, in the library of the Pontifical Institute in Toronto, I was actively assisted by Dr Frank Mantello, and in September 1979 at the Bodleian Library, I was capably guided by another former student, Richard Gerberding. In my search through the reference files to the manuscript holdings at the Bodleian, I found no mention of new editions of their manuscripts of Gilbert of Hoyland, and specifically not of Bodley MS 87, ff. 87v-97v. In concluding this litany, my Lord, let me thank the librarians and their staffs who assisted me in collecting microfilm copies of the MSS mentioned by Fr Edmond Mikkers, plus a few others not mentioned.

5. I am likewise pressed to show, my Lord, that the author of the prologue (P) and of the two sermons (to be referred to as A and B) in Bodley MS 87, namely Master Gilbert abbot (M) is really Gilbert of Hoyland (H). Fr Edmond Mikkers in 1963 wrote that the title of P and the style of A suggest the identity of M and H, but the title: *Item sermo de eodem martyre incipit a Magistro G. editus,* suggests that B was not written by H. The text of A and B, however, more important than the title, clearly shows a single author. A ends and B resumes with comment on the text of Matthew 10:38, and in the second paragraph B notes: 'from this verse we should begin, because with this verse yesterday we came to an end'. The rubrics of A and B: *de eodem martyre,* and the texts of A (paragraph 26) and of B (paragraph 1) presuppose a

previous sermon on St Stephen the protomartyr. Let us examine in turn P, A, and B.

THE PROLOGUE (P)

6. On receipt of a friend's commentary on Matthew, M consents to add supplementary comments of his own, but as reluctantly as H had consented in his fifth and sixth Treatises to a similar request. M's self-deprecatory and playful style and his use of metaphors from harvesting grain and grapes, and the sea, are reminiscent of H, who not only delivered a sermon on the Word of God as a seed but used the metaphor in M's objections to gleaning where his correspondent had harvested, to gathering scarce grapes after the vintage, and to fishing with a line where his correspondents had gathered into a net a whole school of fish.

7. Several unresolved questions surface here, my Lord. Did P introduce only the two sermons immediately following or a lengthier commentary on Matthew? A and B are in fact a running commentary on Matthew 10:34-41, and show evidence of being adapted from a commentary for a special occasion. Did P also introduce the remaining five unidentified sermons on Matthew in this manuscript? Of these, one on Mt 4:18 begins at f. 51v, another on 6:24 begins at f. 142v, and three on the Canaanite woman, 15:21-24, begin successively at ff. 145r, 145v, and 146v. Again, could P be the prologue to the volume on Matthew which John Boston of Bury claimed he had seen at the cistercian monastery of New Minster and attributed to H? At the same monastery he had seen another volume, *De casu diaboli,* which he also attributed to H; in Bodley MS 87, at ff. 131r, 132v, 134v, 136r and 140r, a series of five sermons on Luke 11:14-24, could well be entitled *De casu diaboli* and attributed to H.

USE OF SCRIPTURE IN A AND B

8. The opening texts of A and B, *de eodem martyre,* are not taken from the Mass of St Stephen, 26 December, but from the Mass of the Common of Martyrs outside Paschal Time, Mt 10:34-42. A and B seem to be part of a commentary adapted by M to a particular audience on a special occasion, just as H adapted his commentary on the Song of Songs for an audience of nuns. M and H use the literal–historical and the mystical sense of Scripture in the same way, as may be seen from

a brief quotation from each. M: ' . . . in my view Christ is presenting mysteries in these words. History and mystery are not at odds, for the sequence of the literal sense does not exclude hidden meanings' (A:17). H: ' . . . I know full well that the mysteries hidden beneath the words are more wonderful. I am thunderstruck by the mysteries, full of affection at the words, deeply inspired by the wooing of love' (*Mira Simplicitas*, 1, p. 577) M confines his quotations to sacred Scripture, which he uses with the frequency and variety of H. Of the twenty-nine verses from the Old Testament quoted elsewhere at least four times by H, four are found in A and B, two from the Psalms and two from the Song of Songs. Of the twenty-nine verses from the New Testament quoted elsewhere at least four times by H, nine are found in A and B, one from the Gospel of St John and eight from St Paul. The single verse most often quoted by H, at least fifteen times: 'He who clings to the Lord, becomes one spirit with him' (1 Co 6:17), appears twice in A and B. In the use of Scripture, my Lord Abbot, is it an exagerration to equate M and H?

CHARACTERISTIC WORDS IN A AND B

9. The high frequency of characteristic words again links M and H. At least three times M uses the favorite invocation of H: 'O good Jesus' (A:10, 23, 26). In five paragraphs M breaks into prayer as readily as H (A:10-12, 23, 26). Proportionately M calls as many things 'good' as does H: a crust of bread (A:6), separation (A:12), origin (A:22), elevation (B:7), taste and fruit (B:8), the sword (B:12) and even death (B:14). M and H share the next favorite adjective, 'happy', *felix*: O happy soul (A:11), O happy man, *O felicem virum* (A:26), and *O felicem hominem* (B:12) and also twice in M's final paragraph (B:17):

> Happy is the heartland which gathers up the kernels of this faith and cherishes them, so to speak, in the believing bosom of a devout affection. Clearly happy is one who welcomes both groups of Christ's disciples in such a way as to grant a devout receptivity to their work and to maintain towards them the graciousness their honor deserves.

Undoubtedly, my Lord Abbot, you appreciated that familiar word, 'affection', in the last sentences. Words for affection and love, *affectus, affectio, dilectio, amor, caritas,* recur throughout A and B, but especially in three short paragraphs (A:24, B:1 and 3). Would not the frequency of *bonus, felix, affectus* and its variants, also support the equation: M equals H?

SINGULAR AND PLURAL IN A AND B

10. The alternation of singulars and plurals which puzzled me in your 'Song of Songs', my Lord Abbot, recurs in A and B. There you seem to have written a commentary for an individual and later used it for a community or a wider audience. Apparently religious were in the audience of M, for several times he says: 'see, my brothers', or 'see, brethren' (A:8, 19, 23). But often M uses the singular: twice in A, *nonne tibi videtur* (A:9), followed closely by *videte* (A:10), and more often in B: *vides . . . vereris . . . suspendis . . . suspendis . . . suspende* (B:8), *exspolia . . . exue* and four other singulars (B:9), *vides* (B:12), *pone, repone, depone* (B:14) and *vide* (B:15). Whether M was adapting a previously prepared commentary or using the singular for emphasis: 'Let each one of you notice', or whatever the explanation, the alternation of singulars and plurals occurs with an arresting similarity in both M and H.

FIGURES OF WORDS AND FIGURES OF SPEECH IN A AND B

11. The presence and frequency of literary figures in M, my Lord, remind me of what you will pardon me for calling the verbal virtuosity of H. Please excuse my quoting examples whenever possible, my Lord, in my own impoverished vernacular version:

alliteration: *ubi plena pax est et si quid potest dici plus pace* (A:4);
so hang up your animality . . . do not stow it away but sow it unsparingly (B:8);

anaphora: *Quis . . . ? Quis . . . ? Quis . . . ?* (A:1); *Seminatur . . . Seminatur . . . Seminatur . . .* (B:7);

chiasm: *scientis peritiam . . . experientiam sentientis* (A:6);
affectus cohaerens violenti glutino (A:8);
pacata communio et . . . unio plena (A:5);
two swords, one a persecutor's, a lover's the other (B:7);

metaphors: metaphors abound in A and B as in P:

metathesis: *patrem* and *partem, patre* and *parte* (A:19);

oxymoron: gentle violence (A:12);
degenerate generation (A:18);
pious cruelty (B:12);

paradox: carnal peace is tenacious, stuck with the glue of passionate affection (A:8);
with the sword he vaulted into glory (B:1);
your persecutor is your benefactor, your host is his own benefactor (B:15);

rime: *pater, mater, frater* (A:23);
      effusio illa amoris est, ista cruoris (B:7);
sententia: where love is, there is peace (A:11);
      hatred is love in disarray (A:22);
traductio: *affectum affectibus* (A:6); *affectus affectum superat* (B:7);
word-play: the peace Jesus previously commanded and recommended,
      he now seems to countermand (A:1);
      subducit . . . dicit . . . ducere . . . dicere (A:20);
      the penalty he does not impose on you (tibi, singular),
      but the reward he proposes (A:25);
      The martyr's flesh was consumed by torture (consumpta),
      and he was himself consummated in justice (consumma-
      tus, B:1);
      The sower appears prodigal, but is provident (B:8);
      Lay down your soul for Christ *(pone),* but first lay it
      by *(repone)* in Christ; in his keeping lay aside your will
      (depone, B:14);
      Usefully (P:1), uselessly (A:19, 21), useful (B:15).

You suggest that disaffection most frequently results from tedium, my Lord. Am I running the risk of losing your affection by suggesting that M matches the verbal virtuosity of H, as he rings the changes on a favorite word of H, 'order' (A:22)? Need I add that M and H follow the mediaeval *cursus: plenus, tardus* and *velox*?

M RESUMES THE THEMES OF H

12. The cumulative index in this volume, my Lord Abbot, allows a comparison of some forty key words in M and H, where one will find harmonious parallels. In spiritual psychology, M and H both follow the pauline rather than the augustinian trinity in man: *caro/corpus, anima, spiritus* (1 Th 5:23, A:12, B:5). Following Paul, both speak of Christ as father, mother, brother, son. They have complementary passages on peace and the sword, fear and love, martyrdom and joy, glory and divinization. A is addressed to religious, as Jean Leclercq pointed out, for M speaks of the entry into religion which separates a religious from kith and kin, of the common life which his hearers have professed, and particularly of the *morbum singularitatis* (a vivid expression, though the MS has *cor malum singularitatis*). This very Cistercian reflection was developed by H, for he saw singularity as opposed to unity, community and charity (see pp. 561, 16, and 431-3 on the pomegranate). In my opinion, my Lord, the powerful paragraphs of M on kinship (A:14-16) and on the prodigal (A:18-23) could only have been written by one who had reflected for a religious lifetime on these

scriptural passages. What greater incentive for such a lifetime of reflection could be imagined than the vocation letter of Roger of Byland to H? In an uncompromising paragraph (no. 15, pp. 118f), Roger counsels: 'Let neither father nor mother, nor all the bonds of friendship prevent your coming to religious life'. After quoting this very passage in Matthew (10:36f), Roger continues: 'let no ambition for wealth delight you, because your fathers possessed churches by hereditary right. Listen to the psalmist: 'All who said: "for inheritance, let us possess the sanctuary of God", O my God, . . . you will pursue them in your tempest and you will terrify them in your anger' (Ps 82:12-16). Do you see how the universal Church curses owners of this kind, as often as she sings this psalm?''

M EQUALS H

13. Let us finish, my Lord, before the accumulated evidence requires a cumulative index, and before I capitulate to the computer to solve questions of the spirit: humor, poetry and style. Some friends appreciate your humility, my Lord, at the expense of your ability. Earlier your Sermons on the Song of Songs were attributed to Guarinus of St Victor, Gilbert of Cluny, Gilbert Foliot, Gilbert of Poitiers and, happily, to St Bernard of Clairvaux. Would you be surprised or delighted, my Lord, if someone on reading or hearing a literary sermon of yours, should ask you: 'did you really write that yourself? or did Gilbert of Stanford or some other Gilbert?' You disliked rashness and appreciated caution. This may explain how you or a friend preserved for our time your tribute to Thomas Becket. Is the discovery of this tribute a literary or an historical event? Yet caution does not explain how you came to give this tribute. I suspect that with little notice you were asked to give a triduum before the first anniversary of the murder of the English Cistercians' protomartyr, and that you adapted the appropriate passage from your commentary on Matthew and delivered it just five months before your own death. Thus A and B, both attributed to M, belong also to H. However incomplete the evidence given here, my Lord, the use of Scripture, of characteristic words, of singulars and plurals, of figures of word and speech, and of parallel themes, proves that M equals H. Just as I would not separate these Members from their Head, my Lord, so I would not claim that all your written relics have been rediscovered and collected in these volumes.

Your devoted servant and translator

L. Braceland, SJ

ABBREVIATIONS

ABR	*American Benedictine Review*. Newark, New Jersey, 1950-.
ASOC	*Analecta Sacri Ordinis Cisterciensis; Analecta Cisterciensia*. Rome, 1945-.
B	Bodleian Library Ms. Bodley G. 24.
CC	Corpus Christianorum series. Turnhout, Belgium, 1953-.
CF	Cistercian Fathers Series. Spencer, Mass., Washington, D.C., Kalamazoo, Mich., Cistercian Publications, 1970-.
CS	Cistercian Studies Series. Spencer, Mass., Washington, D.C., Kalamazoo, Mich., Cistercian Publications, 1969-.
CSt	*Cistercian Studies*. Chimay, Belgium, 1961-.
Cîteaux	*Cîteaux: Commentarii cistercienses; Cîteaux in de Nederlanden*. Westmalle, Belgium, 1950-.
Coll.	*Collectanea o.c.r.; Collectanea cisterciensia*. Rome, 1934-.
de Lubac	De Lubac, Henri, *Exégèse Médiéval*. Paris, Aubier, 1959-64.
DSp	*Dictionnaire de Spiritualité*, Paris, 1932-.
Dion	*Oeuvres Complètes de Saint Bernard*, V:1-319, Latin text and French tr. of Gilbert of Hoyland, P. Dion. Paris: Vivès, 1873.
E	Epistle of Gilbert of Hoyland, cited by number and paragraph.
Flor.	*Sermones super Cantica Canticorum, Editio princeps* [of Gilbert of Hoyland]. Florence, Nicolaus Laurenti, 1485.
G.	Gilbert of Hoyland.
Gilson	Gilson, Etienne, *The Mystical Theology of Saint Bernard*, tr. A. H. C. Downes. London: Sheed and Ward, 1940.
Lam	M. Jean Vuong-dinh Lam, 'Le Monastère: Foyer de Vie Spirituelle d'après Gilbert de Hoyland' and 'Les observances monastiques: instruments de Vie Spirituelle d'après Gilbert de Hoyland', Coll. 26 (1964) 5-21, 169-199.
Leclercq	Leclercq, Jean, *The Love of Learning and the Desire for God: A Study of Monastic Culture*, translated C. Misrahi, New York: Fordham Press, 1961.

Miquel	Miquel, Pierre, 'Les Caractères de l'expérience religieuse d'après Gilbert de Hoyland', Coll. 27 (1965) 150-159.
Morson	Morson, John, 'The English Cistercians and the Bestiary', *Bulletin of John Rylands Library* 39 (1956) 146-172.
MS	*Mediaeval Studies.* Toronto, 1939-.
R	Bodleian Library MS. Rawlinson G. 38.
Ro	Roger of Byland, 'Lac Parvulorum', *ASOC* 7 (1951) 218-231.
RAM	*Revue d'Ascétique et de Mystique.* Toulouse, 1920-.
RB	*St. Benedict's Rule for Monasteries.* Tr. Leonard Doyle, Collegeville: Liturgical Press, 1948. *La règle de S. Benoît.* Sources chrétiennes 181-183, ed. Adalbert de Vogüé (1972).
R. Ben.	*Revue Bénédictine.* Maredsous, Belgium, 1899-1910; 1911-.
S	Gilbert of Hoyland, *Sermons on the Canticle,* cited by number and paragraph.
SAn	*Studia Anselmiana* series. Rome, 1933-.
SBOp	*Sancti Bernardi Opera,* ed. J. Leclercq, C. H. Talbot, H. M. Rochais. Rome: Editiones Cistercienses, 1957-.
SC	Bernard of Clairvaux, *Sermons on the Song of Songs.* SBOp 1-2, tr. Kilian Walsh, The Works of Bernard of Clairvaux, CF 4, 7, [31, 40].
Ser	Gilbert of Hoyland, Sermon on the Word of God, cited by paragraph.
SMC	*Studies in Medieval Culture.* Kalamazoo, Mich., 1964-.
T	Gilbert of Hoyland, Ascetical Treatise, cited by number and paragraph.
Talbot	Talbot, C. H., 'A Letter of Roger, Abbot of Byland', ASOC 7 (1951) 218-231.
VCH	*The Victoria History of the Counties of England,* ed. William Page. II, *A History of Lincolnshire,* 22. The Abbey of Swineshead, pp. 145-46.
Vulg.	Vulgate. Psalms follow Vulgate enumeration; abbreviations, the *Jerusalem Bible;* translation, generally, the *Revised Standard Version, Catholic Edition.*
White	White, Terence Hanbury, *The English Bestiary.* New York: Putnam, 1960.

Psalms have been cited according to the Vulgate enumeration. Abbreviations and nomenclature conform to that of the Jerusalem Bible.

A SELECTED BIBLIOGRAPHY

A Lapide, Cornelius. *Commentaria in Scripturam Sacram,* re-ed., Augustine Crampon. Paris: Vivès, 1860.

Blaise, Albert. *Corpus Christianorum Continuatio Medieualis, Lexicon Latinitatus Medii Aevi.* Turnhout: Brepols, 1975.

Bouyer, Louis. *The Cistercian Heritage,* tr. Elizabeth A. Livingstone, Westminister, Md.: Newman, 1958.

Buhot, Jacqueline. 'L'Abbaye Normande de Savigny'. *Moyen Age,* 46 (1936) 1-19, 104-121, 178-190, 249-272.

Cabussut, A., Olphe-Gaillard M., 'Cantique des cantiques au Moyen Age.' DSp 2 (1953) 101-102.

―――― 'Une dévotion médiévale peu connue: la dévotion à Jésus notre Mère'. RAM 25 (1949) 234-245.

Chatillon, Jean. 'Cordis Affectus au Moyen Age'. DSp 2 (1953) 2287-2300.

―――― 'Hic, ibi, interim'. RAM (1949) 194-199.

Cheney, C.R. 'Les Bibliothèques cisterciennes en Angleterre au XIIe siècle'. *Mélanges de Saint Bernard.* Dijon (1953) 375-382.

Chenu, M.D. *La théologie au douzième siècle.* Paris, 1957.

Cloes, H. 'La systematisation théologique pendant la 1ère moitié de XIIe siècle'. *Ephemerides Theologicae* 34 (1958) 277-328.

Colombas, G.M. 'Paradis et vie angélique, Le sens eschatologique de la vocation chrétienne'. *Spiritualité monastique.* Paris, 1961.

Costello, Hilary, 'Gilbert of Hoyland'. *Cîteaux* 27 (1976) 109-121.

Déchanet, J.M. 'Amor ipse intellectus est'. *Revue du Moyen Age Latin* 1 (1945) 349-374.

―――― 'La contemplation au XIIe siècle'. DSp 2 (1953) 1948-66.

―――― 'Les fondements et les bases de la spiritualité bernardine'. *Cîteaux* 4 (1953) 292-313.

De Clerck, E. 'Droits du démon et nécessité de la Rédemption'. RTAM 14 (1947) 32-64.

———— 'Questions de sotériologie médiévale'. RTAM 13 (1946) 150-184.

Delatte, Paul. *The Rule of Saint Benedict,* tr. Justin McCann. London: Burns and Oates, 1921.

Delfgaauw, P. 'An approach to saint Bernard's sermons on the Song of songs'. Coll. 23 (1961) 148-161.

———— 'La lumière de la charité chez S. Bernard'. Coll. 18 (1956), 42-69, 306-320.

De Lubac, H. *Exégèse médiévale: Les quatre sens de l'Ecriture.* Paris: Aubier, Coll. *'Théologie',* 1959-64.

Didier, J.C. 'L'ascension mystique et l'union mystique par l'Humanité du Christ selon saint Bernard.' *La vie spirituelle, Supplément* 5 (1930) 140-155.

Dimier, A. 'Les concepts de moine et de vie monastique chez les premiers Cisterciens'. *Studia Monastica* 1 (1959) 399-418.

———— 'Ménagerie Cistercienne' and 'Héraldique Cistercienne'. *Cîteaux* 24 (1973) 5-30, 267-282.

———— 'Observances monastiques'. ASOC 11 (1955) 149-198.

Dugdale, G. *Monasticon Anglicanum.* London: 1846-1855.

Dumeige, Gervais. 'Dissemblance'. DSp 3 (1957) 1330-43.

Dumont, C. 'L'équilibre humain de la vie cistercienne d'après le bien-heureux Aelred de Rievaulx'. Coll. 18 (1956) 177-189.

Dumontier, M. *Saint Bernard et la Bible.* Paris, 1953.

Foreville, Raymonde, 'Gilbert de Sempringham'. DSp 6 (1967) 374-375.

Gilson, Etienne, *The Christian Philosophy of Saint Augustine,* tr. L.E.M. Lynch. London: Gollancz, 1961.

———— *History of Christian Philosophy in the Middle Ages.* New York: Random House, 1954.

———— *The Mystical Theology of Saint Bernard.* Tr. A. H. C. Downes. London: Sheed and Ward, 1955.

Hallam, H. E. *Settlement and Society.* Cambridge U. Press, 1965.

Hallier, Amédée. *The Monastic Theology of Aelred of Rievaulx,* tr. Columban Heaney, CS2. Spencer, Mass., 1969.

Hill, Bennet D. *English Cistercian Monasteries and their patrons in the Twelfth Century.* Urbana: U. of Illinois Press, 1968.

Histoire Littéraire de la France. Edd. Benedictines of St. Maur and L'Institut des Inscriptions et Belles Lettres. Paris: Imprimerie Nationale, 1733-19--; 'Gilbert de Hoylandia', 13 (1814) 461-69.

Ioannis de Forda. *Super extremam partem cantici canticorum sermones CXX,* edd. Edmond Mikkers and H. Costello. *CC Continuatio Mediaeualis* 17-18. Turnhout: Brepols, 1970.

Javelet, Robert, 'Contemplation et vie contemplative aux VIe-XIIe siècles'. DSp 2 (1953) 1929-1948.

—— 'Exercises spirituels dans le Haut Moyen Age'. DSp 4 (1961) 1905-1908.

—— 'L'extase chez les spirituels du XIIe siècle'. DSp 4 (1961) 2113-2120.

—— 'Image et Ressemblance aux 11e et 12e siècles'. DSp 7 (1971) 1425-1434.

—— 'Intelligence et amour chez les auteurs spirituels du XIIe siècle'. RAM 37 (1961) 273-290, 429-450.

—— *Psychologie des auteurs spirituels du XIIe siècle.* Strassbourg 1959.

—— *Saint Bernard mystique.* Paris, 1948.

Knowles, David. *The English Mystical Tradition.* New York: Harper Torchbook, 1961.

—— *The Episcopal Colleagues of Archbishop Thomas à Becket.* Cambridge University Press, 1951.

—— *The Monastic Order in England.* Cambridge University Press, 1950.

—— *The Nature of Mysticism.* New York: Hawthorne, 1966.

—— *The Religious Orders in England,* 3 vols. Cambridge University Press, 1950.

Knowles, David, C.N.K. Brooke, Vera C.M. London, *The Heads of Religious Houses: England and Wales, 940-1216.* Cambridge U. Press, 1972.

Knowles, David and R. Neville Hadcock. *Medieval Religious Houses in England and Wales.* New York: Longmans, Green, 1953.

Knowles, David, and J.K.S. St. Joseph. *Monastic Sites from the Air.* Cambridge University Press, 1952.

Lambert, M. 'La date de l'affiliation de Savigny et de la Trappe à l'Ordre de Cîteaux'. Coll. 3 (1936) 231-233.

Lebreton, M. 'Christ and the christian faith according to St. Bernard'. *Cîteaux* 12 (1961) 105-119.

—— 'Recherches sur les principaux thèmes théologiques traités dans les sermons du XIIe siècle'. RTAM 23 (1956) 5-18.

Leclercq, Jean. 'Disciplina'. DSp 3 (1957) 1291-1302.

—— 'Les écrits de Geoffroy d'Auxerre, Appendices, II: La première rédaction des Sermones in Cantica de Gilbert de Hoyland'. *Revue Bénédictine* 62 (1952) 289-290.

—— 'Ecrits monastiques sur la Bible aux XIe–XIIIe siècles'. MS 15 (1953) 95-106.

—— 'Etudes sur le vocabulaire monastique du moyen âge', SAn 48 (1961).

—— 'Le genre épistolaire au moyen âge'. *Revue du Moyen Age latin,*

2 (1955).

—— *The Love of Learning and the Desire of God,* tr. Catherine Misrahi. New York: Fordham University Press, 1961.

—— 'Monachisme et pérégrination du IXe au XIIe siècle'. *Studia Monastica* 3 (1961) 33-52.

—— *Otia Monastica.* SAn 51 (1963).

Leclercq, Jean, François Vandenbroucke, Louis Bouyer. *The Spirituality of the Middle Ages.* London: Burns and Oates, 1968.

Lekai, Louis. *The White Monks.* Our Lady of Spring Bank, Okauchee. Wis.: Cistercians, 1953.

—— *The Cistercians: Ideals and Reality.* Kent, Ohio: Kent State Univ. Press, 1977.

Loomis, Roger Sherman. *The Grail, from Celtic Myth to Christian Symbol.* New York: Columbia U. Press, 1963.

Marié, G. 'Familiarité avec Dieu, Courant bénédictin et cistercien'. DS 5 (1962) 50-53.

Manrique, A. *Annales Cistercienses,* 4 vols. Lyons, 1642-1649.

Merton, L. 'Action and contemplation in St. Bernard', Coll. 15 (1953) 26-31, 203-216; 16 (1954) 105-121.

Mikkers, E. 'De vita et operibus Gilbert de Hoylandia', *Cîteaux* 14 (1963) 33-43, 265-279.

—— 'Les sermons inédits de Jean de Ford sur le Cantique des cantiques'. Coll. 5 (1938) 250-261.

Miquel, Pierre. 'Les Caractères de l'Expérience Religieuse d'après Gilbert de Hoyland'. Coll. 27 (1965) 150-159.

Morson, John. 'The English Cistercians and the Bestiary'. *Bulletin of the John Rylands Library* 39 (1956) 146-170.

Migne, J.P., ed. *Patrologia Graeca.* Paris: 161 vols., 1857-1876. The volume number precedes the colon; the column number follows it.

—— *Patrologia Latina.* Paris: 222 vols., 1841-1864. The volume number precedes the colon; the column number follows it.

Prayers and Meditations of St. Anselm, tr. Benedicta Ward, Harmondsworth: Penguin, 1973.

Le règle de saint Benoît. Sources chrétiennes 181-183. Ed. Adalbert de Vogüé. Paris: Cerf, 1972.

Reypens, Leonce. 'Connaissance mystique de Dieu, au 12e et 13e siècles.' DSp 3 (1957) 829-901.

Riedlinger, H. 'Gilbert v. Hoyland.' *Lexikon für Theologie und Kirche,* B. IV (1960) 890.

Robert, A., Tournay, R., Feuillet, A. *Le cantique des Cantiques.* Paris: Gabalda, 1963.

The Rule of Saint Benedict. Edited by Justin McCann. London: Burns

Oates, 1952.

St. Benedict's Rule for Monasteries. Tr. Leonard Doyle, Collegeville: Liturgical Press, 1948.

Sancti Bernardi Opera, edd. J. Leclercq, C.H. Talbot, H.M. Rochais. Rome: Editions Cistercienses, 1957-.

Sancti Bernardi Opera Omnia, ed. Jean Mabillon. Milan: Gnocchi, 1690, rpt. 1850-52.

Smalley, Beryl. *The Study of the Bible in the Middle Ages.* Oxford, 1952, 2nd ed.

Squire, Aelred. *Aelred of Rievaulx: a study.* London, SPCK, 1969.

Standaert, Maur. 'La doctrine de l'image chez saint Bernard'. *Ephemerides Theologicae* 23 (1947) 70-129.

―――― 'Le principe de l'ordination dans la théologie spirituelle de S. Bernard'. Coll. 8 (1946) 178-216.

Talbot, C.H. 'A Letter of Roger, Abbot of Byland'. ASOC 7 (1951) 219-221.

Valléry-Radot, Irénée. 'La Queste del Saint Graal'. Coll. 17 (1956) 3-20, 199-213, 321-332.

Van den Bosch, Amatus. 'Intelligence de la Foi chez Saint Bernard'. *Cîteaux* 8 (1957) 85-108.

Vandenbroucke, François. 'Direction spirituelle en Occident, au Moyen Age'. DSp 3 (1957) 1083-1098.

Vuong-dinh-Lam, M. Jean. *Doctrine Spirituelle de Gilbert de Hoyland, d'après son Commentaire sur le Cantique des cantiques.* Diss., Rome: Collegium Anselmeanum, 1963.

―――― 'Le Monastère: foyer de vie spirituelle d'après Gilbert de Hoyland', Coll. 26 (1964) 5-21.

―――― 'Les Observances Monastiques: instruments de vie spirituelle d'après Gilbert de Hoyland', Coll. 26 (1964) 169-199.

―――― 'Gilbert de Hoyland', DSp 6 (1967) 371-374.

White, Terence Hanbury. *The English Bestiary.* New York: Putnam, 1960.

William of St Thierry. *Exposition on the Song of Songs.* CF 6. Spencer, Mass., 1970.

CUMULATIVE INDEX
TO THE WORKS OF
GILBERT OF HOYLAND

Numbers in italic print (e.g. *69*) indicate pages in volume IV; notes are indicated by 'n' or 'nn' (e.g. 37n39 means page 37 note 39; *66n2, 4, 11,* means page 66, notes 2, 4, 11 in volume IV).

SCRIPTURAL INDEX

Column one indicates the scriptural book and its abbreviations. Column two indicates the run-on pages of the first three volumes and in bold face the pages of volume four. Pages **109-123** refer to the *Lac Parvulorum* of Roger of Byland. Psalms have been cited according to the Vulgate enumeration.

Genesis (Gen, Gn)

1:3	276
2:6f	**28**
2:6	430
2:8-3:23	**58**
2:8	426
2:9	220, 427
2:10-14	**28**
2:15	426
2:23	170
2:24	258, 510, **166**
3:1	83
3:2	427
3:7	48, 583
3:8	71
3:15	**140**
3:18f	**26**
3:24	207, 209, 428, **142**
4:12	**6, 26**
4:14	98
8:16	252
8:21	302
9:21	135
9:24	**158**
12-17	137
12:1	252
12:6	**104**
16:14	450
18:1-8	128
20	**104**
20:1-18	**104**
21	**104**
21:30f	449
22:30	**104**
26	**104**
26:1-35	**104**

Genesis (Gen, Gn) (contd.)

26:14-22	**41**
26:18	131
26:20-23	450
26:20	**40**
27:27	179, 426, **17**
27:28	**40**
27:39	416
28:12f	128
29	**75**
29:31	68
30:36	118, 349
31:19	**76**
31:32	**77**
31:34f	**77**
31:40	**75**
32:10	**75**
32:24-9	128
32:24-6	**77**
32:31	101
34:1	251
35	**168**
35:4	**77**
39:6-23	**69**
39:12-14	**70**
39:12	546
41:6	492
45:1-3	67
49:7	316
49:12	298
49:25	**40**

Exodus (Ex)

3:3	252
3:5	233
3:14	**34**

Romans (Rm) (contd.)
11:20	220, 285, 331, **61**
11:25	157, **64**
11:29	368
11:33	453
11:36	**44**
12:1	318, 523
12:2	**5, 77**
12:3	212
12:6	301
12:8	376, 449
12:9	**122**
12:12	57, 89, 595, **27, 52**
12:15	259
12:16	58, 331, 485, **61, 64**
13:1	**69**
13:2	174
13:10	352, 428
13:12	50
13:13	355
13:14	130, 166
14:2	**76**
14:4	174
14:5	219, 292
14:7f	571
14:8	505
14:17	57, 150
14:23	227
15:3	**158**

1 Corinthians (1 Co)
1:3	332
1:19	428
1:20	507
1:23	159
1:24	320
1:26	256
1:30	62, 129, **51**
2:2	332, 416
2:6	418, 448, **44**
2:7	336, 416, 493
2:9	**122**
2:10	297, 309, 449, 474, 487, **49**
2:11	308, 449
2:12	308
2:13	422
2:14	54, 448, 591, **146, 168**
2:15	448
2:20	**51**
3:1f	418, **44**
3:2	448, **110**
3:11	**74**
3:12f	256
3:17	528
3:19	**62**

1 Corinthians (1 Co) (contd.)
4:3-5	174
4:4	58
4:5	174
4:7	150, 220, 308, **43**
4:9	159
4:15	**77**
5:6	277
5:7	**78**
5:12	**71**
6:10	**113**
6:11	245, 354f
6:17	47, 51, 66, 158, 169, 205, 210, 214, 258, 316, 324, 408, 591, **54, 166, 170**
6:20	219
7:5f	448
7:5	**142**
7:7	**44**
7:18	**54**
7:32	224, 306, 420
7:34	222
8:1	473
8:10f	243
8:12	50, 455
9:8-10	498
9:11	376
9:20-22	330, 375
9:22	170
9:24-7	**28**
9:24	**19**
9:25	54
10:4	166
10:13	463
10:14	150
10:22	208
10:29	587
10:33	161, 401
11:7	**6, 7, 10**
11:15	365f
11:19	156
11:23	404
12:1	495
12:4-11	402
12:4	518
12:7-10	210
12:10	523
12:27	270
12:31	237f, 240f, 247, 322
13:1	209, 241
13:2	241
13:3	234, 241, 484
13:4-8	323
13:4	241, 589
13:5-6	242
13:6	244